New Perspectives on

MICROSOFT® POWERPOINT® 2000

Comprehensive

S. SCOTT ZIMMERMAN
Brigham Young University

BEVERLY B. ZIMMERMAN
Brigham Young University

D1456464

APPROVED COURSEWARE

COURSE TECHNOLOGY
THOMSON LEARNING™

Australia • Canada • Mexico • Singapore • Spain • United Kingdom • United States

New Perspectives on Microsoft® PowerPoint® 2000—Comprehensive is published by Course Technology.

Managing Editor	Greg Donald	**Developmental Editor**	Rose Marie Kuebbing
Senior Editor	Donna Gridley	**Production Editor**	Christine Spillett
Series Technology Editor	Rachel A. Crapser	**Text Designer**	Meral Dabcovich
Product Manager	Catherine V. Donaldson	**Cover Designer**	Douglas Goodman
Associate Product Manager	Melissa Dezotell		

© 2001 by Course Technology, a division of Thomson Learning

For more information contact:
Course Technology
25 Thomson Place
Boston, MA 02210
Or find us on the World Wide Web at: http://www.course.com

For permission to use material from this text or product, contact us by

- **Web: www.thomsonrights.com**
- **Phone: 1-800-730-2214**
- **Fax: 1-800-730-2215**

All rights reserved. This publication is protected by federal copyright law. No part of this publication may be reproduced, stored in a retrieval system, or transmitted in any form or by any means, electronic, mechanical, photocopying, recording, or otherwise, or be used to make a derivative work (such as translation or adaptation), without prior permission in writing from Course Technology.

Trademarks
Course Technology and the Open Book logo are registered trademarks and CourseKits is a trademark of Course Technology. Custom Edition is a registered trademark of Thomson Learning.

The Thomson Learning logo is a registered trademark used herein under license.

Some of the product names and company names used in this book have been used for identification purposes only and may be trademarks or registered trademarks of their respective manufacturers and sellers.

Microsoft and the Office logo are either registered trademarks or trademarks of Microsoft Corporation in the United States and/or other countries. Course Technology is an independent entity from the Microsoft Corporation, and not affiliated with Microsoft in any manner. This text may be used in assisting students to prepare for a Microsoft Office User Specialist Exam for PowerPoint 2000. Neither Microsoft Corporation, its designated review company, nor Course Technology warrants that use of this text will ensure passing the relevant exam.

Use of the Microsoft Office User Specialist Approved Courseware Logo on this product signifies that it has been independently reviewed and approved in complying with the following standards: Acceptable coverage of all content related to the Microsoft Office Expert Exam entitled *Microsoft PowerPoint 2000*; and sufficient performance-based exercises that relate closely to all required content, based on sampling of text.

Disclaimer
Course Technology reserves the right to revise this publication and make changes from time to time in its content without notice.

ISBN 0-619-01977-8

Printed in the United States of America

1 2 3 4 5 6 7 8 9 10   BM 05 04 03 02 01

PREFACE

The New Perspectives Series

About New Perspectives

Course Technology's **New Perspectives Series** is an integrated system of instruction that combines text and technology products to teach computer concepts, the Internet, and microcomputer applications. Users consistently praise this series for innovative pedagogy, use of interactive technology, creativity, accuracy, and supportive and engaging style.

How is the New Perspectives Series different from other series?

The **New Perspectives Series** distinguishes itself by **innovative technology**, from the renowned Course Labs to the state-of-the-art multimedia that is integrated with our Concepts texts. Other distinguishing features include **sound instructional design**, **proven pedagogy**, and **consistent quality**. Each tutorial has students learn features in the context of solving a realistic case problem rather than simply learning a laundry list of features. With the **New Perspectives Series**, instructors report that students have a complete, integrative learning experience that stays with them. They credit this high retention and competency to the fact that this series incorporates critical thinking and problem-solving with computer skills mastery. In addition, we work hard to ensure accuracy by using a multi-step quality assurance process during all stages of development. Instructors focus on teaching and students spend more time learning.

Choose the coverage that's right for you

New Perspectives applications books are available in the following categories:

Brief
2-4 tutorials

Brief: approximately 150 pages long, two to four "Level I" tutorials, teaches basic application skills.

Introductory
6 or 7 tutorials, or Brief + 2 or 3 more tutorials

Introductory: approximately 300 pages long, four to seven tutorials, goes beyond the basic skills. These books often build out of the Brief book, adding two or three additional "Level II" tutorials.

Comprehensive
Introductory + 4 or 5 more tutorials. Includes Brief Windows tutorials and Additional Cases

Comprehensive: approximately 600 pages long, eight to twelve tutorials, all tutorials included in the Introductory text plus higher-level "Level III" topics. Also includes two Windows tutorials and three or four fully developed Additional Cases. The book you're holding is a Comprehensive book.

Advanced
Quick Review of basics + in-depth, high-level coverage

Advanced: approximately 600 pages long, covers topics similar to those in the Comprehensive books, but offers the highest-level coverage in the series. Advanced books assume students already know the basics, and therefore go into more depth at a more accelerated rate than the Comprehensive titles. Advanced books are ideal for a second, more technical course.

Office

Quick Review of basics + in-depth, high-level coverage

Custom Editions

Choose from any of the above to build your own Custom Editions or CourseKits

Office: approximately 800 pages long, covers all components of the Office suite as well as integrating the individual software packages with one another and the Internet.

Custom Books The New Perspectives Series offers you two ways to customize a New Perspectives text to fit your course exactly: *CourseKits*™ are two or more texts shrinkwrapped together, and offer significant price discounts. *Custom Editions*®, offer you flexibility in designing your concepts, Internet, and applications courses. You can build your own book by ordering a combination of topics bound together to cover only the subjects you want. There is no minimum order, and books are spiral bound. Contact your Course Technology sales representative for more information.

What course is this book appropriate for?

New Perspectives on Microsoft PowerPoint 2000—Comprehensive can be used in any course in which you want students to learn the most important topics of PowerPoint 2000, including creating special types of presentations, using a film recorder to prepare 35mm slides, publishing a web presentation with Custom Action Buttons, applying advanced special effects, inserting a CD audio track into a slide, and setting up a self-running presentation. It is particularly recommended for a full-semester course on PowerPoint 2000, or as part of a course on presentation skills. This book assumes that students have learned basic Windows navigation and file management skills from Course Technology's *New Perspectives on Microsoft Windows 95—Brief,* or the equivalent book for Windows 98, 2000, or NT.

What is the Microsoft Office User Specialist Program?

The Microsoft Office User Specialist Program provides an industry-recognized standard for measuring an individual's mastery of an Office application. Passing one or more MOUS Program certification exam helps your students demonstrate their proficiency to prospective employers and gives them a competitive edge in the job marketplace. Course Technology offers a growing number of Microsoft-approved products that cover all of the required objectives for the MOUS Program exams. For a complete listing of Course Technology titles that you can use to help your students get certified, visit our Web site at **www.course.com**.

New Perspectives on Microsoft PowerPoint 2000—Comprehensive has been approved by Microsoft as courseware for the Microsoft Office User Specialist (MOUS) program. After completing the tutorials and exercises in this book, students may be prepared to take the MOUS expert exam for PowerPoint 2000. For more information about certification, please visit the MOUS program site at **www.mous.net**.

Proven Pedagogy

CASE

Tutorial Case Each tutorial begins with a problem presented in a case that is meaningful to students. The case turns the task of learning how to use an application into a problem-solving process.

45-minute Sessions Each tutorial is divided into sessions that can be completed in about 45 minutes to an hour. Sessions allow instructors to more accurately allocate time in their syllabus, and students to better manage their own study time.

1.

2.

3.

Step-by-Step Methodology We make sure students can differentiate between what they are to do and what they are to read. Through numbered steps—clearly identified by a gray shaded background—students are constantly guided in solving the case problem. In addition, the numerous screen shots with callouts direct students' attention to what they should look at on the screen.

TROUBLE?

TROUBLE? Paragraphs These paragraphs anticipate the mistakes or problems that students may have and help them continue with the tutorial.

Tutorial Tips Page This page, following the Table of Contents, offers students suggestions on how to effectively plan their study and lab time, what to do when they make a mistake, and how to use the Reference Windows, MOUS grids, Quick Checks, and other features of the New Perspectives series.

"Read This Before You Begin" Page Located opposite the first tutorial's opening page for each level of the text, the Read This Before You Begin Page helps introduce technology into the classroom. Technical considerations and assumptions about software are listed to save time and eliminate unnecessary aggravation. Notes about the Data Disks help instructors and students get the right files in the right places, so students get started on the right foot.

Quick Check Questions Each session concludes with meaningful, conceptual Quick Check questions that test students' understanding of what they learned in the session. Answers to the Quick Check questions are provided at the end of each tutorial.

Reference Windows Reference Windows are succinct summaries of the most important tasks covered in a tutorial and they preview actions students will perform in the steps to follow.

Task Reference Located as a table at the end of the book, the Task Reference contains a summary of how to perform common tasks using the most efficient method, as well as references to pages where the task is discussed in more detail.

End-of-Tutorial Review Assignments, Case Problems, Internet Assignments, and Lab Assignments Review Assignments provide students with additional hands-on practice of the skills they learned in the tutorial using the same case presented in the tutorial. These Assignments are followed by three to four Case Problems that have approximately the same scope as the tutorial case but use a different scenario. In addition, some of the Review Assignments or Case Problems may include Exploration Exercises that challenge students and encourage them to explore the capabilities of the program they are using, and/or further extend their knowledge. Each tutorial also includes instructions on getting to the text's Student Online Companion page, which contains the Internet Assignments and other related links for the text. Internet Assignments are additional exercises that integrate the skills the students learned in the tutorial with the World Wide Web. Finally, if a Course Lab accompanies a tutorial, Lab Assignments are included after the Case Problems.

File Finder Chart This chart, located in the back of the book, visually explains how a student should set up their data disk, what files should go in what folders, and what they'll be saving the files as in the course of their work.

MOUS Certification Chart In the back of the book, you'll find a chart that lists all the skills for the Microsoft Office User Specialist Expert Exam on PowerPoint 2000. With page numbers referencing where these skills are covered in this text and where students get hands-on practice in completing the skills, the chart can be used as an excellent study guide in preparing for the Microsoft PowerPoint 2000 expert exam.

APPROVED COURSEWARE

New Perspectives on Microsoft® PowerPoint® 2000—Comprehensive Instructor's Resource Kit contains:

- Electronic Instructor's Manual in Word 97 format
- Data Files
- Solution Files
- Course Labs

- Course Test Manager Testbank
- Course Test Manager Engine
- Figure Files
- Sample Syllabus

These supplements come on CD-ROM. If you don't have access to a CD-ROM drive, contact your Course Technology customer service representative for more information.

The New Perspectives Supplements Package

Electronic Instructor's Manual Our Instructor's Manuals include tutorial overviews and outlines, technical notes, lecture notes, solutions, and Extra Case Problems. Many instructors use the Extra Case Problems for performance-based exams or extra credit projects. The Instructor's Manual is available as an electronic file, which you can get from the Instructor Resource Kit (IRK) CD-ROM or download it from **www.course.com**.

Data Files Data Files contain all of the data that students will use to complete the tutorials, Review Assignments, Case Problems and Additional Cases. A Readme file includes instructions for using the files. See the "Read This Before You Begin" page for more information on Data Files.

Solution Files Solution Files contain every file students are asked to create or modify in the tutorials, Review Assignments, Case Problems, Extra Case Problems and Additional Cases. A Help file on the Instructor's Resource Kit includes information for using the Solution files.

Course Labs: Concepts Come to Life These highly interactive computer-based learning activities bring concepts to life with illustrations, animations, digital images, and simulations. The Labs guide students step-by-step, present them with Quick Check questions, let them explore on their own, test their comprehension, and provide printed feedback. Lab icons at the beginning of the tutorial and in the tutorial margins indicate when a topic has a corresponding Lab. Lab Assignments are included at the end of each relevant tutorial. The Labs available with this book and the tutorials in which they appear are:

TUTORIAL 3   TUTORIAL 4

Figure Files Many figures in the text are provided on the IRK CD-ROM to help illustrate key topics or concepts. Instructors can create traditional overhead transparencies by printing the figure files. Or they can create electronic slide shows by using the figures in a presentation program such as PowerPoint.

Course Test Manager: Testing and Practice at the Computer or on Paper Course Test Manager is cutting-edge, Windows-based testing software that helps instructors design and administer practice tests and actual examinations. Course Test Manager can automatically grade the tests students take at the computer and can generate statistical information on individual as well as group performance.

More innovative technology

Course CBT

Enhance your students' Office 2000 classroom learning experience with self-paced computer-based training on CD-ROM. Course CBT engages students with interactive multimedia and hands-on simulations that reinforce and complement the concepts and skills covered in the textbook. All the content is aligned with the MOUS (Microsoft Office User Specialist) program, making it a great preparation tool for the certification exams. Course CBT also includes extensive pre- and post-assessments that test students' mastery of skills. These pre- and post-assessments automatically generate a "custom learning path" through the course that highlights only the topics students need help with.

Skills Assessment Manager (SAM)

How well do your students *really* know Microsoft Office? SAM is a performance-based testing program that measures students' proficiency in Microsoft Office 2000. SAM is available for Office 2000 in either a live or simulated environment. You can use SAM to place students into or out of courses, monitor their performance throughout a course, and help prepare them for the MOUS certification exams.

CyberClass

CyberClass is a Web-based tool designed for on-campus or distance learning. Use it to enhance how you currently run your class by posting assignments and your course syllabus or holding online office hours. Or, use it for your distance learning course, and offer mini-lectures, conduct online discussion groups, or give your mid-term exam. For more information, visit our Web site at: **www.course.com/products/cyberclass/index.html**.

WebCT

WebCT is a tool used to create Web-based educational environments and also uses WWW browsers as the interface for the course-building environment. The site is hosted on your school campus, allowing complete control over the information. WebCT has its own internal communication system, offering internal e-mail, a Bulletin Board, and a Chat room. Course Technology offers pre-existing supplemental information to help in your WebCT class creation, such as a suggested Syllabus, Lecture Notes, Figures in the Book / Course Presenter, Student Downloads, and Test Banks in which you can schedule an exam, create reports, and more.

Acknowledgments

The authors would like to thank the following reviewers for their valuable feedback on this project: Janette Moody, The Citadel, and Linda Reis, Garland County Community College. Also we give special thanks to Melissa Dezotell, Associate Product Manager; Christine Spillett, Senior Production Editor; Rachel Crapser, Series Technology Editor; Greg Donald, Managing Editor; Donna Gridley, Senior Editor; Catherine Donaldson, Product Manager; John Bosco, Quality Assurance Project Leader; John Freitas and Andrew Schiarretta, QA testers; and the staff at GEX. Thank you all for your expertise, enthusiasm, and vision for this book. Finally, we would like to thank Rose Marie Kuebbing, our developmental editor, for her expert assistance and friendly support.

S. Scott Zimmerman
Beverly B. Zimmerman

BRIEF CONTENTS

TABLE OF CONTENTS

Tutorial 2   PPT 2.01

Creating and Modifying Text and Graphic Objects

Preparing a Sales Presentation

Tutorial 3   PPT 3.03

Preparing and Presenting a Slide Show

Annual Report of Inca Imports International

Reference Window List

Tutorial Tips

These tutorials will help you learn about Microsoft PowerPoint 2000. The tutorials are designed to be worked through at a computer. Each tutorial is divided into sessions. Watch for the session headings, such as Session 1.1 and Session 1.2. Each session is designed to be completed in about 45 minutes, but take as much time as you need. It's also a good idea to take a break between sessions.

To use the tutorials effectively read the following questions and answers before you begin.

Where do I start?

Each tutorial begins with a case, which sets the scene for the tutorial and gives you background information to help you understand what you will be doing. Read the case before you go to the lab. In the lab, begin with the first session of a tutorial.

How do I know what to do on the computer?

Each session contains steps that you will perform on the computer to learn how to use Microsoft PowerPoint 2000. Read the text that introduces each series of steps. The steps you need to do at a computer are numbered and are set against a shaded background. Read each step carefully and completely before you try it.

How do I know if I did the step correctly?

As you work, compare your computer screen with the corresponding figure in the tutorial. Don't worry if your screen display is somewhat different from the figure. The important parts of the screen display are labeled in each figure. Check to make sure these parts are on your screen.

What if I make a mistake?

Don't worry about making mistakes—they are part of the learning process. Paragraphs labeled "TROUBLE?" identify common problems and explain how to get back on track. Follow the steps in a TROUBLE? paragraph only if you are having the problem described. If you run into other problems:

- Carefully consider the current state of your system, the position of the pointer, and any messages on the screen.

- Complete the sentence, "Now I want to…" Be specific, because identifying your goal will help you rethink the steps you need to take to reach that goal.

- If you are working on a particular piece of software, consult the Help system.

- If the suggestions above don't solve your problem, consult your technical support person for assistance.

How do I use the Reference Windows?

Reference Windows summarize the procedures you will learn in the tutorial steps. Do not complete the actions in the Reference Windows when you are working through the tutorial. Instead, refer to the Reference Windows while you are working on the assignments at the end of the tutorial.

How can I test my understanding of the material I learned in the tutorial?

At the end of each session, you can answer the Quick Check questions. The answers for the Quick Checks are at the end of that tutorial.

After you have completed the entire tutorial, you should complete the Review Assignments and Case Problems. They are carefully structured so that you will review what you have learned and then apply your knowledge to new situations.

What if I can't remember how to do something?

You should refer to the Task Reference at the end of the book; it summarizes how to accomplish tasks using the most efficient method.

Before you begin the tutorials, you should know the basics about your computer's operating system. You should also know how to use the menus, dialog boxes, Help system, and My Computer.

How can I prepare for MOUS Certification?

The Microsoft Office User Specialist (MOUS) logo on the cover of this book indicates that Microsoft has approved it as a study guide for Microsoft PowerPoint 2000. At the back of this text, you'll see a chart that outlines the specific Microsoft certification skills for Microsoft PowerPoint 2000 that are covered in the tutorials. You'll need to learn these skills if you're interested in taking a MOUS exam. If you decide to take a MOUS exam, or if you just want to study a specific skill, this chart will give you an easy reference to the page number on which the skill is covered. To learn more about the MOUS certification program refer to the preface in the front of the book or go to **http://www.mous.net**.

Now that you've read the Tutorial Tips, you are ready to begin.

New Perspectives on

PRESENTATION CONCEPTS

TUTORIAL 1   PRES 1.03

Planning and Developing Your Presentation

Presentations for Youth Essential Services (YES!), a Nonprofit Service Agency

TUTORIAL 2   PRES 2.01

Giving Your Presentation

Presentation to the Student Senate at Rocky Mountain State College

OBJECTIVES

In this tutorial you will:

- Write a statement of purpose for your presentation

- Analyze the needs and expectations of your audience

- Assess the situation in which you'll give your presentation

- Select an appropriate medium for your presentation

- Limit your topic to provide focus

- Outline the general organization of a presentation

- Develop an effective introduction, body, and conclusion

PLANNING AND DEVELOPING YOUR PRESENTATION

Presentations for Youth Essential Services (YES!), a Nonprofit Service Agency

Giving Presentations for YES!

As a student at Rocky Mountain State College, you recently obtained an internship with Youth Essential Services (YES!), a private, nonprofit organization serving school-aged children with physical and mental disabilities in the Colorado Springs area. The mission of YES! is to provide developmentally challenged youth with training and motivational programs to help them function effectively in society. Presently, the organization serves between 1100 and 1300 young people each month.

Kenna McNaughton, executive director of YES!, says that you'll make many oral presentations as part of your internship. Some of these presentations will be brief and informal, such as communicating pertinent information to the YES! staff, or providing training to volunteers. Other presentations will be lengthy and formal, such as reporting on the status of programs to the Board of Directors, or requesting funds from potential donors. Sometimes you'll need to convey your entire message in an oral format; other times your presentation might supplement a written document, such as a financial statement or a wrap-up report for a successful project. Sometimes you'll give your presentation as part of a group or team; other times you'll give your presentation alone. The success of your internship—and of many of the organization's programs—will depend upon the quality of your presentations.

SESSION 1.1

In this session, you'll learn the skills for planning a presentation: determining the purpose of your presentation, analyzing the needs and expectations of your audience or listeners, assessing the situation (environment) for your presentation, and choosing an appropriate medium. Regardless of the type of presentation you give, its effectiveness will be determined by how well you plan your presentation.

Planning Your Presentation

Plan your oral presentation the same way you would plan a written document—consider your purpose, audience, and situation. Oral presentations, however, differ from written documents in the demands placed upon your audience, so you'll need to apply special techniques to ensure a successful presentation.

Planning a presentation in advance will improve the quality of your presentation, make it more effective and enjoyable, and, in the long run, save you time and effort. As you plan your presentation, you should determine why you're giving the presentation, who will be listening to the presentation, and where the presentation will take place.

Figure 1-1	PLANNING SAVES TIME

Specific questions you should ask yourself about the presentation include:

- What is the purpose of this presentation?
- What type of presentation do I need to give?
- Who is the audience for my presentation, and what do they need and expect?
- What is the situation (location and setting) for my presentation?
- What is the most appropriate media for my presentation?

Answering these questions will help you create a more effective presentation, and will enable you to feel confident in presenting your ideas. The following sections will help you answer these questions in planning your presentation.

Determining the Purpose of Your Presentation

■ Your purpose in giving a presentation will vary according to each particular situation, so the best way to determine your purpose is to ask yourself why you're giving this presentation and what you expect to accomplish. Common purposes for giving presentations include to inform, to persuade, and to demonstrate or train. We'll now consider these types of presentations.

Giving Informative Presentations

Informative presentations provide your audience with background information, knowledge, and specific details about a topic that enable them to make informed decisions, form attitudes, or increase their expertise on a topic.

Examples of informative presentations include:

■ Academic or professional conference presentations

■ Briefings on the status of projects

■ Reviews or evaluations of products and services

■ Reports at company meetings

■ Luncheon or dinner speeches

■ Informal symposia

| Figure 1-2 | PROVIDE BACKGROUND AND DETAILS |

Informative presentations can address a wide range of topics and are given to a wide range of audiences. For example, you might want to educate students at Rocky Mountain State College about the goals and programs of YES!, or you might want to inform YES! staff members about plans for next month's sports activity. Or, you might want to tell parents of youth participating in YES!-sponsored activities about the organization of the Board of Directors. Your main goal in each instance is to provide useful and relevant information to your intended audience.

Giving Persuasive Presentations

Although every presentation involves influencing an audience to listen and be interested in a specific topic, some presentations are more persuasive than others. Presentations with the specific goal of persuasion attempt to influence how an audience feels or acts regarding a particular position or plan.

Examples of persuasive presentations include:

- Recommendations
- Sales presentations
- Action plans and strategy sessions
- Motivational presentations

Figure 1-3   INFLUENCE YOUR AUDIENCE

Persuasive presentations also cover a wide range of topics and are given to a wide range of audiences. In addition, persuasive presentations are usually designed as balanced arguments involving logical as well as emotional reasons for supporting an action or viewpoint. For example, you might want to persuade students at Rocky Mountain State College to volunteer their time in community service. Or, you might want to recommend a particular fundraising activity to YES! administrators. Or, you might want to motivate parents of YES! participants to apply for additional services for their children. Your goal in each of these persuasive presentations is to convince your audience to accept a particular plan or point of view.

Giving Demonstrations or Training Presentations

Audiences attend demonstrations to see how something works or to understand a process or procedure. Examples of demonstration presentations include:

- Overviews of products and services
- Software demonstrations
- Process explanations

For example, you might want to demonstrate to volunteers from Rocky Mountain State College how to give encouragement and support to handicapped youth at athletic events. Or, you might want to show YES! staff members how the new accounting software handles reimbursements. Or, you might want to show parents of YES! participants how to fill out a transportation release form. In each of these presentations, your goal is to show how something works so your audience understands the process.

Training presentations provide audiences with an opportunity to learn new skills, or to educate themselves on how to perform a task, such as how to operate a piece of equipment. Training presentations usually differ from demonstrations by providing listeners with hands-on experience, practice, and feedback, so they can correct their mistakes and improve their performances. Examples of training presentations include:

- Employee orientation (completing job tasks such as running the copy machine)
- Seminars and workshops
- Educational classes and courses

| Figure 1-4 | SHOW HOW TO PERFORM A TASK |

For example, you might want to provide training to volunteers from Rocky Mountain State College on how to manage conflict during team sports. Or, you might want to present a seminar to the YES! staff on how to write an effective grant proposal. Or, you might want to teach parents of YES! participants how to help their children with basic life skills, such as counting money. In all of these presentations, your goal is to assist your audience in learning and practicing new abilities and skills.

Sometimes you may have more than one purpose for your presentation. For instance, you need to inform the YES! staff of the newly revised policy on transporting participants to organized activities. In addition to explaining the new policy, you'll need to persuade your co-workers of the importance of following the new guidelines. You might also need to answer any questions they have about how to implement certain aspects of the policy.

Having too many purposes can complicate your presentation and keep you from focusing on the specific needs of your audience. For that reason, you should try to limit your presentation to one main purpose, and one or two secondary purposes.

Next you'll analyze what your audience will need and expect from your presentation.

Analyzing **Your Audience's Needs and Expectations**

The more you know about your listeners, the more you'll be able to adapt your presentation to their needs. By putting yourself in your listeners' shoes, you'll be able to visualize your audience as more than just a group of passive listeners, and anticipate what they need and expect from your presentation. Anticipating the needs of your audience will also increase the chances that your audience will react favorably to your presentation.

When you give a presentation to YES! employees, your audience consists of professionals, such as counselors, therapists, and support staff. Audiences in these categories typically are interested in specifics related to their job functions, as well as how your desired outcomes will impact their workload, fulfill their goals and objectives, and affect their budget. In addition, YES! coworkers usually want a less formal presentation than audiences outside your organization.

When you give your presentation at Rocky Mountain State College, your audience will consist of other students and interested faculty and administrators. They will expect to learn: how student involvement in community service benefits the campus community; how community service experiences can supplement what students learn in the classroom; how a partnership between YES! and Rocky Mountain State College would function; and what the administrative costs would be for the university.

Other characteristics of your audience that you'll want to consider include demographic features such as age, gender, level of education, and familiarity with your topic.

Figure 1-6	ADAPT TO THE NEEDS OF YOUR AUDIENCE

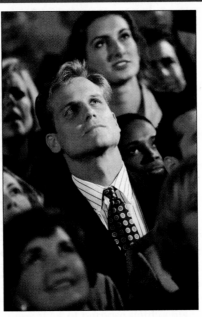

Examples of how demographic characteristics can affect your presentations include:

■ **Age:** People of different age groups may vary in terms of attention span and the way they relate to examples. A presentation on the educational impact of student involvement in community service would be appropriate for college students, but probably not for elementary-school students. Moreover, young children have shorter attention spans and generally can't sit for as long as adults. Presentations to young children should be divided into short sessions interspersed with physical activity.

- **Gender:** It's important to fairly represent both genders by avoiding male pronouns (he, his) to represent both sexes, and by using examples that show both men and women performing all jobs at work and at home.

- **Education:** Audiences with specialized training expect examples that use terms and concepts from their field. Audiences with more education expect a higher level of technicality than audiences with less education.

- **Familiarity with the topic:** Audiences familiar with your topic won't need as many definitions and explanations as audiences not familiar with your topic.

In addition to analyzing general features and characteristics of your audience, you should also consider how your audience will use the information that you present. YES! administrators attending a presentation on potential fundraising activities need to know how much money other organizations have raised, and how much the fundraising activity itself would cost, in order to estimate their net profit.

Understanding the needs and expectations of your audience helps you adapt the content of your presentation to a particular audience, and enables you to address their concerns. By anticipating questions your listeners might ask about your topic, you can address those questions and concerns in your presentation. Finally, understanding the needs and concerns of your audience assures that your presentation is useful, interesting, and relevant.

REFERENCE WINDOW   RW

Questions for Analyzing Your Audience

- Who will be listening to my presentation (peers, superiors, subordinates, strangers)?
- What do they expect me to talk about?
- What general characteristics do I know about the audience (age, gender, education level, knowledge of the topic)?
- What do they need to know about the topic (general background or overview, details, cost estimates)?
- How will my listeners use this information (make decisions, perform a task)?
- What are my audience's major concerns or objections (too expensive, too difficult)?
- What do I want my audience to think, know, or do as a result of this presentation?

In your presentation about YES!, you realize that your audience will be your peers. They will vary in their experience with your topic, but most of them will be familiar with volunteerism. The biggest concern of college students is that involvement in service activities with YES! might be too time-consuming. You'll need to address that concern in your presentation.

Figure 1.7 provides a basic worksheet for helping you analyze the needs and expectations of your audience for this and other presentations.

Figure 1-7	AUDIENCE ANALYSIS WORKSHEET

Audience Analysis
Worksheet

Who will be listening to your presentation? Check all that apply.
☐ Peers
☐ Superiors
☐ Subordinates
☐ Strangers

What do they expect you to talk about?
_____
_____

What general characteristics do you know about the audience?
Age _____
Gender _____
Education _____
Experience with topic _____
Other _____

What does your audience need to know about the topic? Check and explain all that apply.
☐ General background or overview _____
☐ Details _____
☐ Cost estimates _____
☐ Other _____

How will your listeners use this information? Check and explain all that apply.
☐ Make decisions _____
☐ Perform a task _____
☐ Form an opinion _____
☐ Increase understanding _____
☐ Other _____

What are your audience's biggest concerns or objections? Check and explain all that apply.
☐ Too expensive _____
☐ Too difficult _____
☐ Other _____

What do you want your audience to think, know, or do as a result of this presentation?
_____
_____
_____

Assessing the Situation for Your Presentation

Many of your presentations will involve speaking on the same subject to different audiences and in different settings. Planning an effective presentation will be a matter of learning to adapt your content to each unique situation. The more you know about the circumstances, the better you can adapt your presentation to different audiences.

Probably the most important aspect to consider is how much time you'll have, and whether someone else will speak before or after you. Speaking with others means you'll have to watch your time closely so you don't infringe on someone else's time. It can also mean that you'll have to cut your presentation short because someone has used part of your time. Even if you're the sole speaker, it's wise to make back-up plans in case your time limit changes just before you speak.

Figure 1-8 SETTING AND LOCATIONS AFFECT EXPECTATIONS

The setting for a presentation can affect audience expectations, and hence will dictate the appropriate level of formality. That's why it's important to know where your presentation will occur, including the size and shape of the room, and the seating arrangement. The small conference room with a round table and moveable chairs at YES! headquarters would call for a much more informal presentation than the large rectangular lecture hall with fixed seating at Rocky Mountain State College.

You'll also need to adapt your presentation according to the size of your audience. Four or five co-workers at YES! would probably expect to be able to interrupt your presentation and ask questions or express their own views, versus the expectations of a large audience at Rocky Mountain State College. The setting for your presentation and size of your audience also influence the type of medium you can use, and the size of your visuals. Students in large rooms often sit toward the back of the room, far away from your visuals. You will need to increase the size of your visuals in your presentation at Rocky Mountain State College, or use an overhead, slide, or computer projection system. On the other hand, if your audience at YES! is fewer than ten people, you might be able to use a laptop computer screen for your visuals.

REFERENCE WINDOW **RW**

Questions For Analyzing Your Presentation Situation

- How much time will I have for my presentation?
- Will I be speaking alone or with other people?
- How large will the audience be?
- How formal or informal will the setting be?
- What will the room be like, and how will it be arranged?
- What equipment will be available for my presentation (chalkboard, overhead projector, slide projector, computer projection system)?
- Do I have the skills to operate available equipment?
- Who will be available to assist me in case of an equipment failure?
- How much time will I have to set up for my presentation?
- What other aspects must I consider (temperature, extraneous noises)?
- Who will be available to assist me with room temperature, lights, or extraneous noise problems?
- How should I introduce myself and my qualifications?

Now you need to decide what kind of media you'll use in your presentation.

Selecting Appropriate Media

As you plan your presentation, you'll need to select the media you'll use to support and clarify your presentation. Media commonly used for oral presentations include:

- Chalkboard
- Whiteboard
- Notepad and easel
- Flip chart
- Posters
- Black-and-white or color overheads
- Handouts
- 35mm slides
- Computer-projected visuals, such as PowerPoint slides.

In selecting appropriate media for your presentation, it's important to fit the media to your particular purpose, audience, and situation. Every medium allows you to provide support for the points you'll make in your presentation, and help your audience see and hear your ideas. Each medium, however, has its own strengths and limitations. We'll consider those now.

Using a Chalkboard, Whiteboard, or Notepad

Chalkboards, whiteboards, or large paper notepads work well for small meetings and informal discussions, and are especially helpful in stressing important points from your presentation, or in recording comments from the audience. These media usually require little advance preparation, other than bringing along a piece of chalk or a marker, and they come in portable forms.

Figure 1-9   **CHALKBOARDS EMPHASIZE MAIN POINTS**

On the other hand, these media have disadvantages, including the difficulty of speaking to your audience while you write or draw. If your handwriting is difficult to read, it can detract from your presentation, as can poor spelling. In addition, these media are only effective for writing a few words or short phrases, or making simple drawings.

Using a Flip Chart

Flip charts can be used in both formal and informal settings. Using a flip chart with previously prepared pictures and visuals allows you to highlight the main points of your presentation, and present information in an appropriate sequence. Flip charts work best when used in a small, well-lighted room.

Figure 1-10	FLIP CHARTS SHOW SEQUENCE

The disadvantages of flip charts are that they are too small to be seen in large rooms or by large audiences, they require significant advance preparation, and they are cumbersome.

Using Posters

Posters or written summaries of your presentation that can be displayed on stationary blackboards or attached to the walls of a room are effective for letting audiences refer to your presentation before or after the event. Posters are especially prevalent at academic or professional conferences, and presenters often stand by their posters to answer questions from the audience.

Figure 1-11	POSTERS PROVIDE VISUAL SUMMARIES

Because posters usually contain professional lettering, as well as technical graphics and illustrations, they can't be easily revised, and they do require advance preparation.

Using Black-and-White or Color Overheads

Overheads are used a lot so required equipment is usually accessible. Creating overheads can be as simple as copying your presentation notes onto overhead transparencies. Overheads do require some advance preparation, however, or they look amateurish or uninteresting. In addition, overheads are ineffective if the lettering is too small or too dense.

Figure 1-12	OVERHEADS FOCUS ATTENTION

Overheads allow for flexibility in your presentation as they can quickly be reordered or adjusted, as necessary. You can also draw on overheads using a transparency marker during your presentation.

Using Handouts

Handouts give your listeners something to take with them following your presentation, such as a summary of key points or numerical data. Handouts can assist your listeners in understanding difficult concepts, and can also alleviate the difficulties of taking notes.

Figure 1-13	HANDOUTS ALLEVIATE NOTE TAKING

Although handouts are helpful, they require advance preparation to look professional. Also, be careful that your handouts don't detract from your presentation by enticing your audience to pay more attention to them than your presentation.

Using 35mm Slides

Using 35mm slides requires advance preparation, so you must allow enough time to take pictures, and have them developed into professional-looking slides. Slides are especially good for presentations in a formal setting, in large rooms, or with large audiences. Slides require that you turn the lights down, however, which makes it difficult for you to see your presentation notes, for the audience to take notes, and for some people to stay awake. In addition, using slides forces you to choose between facing your audience and standing at a distance from the slide projector, or standing behind the slide projector and talking to the backs of your audience.

Figure 1-14	SLIDES HELP LARGE AUDIENCES

You can increase the effectiveness of your slide presentation by using a hand-held remote to advance your slides, and a laser pointer to draw attention to important aspects of the slides. Or, you could give the presentation in tandem with someone else—you as the presenter and the other person as the operator of the equipment.

Using Electronic On-Screen Presentations

Electronic on-screen presentations (such as those created with Microsoft PowerPoint, Corel Presentations, or some other presentation software package) allow you to create professional-looking presentations with a consistent visual design. They also enable you to incorporate other media into your presentations, such as photographs, sound, animation, and video clips. Electronic on-screen presentations are also easy to update or revise on the spot, and can easily be converted into other media, such as overheads, posters, or 35mm slides.

| Figure 1-15 | INCORPORATE OTHER MEDIA |

Electronic on-screen presentations require special equipment such as a computer projection system which may not always be available. And, sometimes you must present your computer presentation in a darkened room, making it difficult for you to see your notes and for your listeners to take notes. You can reduce the difficulty by asking someone else to operate the computer equipment for you.

In addition, electronic on-screen presentations require advance preparation and set up to ensure compatibility of the computer, the projection system, and the disk containing your presentation files. Moreover, many presenters create on-screen presentations that are too elaborate, rather than simple and straightforward.

REFERENCE WINDOW | **RW**

Strengths and Weaknesses of Presentation Media

Type of Medium	Strengths	Weaknesses	Audience Size	Advance Preparation	Formality
Chalkboard Whiteboard Notepad	Enables audience input; good for summarizing; adaptable	Must write and talk simultaneously; requires good handwriting and spelling	Small	None required	Informal
Flip chart	Can highlight main points and sequence information	Too small to be seen in large room; cumbersome	Small	Required	Formal and Informal
Posters	Can be referred to following your presentation; good for displaying other materials	Can't be easily revised; needs explanation	Medium, Large	Required	Formal and Informal
Overheads	Equipment readily available; adaptable; can draw on	Often boring, uninteresting, or ineffective	Medium, Large	Required	Formal and Informal
Handouts	Alleviates taking notes; can be referred to later	Can distract from your presentation	Small, Medium, Large	Required	Formal and Informal
35mm slides	Good for formal presentations in large rooms	Difficult to see your notes and to advance slides; require special equipment	Large	Extensive preparation required	Formal
Electronic on-screen slides	Incorporates media; good for formal presentations in large rooms	May be too elaborate or distracting; require special equipment	Small, Large	Extensive preparation required	Formal

Since every medium has its disadvantages, you might want to use more than one medium in your presentation. At the college you'll give your presentation in a room that isn't equipped with a computer projection system, but does have a large chalkboard and overhead projector. So you might want to create a poster displaying photographs of YES! activities and participants, show an overhead transparency explaining how the partnership between YES! and the university would work, and prepare a handout containing information on YES! service projects.

No matter what media you use, your goal should be to keep your presentation simple and to adapt it to the purpose, audience, and situation of each unique situation.

Figure 1.16 provides a basic worksheet for helping you assess the situation and media for this and other presentations.

Figure 1-16 ○ **SITUATION ASSESSMENT WORKSHEET**

Situation and Media Assessment
Worksheet

How much time will you have for your presentation and the setup? _____

How large will your audience be? _____

How formal will the setting be? _____

What will the room be like and how will it be arranged? _____

What equipment will be available for your presentation? Check all that apply.
☐ Chalkboard
☐ Whiteboard
☐ Notepad and easel
☐ Stationary posterboard
☐ Overhead projector
☐ Slide projector
☐ Computer projection system

What other aspects must you consider for your presentation?
Temperature _____
Lighting _____
Noise and distractions _____
Other _____

Who will assist you with the equipment and other situational aspects?
Friend or colleague _____
Media or custodial staff _____
Other _____

How will you introduce yourself and your qualifications?
_____
_____
_____

What media will be appropriate for your presentation? Check appropriate media and explain.
☐ Chalkboard _____
☐ Whiteboard _____
☐ Notepad and easel _____
☐ Flip chart _____
☐ Poster _____
☐ Black-and-white or color overheads _____
☐ Handouts _____
☐ 35mm slides _____
☐ Computer Projected visuals, such as PowerPoint slides _____

Session 1.1 QUICK CHECK

1. Define and give examples for the following types of presentations:

   a. informative presentation

   b. persuasive presentation

   c. demonstration or training session

2. In two or three sentences, describe how knowing the education level of an audience would affect a presentation on trademarks and copyright laws.

3. List at least two important questions you should ask as part of assessing the presentation situation.

4. Consider the following presentations. In each instance list two media that would be effective for that presentation, and explain why you think those media would be effective. Then list two media that would be ineffective for that presentation and explain why.

   a. a presentation at the local hardware store to eight to 10 homeowners on how to successfully remodel a kitchen

   b. a presentation at a hotel ballroom to 40 to 50 convention planners on why they should hold their next convention in Colorado Springs

   c. a presentation to two or three administrative staff at a local business on how to conduct a successful Web conference

5. List two media that are useful for recording comments from the audience.

6. If you want to use sound and animation in your presentation, which medium should you use?

SESSION 1.2

In this session, you'll learn how to focus your presentation, and develop an effective introduction, body, and conclusion for that presentation.

Focusing Your Presentation

Once you determine your purpose, analyze your audience's needs and expectations, and assess the particular situation in which you'll give your presentation, you need to plan the content of your presentation. You should begin by identifying the major points or main ideas that are directly relevant to your listeners' needs and interests, and then focus on those.

One of the biggest problems every presenter faces is how to make the topic manageable. Your tendency will be to want to include every aspect of a topic, but trying to cover every facet usually means that you'll give your audience irrelevant information and lose their interest. Focusing on one aspect of a topic is like bringing a picture into focus with your camera—it clarifies your subject and allows you to emphasize interesting details. Failing to focus, in presentations as in photography, always brings disappointment to you and your audience.

How you focus your topic will depend upon the purpose, audience, and situation for your presentation. Remember, the narrower the topic, the more specific and interesting the information will be. Strategies for limiting your presentation topic are the same as those you would use to limit the scope of any written document—focus on a particular time or chronology, geography or region, category, component or element, segment or portion of a procedure, or point of view.

- Time or chronology: Limiting a topic by time means you focus on a few years, rather than trying to cover the entire history of a topic. Unfocused: The history of Egypt from 640 to 2000. Focused: The history of Egypt during the Nasser years (1952–1970).

- Geography or region: Limiting a topic by geography or region means you look at a topic as it relates to a specific location. Unfocused: Fly fishing. Focused: Fly fishing in western Colorado.

- Category or classification: Limiting a topic by category means you focus on one member of a group or on a limited function. Unfocused: Thermometers. Focused: Using bimetallic-coil thermometers to control bacteria in restaurant-prepared foods.

- Component or element: Limiting a topic by component or element means you focus on one small aspect or part of an organization or problem. Unfocused: Business trends. Focused: Blending accounting practices and legal services, a converging trend in large businesses.

- Segment or portion: Limiting a topic by segment or portion means you focus on one part of a process or procedure. Unfocused: Designing, manufacturing, characterizing, handling, storing, packaging, and transporting of optical filters. Focused: Acceptance testing of optical filters.

- Point of view: Limiting a topic by point of view means you look at a topic from the perspective of a single group. Unfocused: Employee benefits. Focused: How employers can retain their employees by providing child-care assistance and other nontraditional benefits.

REFERENCE   WINDOW   **RW**

Ways to Limit Your Topic
- Time or chronology
- Geography or region
- Category or classification
- Component or element
- Segment or portion of a process or procedure
- Point of view or perspective

In your presentation about YES! at Rocky Mountain State College, you'll need to limit your topic. You decide to discuss only current programs needing volunteers, not past or future programs. You'll also limit your presentation to service opportunities in the Colorado Springs area, and not include opportunities at the YES! satellite programs throughout the state. In addition, you'll only present information on volunteer programs, not fundraising, budgeting, or legal functions. Further, you'll only discuss how student volunteers assist with recreation therapy, not physical therapy. Finally, you'll approach your topic from a student volunteer's perspective.

Identifying Your Main Ideas

As you identify your main ideas, you should phrase them as conclusions you want your audience to draw from your presentation. This helps you to continue to design your presentation with the listener in mind.

Your main ideas for your presentation about YES! at Rocky Mountain State College include:

1. University students and their communities benefit when students volunteer with nonprofit organizations such as YES!.

2. Students learn as they participate in service that meets a community need.

3. Students can apply what they learn in the classroom to help solve many social and economic problems in the community.

4. A formal partnership between YES! and the university would assist students in obtaining course credit for their service with nonprofit organizations.

You're now prepared to consider the content and organization of your presentation. In the sections that follow, you'll formulate the general organization of your presentation.

Organizing Your Presentation

Once you've finished planning your presentation, you'll need to assemble the contents of your presentation, and organize your ideas in a logical manner. There are many different ways to organize or arrange your presentation, depending upon your purpose, the needs of your audience, and a particular speaking situation. In general, all good presentations start with an effective introduction, continue with a well-organized body, and end with a strong conclusion.

The introduction of a presentation enables you to gain your listeners' attention, establish a relationship with your audience, and preview your main ideas. The body of your presentation is where you'll present pertinent information, solid evidence, and important details. The conclusion allows you to restate your main points, suggest appropriate actions, and recommend further resources.

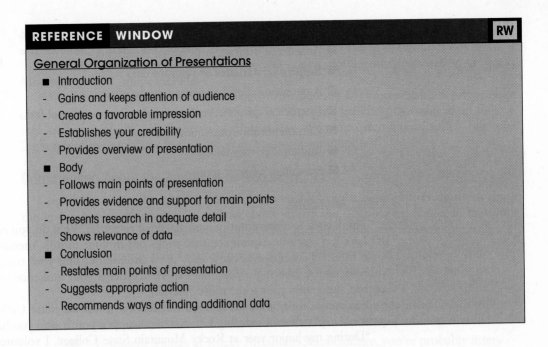

REFERENCE WINDOW | **RW**

General Organization of Presentations

- ■ Introduction
  - Gains and keeps attention of audience
  - Creates a favorable impression
  - Establishes your credibility
  - Provides overview of presentation
- ■ Body
  - Follows main points of presentation
  - Provides evidence and support for main points
  - Presents research in adequate detail
  - Shows relevance of data
- ■ Conclusion
  - Restates main points of presentation
  - Suggests appropriate action
  - Recommends ways of finding additional data

| Figure 1-17 | INTRODUCTION, BODY, AND CONCLUSION |

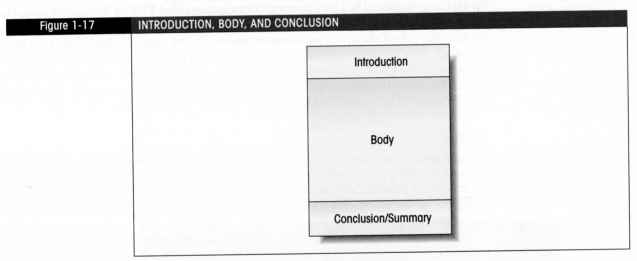

In the next section, you'll learn how to develop the introduction to your presentation.

Developing an Introduction

Your introduction is the most important part of your entire presentation because it provides your listeners' first impression of you and your presentation, and sets the tone for the rest of your presentation. An effective introduction enables you to gain your listeners' attention, establish a rapport with your audience, and provide your listeners with an organizational overview or preview of your presentation.

Gaining Your Audience's Attention

Your first task in giving an effective presentation is to gain and keep your audience's attention. Even if your audience is interested in your topic, they can be easily distracted, so it's important to create an effective introduction that will immediately grab their attention.

In your presentation at Rocky Mountain State College, you might ask a few members of the audience to express their feelings about their volunteer efforts in the past.

Stating Your Purpose Statement

Simply stating your purpose statement works well as an introduction if your audience is already interested in your topic, or your time is limited. Most audiences, however, will appreciate a more creative approach than simply stating, "I'm going to persuade you to support a partnership between Rocky Mountain State University and YES!, a local nonprofit organization." Instead you might say something like, "My purpose is to discuss a situation that affects almost every student at Rocky Mountain State University."

Because you'll be giving many presentations throughout your career, you'll want to be on the lookout for ideas for effective introductions. You might want to keep a presentations file for collecting interesting stories and quotations that you can use in preparing future presentations.

REFERENCE WINDOW   **RW**

Ways to Gain Your Audience's Attention

Method for Gaining Attention	Strength of Method
Anecdote or personal experience	Helps audience relate to you as a real person
Surprising statistic or relevant data	Increases audience interest in topic
Quotation, familiar phrase or definition	Leads in well to remainder of presentation
Rhetorical question or issue	Gets audience thinking about topic
Comment about the audience or occasion	Enables you to show your enthusiasm
Audience participation	Encourages audience to add their own ideas
Statement of the topic	Works well if audience is already interested

---

Establishing a Rapport with Your Audience

The methods you use to gain your audience's attention will establish how the audience responds to you and to your presentation. It's important, then, that whatever you do in your introduction creates a favorable impression with your audience, and helps you establish credibility.

If your audience is unfamiliar with you or no one formally introduces you, you should introduce yourself and provide your credentials to establish a rapport with your audience. Be careful not to spend much time on this, however, or to distance yourself from your audience by over-emphasizing your accomplishments.

In your presentation at Rocky Mountain State College, you might start out by simply saying, "Hi. I'm_____, a Senior at RMSC and a Recreation Management major."

Providing an Overview of Your Presentation

One of the most important aspects of an introduction is to provide your audience with an overview of your presentation. Research indicates that overviews, sometimes called advance organizers, prepare your audience for each point that will follow, and provide them with a structure for plugging in your main points. Overviews help your audience understand and remember your presentation because they provide a road map of it.

Overviews should be brief and simple, stating what you plan to do and in what order. After you've given your audience an overview of your presentation, it's important that you follow that same order.

Avoiding Common Mistakes in an Introduction

An inadequate introduction can ruin the rest of your presentation no matter how well you've prepared. So you should allow yourself plenty of time to carefully plan your introductions. In addition, you should consider these guidelines to avoid common mistakes:

- Don't begin by apologizing about any aspect of your presentation, such as how nervous you are, or your lack of preparation. Apologies destroy your credibility and guarantee that your audience will react negatively to what you present.
- Check the accuracy and currency of your stories, examples, and data. Audiences don't appreciate being misled, misinformed, or manipulated.
- Steer clear of anything potentially vulgar, ridiculing, or sexist. You won't be respected or listened to once you offend your audience.
- Don't use gimmicks to begin your presentation, such as making a funny face, singing a song, or ringing a bell. Members of your audience won't know how to respond and will feel uncomfortable.
- Avoid trite, flattering, or phony statements, such as, "Ladies and gentlemen, it is an unfathomable honor to be in your presence." Gaining respect requires treating your audience as your equal.
- Don't coerce people into participating. Always ask for volunteers. Putting reluctant members of your audience on the spot embarrasses everyone.
- Be cautious when using humor. It's difficult to predict how audiences will respond to jokes and other forms of humor; therefore, you should avoid using humor unless you know your audience well.

Once you've introduced your topic, you're ready to develop the major points or body of your presentation.

Developing **the Body of Your Presentation**

To develop the body of your presentation, you'll need to gather information on your topic, determine the organizational approach, add supporting details and other pertinent information, and provide transitions from one point to the next.

Gathering Information

Most of the time, you'll give presentations on topics about which you're knowledgeable and comfortable. Other times, you might have to give presentations on topics that are new to you. In either case, you'll probably need to do research to provide additional information that is effective, pertinent, and up-to-date.

You can find additional materials on your topic by consulting:

- Popular press items from newspapers, radio, TV, and magazines. This information, geared for general audiences, provides surface-level details and personal opinions that may need to be supplemented by additional research.

| Figure 1-19 | USING NEWSPAPERS AND MAGAZINES |

■ Library resources such as books, specialized encyclopedias, academic jour-
nals, government publications, and other reference materials. You can access
these materials using the library's card catalog, indexes, computer searches,
and professional database services.

| Figure 1-20 | USING INFORMATION IN LIBRARIES |

■ Corporate documents and office correspondence. Since using these materials
might violate your company's nondisclosure policy, you might need to obtain
your company's permission, or get legal clearance.

Figure 1-21	USING CORPORATE DOCUMENTS

■ Experts and authorities in the field, or other members of your organization. Talking to others who are knowledgeable about your topic will give you additional insight.

Figure 1-22	TALKING TO EXPERTS AND AUTHORITIES

■ Interviews, surveys, and observations. If you do your own interviews, surveys, and observations, be prepared with a list of specific questions, and always be respectful of other people's time.

| Figure 1-23 | INTERVIEWING AND SURVEYING |

■ Internet sources. The Web has become an excellent place to find information on any topic. Be sure, however, to evaluate the credibility of anything you obtain from these sources.

| Figure 1-24 | USING THE INTERNET |

For your presentation at Rocky Mountain State College, you located the following additional information: an article from the *Colorado Springs Daily Scribe* entitled, "YES! Helps Children Meet Their Challenges;" a book from the RMSC library entitled, *A Guidebook for Providing Opportunities for Experiential Education in Higher Education*; the YES! organization's latest annual report; an informal survey of 25 current interns showing their attitudes toward establishing a partnership between YES! and RMSC; and printouts of the YES! Web page describing the organization's funding sources and current activities.

After you fully research your topic, you're ready to organize the information in an understandable and logical manner so that your listeners can easily follow your ideas.

Organizing Your Information

You should choose an organizational approach for your information based upon the purpose, audience, and situation of each specific presentation. Sometimes your company or supervisor might ask you to follow a particular pattern or template in giving your presentations. Other times you might be able to choose your own organizational approach. Some common approach options include: inductive, deductive, chronological, spatial, and problem-solution organizational patterns.

Organizing Information Inductively

Organizing information inductively means you begin with the individual facts and save your conclusions until the end of your presentation. Inductively organized presentations usually are more difficult to follow because the most important information may come at the end of a presentation. Inductive organization can be useful, however, when your purpose is to persuade your audience to follow an unusual plan of action, or you feel your audience might resist your conclusions.

Figure 1-25	INDUCTIVE ORGANIZATION

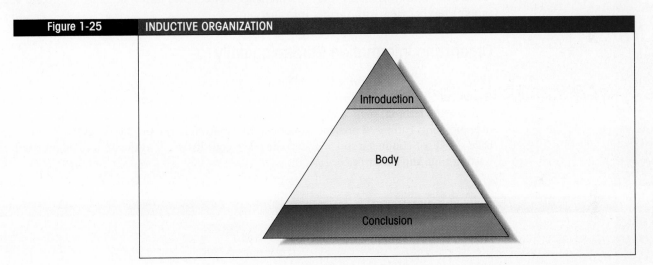

If you thought student leaders at Rocky Mountain State College would resist your recommendation (that $600,000 from student fees be allocated to the operating budget of a new Student Community Involvement Center), you would probably want to first present your reasons for making that recommendation.

Organizing Information Deductively

Organizing information deductively means you present your conclusions or solutions first, and then explain the information that led you to reach your conclusions. Deductive organization is the most common pattern used in business because it presents the most important or bottom-line information first.

Figure 1-26	DEDUCTIVE ORGANIZATION

Introduction/Conclusion

Body

Summary

Deductive organization works well for informative presentations because it allows your audience to know your recommendations at the beginning of the presentation when their attention level is highest. Organizing your presentation at Rocky Mountain State College in a deductive manner would mean that you would begin by stating your opinion that student leaders should support an official partnership between the university and YES!, and then supporting that view with further information.

Organizing Information Chronologically

When you organize information chronologically, you organize things according to a time sequence. Chronological organization works best when you must present information in a step-by-step fashion, such as demonstrating a procedure, or training someone to use a piece of equipment. Failing to present sequential information in the proper order (such as how to bake a cake, or conduct a soil analysis) can leave your listeners confused, and might result in wasting time and resources.

Figure 1-27	CHRONOLOGICAL ORGANIZATION

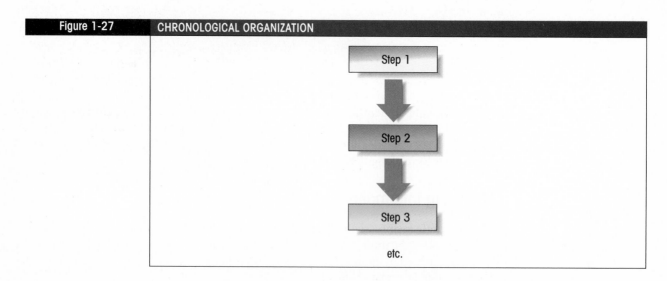

Step 1

Step 2

Step 3

etc.

If you were explaining to administrators how to answer a Request for Proposal (RFP) to obtain government funding for YES! activities, you would need to explain how to complete the process in a specified sequence.

Organizing Information Spatially

Spatial organization is used to provide a logical and effective order for describing the physical layout of an item or system.

Figure 1-28	SPATIAL ORGANIZATION

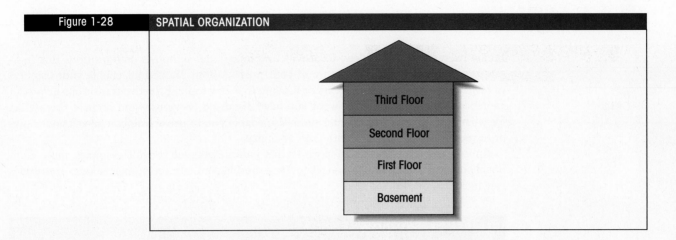

If you were describing the blueprints or plans for a new building for YES!, you would begin by describing all the rooms on the bottom floor, then proceed to the next floor and describe all the rooms on that floor, and so on.

Organizing Information by Problem and Solutions

Using the problem-solution method of organization consists of presenting a problem, outlining various solutions to the problem, and then explaining the solution you recommend. Problem-solution presentations work best when your purpose is to recommend a specific action or solution over several alternative actions or solutions.

REFERENCE WINDOW   **RW**

Ways to Organize Your Presentation

Organizational Pattern	Explanation of Pattern	Type of Presentation
Deductive	Present conclusions or solutions first	Informative presentations
Inductive	Present conclusions or solutions last	Persuasive presentations
Chronological	Order by time sequence	Demonstrations and training
Spatial	Order by space or position	Physical layouts
Problem/Solution	Present problem and various solutions, then recommend solution	Persuasive presentations

Supporting **Your Main Points**

In every presentation, it's important to keep the information simple and relevant. Research has shown that our short-term memory limits what we can recall to a maximum of seven chunks of information, and that we remember specific, concrete details long after we remember generalities or unrelated pieces of information.

You should, therefore, support the main points of your presentation with evidence in the form of specific reasons, explanations, examples, data, or agreement of experts. In addition, you should try to intersperse difficult concepts with easier-to-understand material, and try to move from what your audience already understands to new information.

Providing Transitions

In any presentation, you need to provide organizational signposts or transitions that indicate the organization and structure of your presentation. Transitions enable your listeners to realize that you're shifting gears or moving to a new topic. Effective transitions help your audience mentally summarize what you have discussed previously and prepare themselves for what you'll discuss next. Transitions also enable you to pause briefly to check your notes or to reestablish eye contact with your audience.

Appropriate transitions include words that indicate you will provide examples, make additional points, compare similar concepts, discuss results, or make recommendations. Transitions may include:

REFERENCE WINDOW   RW

Purpose	Word or Phrase
Provide examples	For example, For instance, To illustrate
Make additional points	In addition, Furthermore, Next, Now I will discuss
Establish order	First, Second, Third
Compare	Likewise, In the same manner, Let's consider another
Discuss results	Consequently, Therefore, Thus
Summarize	In brief, To conclude, To move to my last point, Finally
Recommend	I'd like to suggest, What do we do now?

Now that you've developed an effective body for your presentation by supporting your main points with adequate details and creating effective transitions, you're ready to develop a conclusion or summary.

Developing Your Summary or Conclusion

Summaries and conclusions are valuable because they help your listeners remember important information from your presentation and allow you to reemphasize your main points. Your conclusion leaves your audience with a final impression of you and your presentation, so you don't want to leave your conclusion to chance. Plan to spend as much time on the conclusion as you did on your introduction.

The following suggestions will help you create an effective summary or conclusion:

- Use a clear transition to move into your conclusion. This will signal your audience that you're moving from the body of your presentation to the closing statements.

- Recap the key ideas of your presentation. Repeating the main points of your presentation will help your audience remember what you covered.

- Review the relevancy or importance of what you said. Don't introduce new ideas; simply remind your audience why they should care about your topic.

- If appropriate, suggest a clear action step or plan. If your purpose was to persuade your audience to take a specific action, you should use your conclusion to suggest what the audience should do now.

- If possible, suggest where your audience can find additional resources by providing important phone numbers, addresses, e-mail addresses, or Web addresses.

- Relate your conclusion to your introduction. Some experts suggest writing your conclusion at the same time you write your introduction to assure that they both provide the same focus. Whenever you write your conclusion, compare it to your introduction to make sure they are complementary.

- Don't end with an apology or trite statement like "I see my time is up, so I'll quit." When you're finished, say "Thank you," and sit down.

In your presentation at Rocky Mountain State College, you could conclude your presentation by stating, "Now that you've seen how a formal partnership between YES! and the university would work, I'd like to briefly summarize the main points I've made today. First, university students and the communities in which they live both benefit when students volunteer with nonprofit organizations. Second, students become active learners as they apply what they learn in the classroom to help solve community problems. Finally, it's important to establish a formal partnership between these nonprofit organizations and the university so that students can obtain course credit for their work. By allocating $600,000 from student fees toward the operating budget of a new Student Community Involvement Center, you can help students take advantage of opportunities for experiential learning, while helping Chad and the 1300 other young people like him."

Figure 1-29 provides a basic worksheet for helping you determine the focus and organization for this and other presentations.

Figure 1-29	FOCUS AND ORGANIZATION WORKSHEET

**Focus and Organization
Worksheet**

How will you focus your presentation?
Time or chronology _____
Geography or region _____
Category or classification _____
Component or element _____
Segment or portion _____
Point of view _____

What are your main ideas for your presentation?
_____
_____
_____

How will you gain your audience's attention?
Anecdote, story, or personal experience _____
Statistic or relevant data _____
Quotation, familiar phrase, or definition _____
Rhetorical question, issue, or problem _____
Comment about audience or situation _____
Audience participation _____
Statement of topic _____

How will you establish a rapport with your audience?
_____
_____

Where can you find additional information about your presentation?
Newspapers or magazines _____
Library resources _____
Corporate documents _____
Experts and authorities _____
Interviews and surveys _____
Internet sources _____

How will you organize your information? Check one and then explain it.
☐ Inductively ☐ Deductively ☐ Chronologically ☐ Spatially ☐ Problem/Solution
_____
_____

How will you support your main points?
_____
_____

What transitions will you use?
_____
_____

How will you conclude or summarize your presentation?
_____
_____

In this tutorial, you learned how to plan and organize your presentation based upon the needs of your audience and the presentation situation. In Tutorial 2, you'll learn how to use effective visuals in your presentation, and how to deliver your message with confidence and clarity.

Session 1.2 QUICK CHECK

1. List three methods for focusing your topic.

2. Determine which methods have been used to focus the following topics: (a) Creating E-commerce Solutions for Small Business Owners (b) How to Submit Winning Bids: Obtaining Government Contracts.

3. Why should you phrase the main ideas of your presentation as conclusions you want your audience to draw?

4. What are the three basic parts of every presentation, and what is the purpose of each part?

5. List one advantage for each of the following ways to gain your audience's attention: (a) personal experience (b) statistics or data (c) rhetorical questions.

6. List four places to find additional materials on a topic.

7. What is the difference between organizing your presentation deductively and inductively, and when would you use each of these organizational patterns?

8. Give an example of a transitional phrase you could use to indicate that you're moving to your next main point.

REVIEW ASSIGNMENTS

While you're preparing your presentation to student leaders at Rocky Mountain State College, your supervisor, Kenna McNaughton, decides to have you give three presentations at Rampart High School, also in Colorado Springs.

The first presentation will be a 30-minute, informative presentation on the value of community service. You'll give this presentation, as part of a school assembly, to over 200 students in a large, computer-equipped auditorium with fixed seating.

The second presentation will be a 15-minute, persuasive presentation to teachers on giving credit for service assignments. You'll give this presentation as part of a faculty in-service meeting, to approximately 35 teachers in a faculty lounge with small tables and movable chairs.

The third presentation will be a 50-minute presentation for Senior class officers on how to plan a successful service project. You'll give this presentation as part of a leadership training session, to about six students in a medium-sized classroom with movable desks. Do the following:

1. Complete a Purpose and Outcomes Worksheet for the three types of presentations.

2. Explain differences and similarities between the three groups in terms of the following demographic features: age, gender, and level of education. Then complete an Audience Analysis Worksheet for the three types of presentations.

3. Explain how the settings for these presentations will affect your audience's expectations and the appropriate level of formality. Then complete a Situation and Media Assessment Worksheet for the three types of presentations.

4. Determine appropriate and inappropriate media for each of the three presentations.

5. Give an example of how you could focus the topic for the first presentation by limiting it by geography or region.

6. Give an example of how you could focus the second presentation by limiting it by point of view.

7. Give an example of how you could focus the third presentation by limiting it by category or classification.

8. Prepare an introduction for the first presentation using a story or anecdote. (You may create a fictional anecdote.)

9. Prepare an introduction for the second presentation using rhetorical questions.

10. Prepare an introduction for the third presentation using some kind of audience participation.

11. List two places to find additional information on the topics of each of these presentations.

12. Determine an appropriate organizational pattern for each of the three presentations.

13. Complete a Focus and Organization Worksheet for each of the three presentations.

CASE PROBLEMS

Case 1. American Cancer Society The American Cancer Society is a well-known nonprofit organization with chapters in nearly every state and county. Working with another member of the class, create a team presentation to inform your classmates about the goals and programs of the American Cancer Society organization in your area. You should be able to get information about the organization by consulting your local United Way organization, or by searching the Internet.

1. Decide on a type of presentation.

2. Complete a Purpose and Outcomes Worksheet.

3. Define your audience according to their general demographic features of age, gender, level of education, and familiarity with your topic.

4. Explain how the demographic characteristics of your audience will affect your presentation. Then complete an Audience Analysis Worksheet.

5. Describe the setting for your presentation and the size of your audience. Then complete a Situation and Media Assessment Worksheet.

6. Select appropriate media for your presentation and explain why they are appropriate. Explain why other media are inappropriate.

7. Show two ways to focus your presentation and limit the scope of your topic.

8. Each of you should select a method for gaining your audience's attention and write an introduction using that method. Discuss the strengths of each method for your particular audience.

9. Create an advance organizer, or overview.

10. Identify at least two sources for information on your topic and consult those sources. Print out at least one page of information that supports the main points of your presentation.

11. Select an appropriate organizational pattern for your presentation. Explain why that pattern is appropriate.

12. Identify four transitional phrases that you'll use.

13. Write a summary for your presentation recapping the key ideas.

14. Complete a Focus and Organization Worksheet.

Case 2. Safelee Home Security Products Sudhir Raguskus is director of marketing for Safelee Home Security Products. The company currently markets a new line of home security systems that includes hardware (alarms, automated lighting, and deadbolt locks) and monitoring services. Sudhir asks you to help prepare presentations for his company. Do the following:

1. Complete a Purpose and Outcomes Worksheet for each of these audiences: (a) sales personnel (b) potential clients (c) public safety officials who will be notified by Safelee in cases of emergency

2. Explain the differences and similarities between the above three groups in terms of the following demographic features: age, level of education, and familiarity with the subject. Complete an Audience Analysis Worksheet for each of the three presentations.

3. Explain the likely settings for these presentations and how these will affect your audience's expectations and dictate the appropriate level of formality.

4. Determine appropriate and inappropriate media for each of the three presentations. Complete a Situation and Media Assessment Worksheet for each of the three-presentations.

5. Give an example of how to focus or limit each presentation.

6. Identify three main ideas of your presentation to potential clients.

7. Prepare an appropriate introduction for each presentation. (Some of your introductory information may be fictional.)

8. Determine how to establish a rapport with public safety officials.

9. List two places to find additional information on the topics of each of these presentations.

10. Determine an appropriate organizational pattern for each of the three presentations.

11. Write an effective conclusion for each of the three presentations.

12. Complete a Focus and Organization Worksheet for each of the three presentations.

Case 3. EVENTix EVENTix owns and operates transactional kiosks that sell mall gift certificates and event/entertainment tickets. Konda Cameron, marketing director for EVENTix, asks you to prepare several presentations about EVENTix. Do the following:

1. Think of the most recent event (such as a concert, sports event, or movie) that you attended. Complete a Purpose and Outcomes Worksheet for a presentation to participants of the event, trying to convince them that they should purchase future events tickets from EVENTix.

2. Complete a Purpose and Outcomes Worksheet for a presentation to participants of the event, explaining how to obtain tickets from an EVENTix kiosk.

3. Complete a Purpose and Outcomes Worksheet for a presentation to participants of the event, informing them of other events for which EVENTix sells tickets.

4. Konda asks you to present information about EVENTix's gift certificate programs at a retailers convention. You'll give your 15-minute presentation in the ballroom of a hotel to over 300 conference attendees. Describe how your presentation will be influenced by this situation. Complete an Audience Analysis Worksheet.

5. Determine appropriate media for the convention presentation if no on-screen technology is available.

6. Complete a Situation and Media Assessment Worksheet.

7. Give an example of how to focus your topic for this particular audience.

8. Create an appropriate attention-getting introduction for your presentation. Explain why other attention getters might be inappropriate.

9. Determine an appropriate organizational pattern.

10. Complete a Focus and Organization Worksheet.

Case 4. *Analyzing an Oral Presentation* Attend or read a presentation, lecture, or speech and, if possible, obtain a transcript of the presentation. Make copies of your notes or the complete transcript of the presentation for your teacher. Do the following:

1. Complete a Purpose and Outcomes Worksheet.

2. Describe the audience for the presentation, including any general demographics that you can determine. Complete an Audience Analysis Worksheet.

3. Describe where the presentation was given, including the setting and the number of people attending the presentation.

4. Describe the media the speaker used for the presentation. Explain whether or not you feel the media were appropriate, and whether other media would have been more effective. (For instance, if overheads were used, would it have been more effective to use an online electronic presentation?) Complete a Situation and Media Assessment Worksheet.

5. Identify how the speaker established a rapport with the audience.

6. Describe any mistakes the speaker may have made in apologizing to the audience, or failing to consider the needs of the audience. How could these mistakes have been prevented?

7. Determine the structure of the presentation. If you have a written copy of the presentation, mark the introduction, body, and conclusion on the copy.

8. Describe how the speaker gained the audience's attention.

9. Identify whether the speaker provided an overview, or preview, of the presentation. If you have a written copy of the presentation, underline any overviews or previews.

10. Identify the major points in the presentation. If you have a written copy of the presentation, underline the details the presenter used to support these major points.

11. Identify the organizational pattern used in the presentation. Explain whether or not you think the organizational pattern was effective, or if another organizational pattern might have been better.

12. Identify any transitional phrases the speaker used.

13. Describe how the speaker ended the presentation. Explain whether or not you felt the ending was effective.

14. Complete a Focus and Organization Worksheet.

15. Interview a professional in your field and ask about the types of presentations he or she gives. Organize these into the types of presentations given above. Explain your findings.

QUICK | CHECK ANSWERS

Session 1.1

1. (a) explains background information, knowledge, and details about a topic; academic and professional conference presentations, briefings, reviews, reports, meetings, luncheon or dinner speeches, informal symposia. (b) convinces audience to feel or act a certain way; recommendations, sales, action plans, strategy sessions, motivational speeches. (c) demonstrations: show how something works; product and services overviews, computer software demonstrations. Training sessions: give hands-on practice and feedback on performance; employee orientation, seminars, workshops, classes, courses.

2. Audiences with specialized education, such as lawyers, would expect you to use specialized terms; audiences with less education would need more explanations and definitions.

3. How much time will I have? Will I be speaking alone? How large of an audience? How formal or informal of a setting? What will the room be like? How will the room be arranged? What equipment will be available? How much time will I have to set up? What other aspects must I consider? Will I need to introduce myself?

4. (a) effective: flip chart, poster, handout; they work with small informal groups and don't require additional equipment. Ineffective: 35mm slides and computer-projected visuals; they're better for larger, more formal presentations. (b) effective: posters, black-and-white or color overheads, 35mm slides, computer-projected visuals; they're better for large groups where visuals need to be enlarged, and for formal presentations. (c) chalkboard, whiteboard, notepad, handout; they're best for small groups where audience involvement is important.

5. chalkboard, whiteboard, notepad

6. computer-projected slides

Session 1.2

1. by time or chronology, geography or region, category or classification, component or element, segment or portion, point of view.

2. (a) category, component, point of view (b) category, component, segment

3. True

4. introduction (to gain and keep attention, create favorable impression, establish credibility, present overview), body (provide evidence and support for main points, present research, show relevance), conclusion (restate main points, suggest action, recommend additional sources)

5. (a) draw audience into the topic, makes topic more personal and relevant, helps audience relate to you as a person (b) increase interest in topic (c) address thought-provoking and important issues

6. popular press, library resources, corporate documents, experts, interviews, surveys, observations, Internet

7. deductive: presents conclusions first and reasoning second; informative presentations. inductive: presents reasons first, conclusions last; persuasive presentations, or when audience will resist conclusions

8. in addition, furthermore, next, now I will discuss

In this tutorial you will:

- Select and create appropriate and effective visuals

- Present your visuals

- Choose an appropriate delivery method

- Overcome your nervousness and control your speaking anxiety

- Improve your delivery

- Analyze your non-verbal communication

- Set up for your presentation

GIVING YOUR PRESENTATION

Presentation to the Student Senate at Rocky Mountain State College

Giving Your Presentation at Rocky Mountain State College

Joni de Paula, student body president at Rocky Mountain State College (RMSC), invites you to talk about your experiences as a YES! intern with members of the RMSC Student Senate as part of their deliberations over a proposed partnership with local nonprofit organizations. You planned and organized your presentation; now you'll prepare to give it.

In this tutorial, you'll learn the benefits of using visuals in your presentations, and how to select and create appropriate visuals. You'll also choose an appropriate method for delivering your presentation, and learn ways to improve your delivery. Finally, you'll learn how to set up for your presentation.

SESSION 2.1

In this session you'll learn the skills for effectively using visuals in your presentation: how visuals can benefit your presentation; how to select visuals that are appropriate for your purpose, audience, and situation; and how to effectively present those visuals.

Understanding the Benefits of Using Visuals in Your Presentation

It's much more difficult for people to understand and remember what they hear versus what they see. You can help your listeners comprehend and retain the ideas from your presentation by supplementing your presentation with effective visual aids. The old adage, "A picture is worth a thousand words" especially applies to presentations because listeners understand ideas faster when they can see and hear what you're talking about. Using visuals such as tables, charts, and graphs, to supplement your presentation:

- increases your audience's understanding. Visuals are especially helpful in explaining a difficult concept, displaying data, and illustrating the steps in a process.

- helps listeners remember information. Audiences will remember information longer when you use visuals to highlight or exemplify your main points, review your conclusions, and explain your recommendations.

- highlights your organization. Visuals can serve the same purpose as headings in a printed manuscript by allowing your audience to see how all the parts of your presentation fit together. Visuals can also help you preview and review main points, and differentiate between the main points and the sub-points.

- adds credibility to your presentation. Speakers who use visuals in their presentation are judged by their audiences as more professional and better prepared, as well as more interesting.

- stimulates and maintains your listeners' attention. It's much more interesting to see how something functions, rather than just hear about it. Giving your listeners somewhere to focus their attention keeps them from being distracted or bored.

- varies the pace of your presentation. Visuals enable you to provide sensory variety in your presentation, and keep your presentation from becoming monotonous.

- keeps you on track. Visuals not only benefit your audience, but also help you by providing a means for remembering what you want to say, and for staying on track.

In your presentation at Rocky Mountain State College, if you want to present information showing how the number of students involved in internships has dramatically increased in the last few years, you could simply read a summary of the numbers, as shown in Figure 2-1.

| Figure 2-1 | WRITTEN SUMMARY |

Internship Data Presented in Verbal Format

In the fall of 1989, the number of students at Rocky Mountain State College involved in internships, hit an unprecedented peak at 90. Then for the next three years, it fell almost steadily, dropping to 87 in 1990, 76 in 1991, 66 in 1992, and 43 in 1993. There was slight upsurge in 1994 to 50, then another little drop in 1995 to 42. Then in 1996, the tide seemed to turn, as the number of interns began to go up, first to 52, then to 60 in 1997. In the four years from 1998 to 2002, the number of students opting for an internship more than doubled, as the number grew from 66 to 86 in 1998 and 1999. In 2000, the number of interns stood at 95, increasing to 113 in 2001 and 120 in 2002.

But reading a long series of numbers would be difficult for your audience to understand, and it would be boring. By using visuals, you can present the same data in a format that's easier to understand, and more interesting. You can present the data in tabular format, as shown in Figure 2-2.

| Figure 2-2 | TABULAR SUMMARY |

Internship Data Presented in Visual Format

Year	Number of interns
1989	90
1990	87
1991	76
1992	66
1993	43
1994	50
1995	42
1996	52
1997	60
1998	66
1999	86
2000	95
2001	113
2002	120

Or, you might want to create a graph instead, as shown in Figure 2-3.

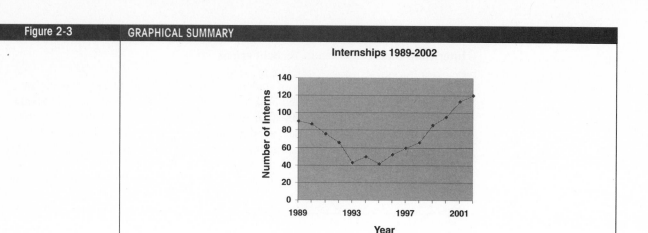

Figure 2-3   GRAPHICAL SUMMARY

Using visuals improves the quality of your presentation, and enables your audience to better understand your presentation. Visuals add information, clarification, emphasis, variety, and even pizzazz to your presentation.

You can choose from many types of visuals for your presentations: tables (text and numerical), graphs (bar and line), charts (pie, organizational, flow), and illustrations (drawings and diagrams, maps, and photographs). In the past, creating visuals was expensive, but the recent development of inexpensive computer software allows you to quickly and inexpensively create tables and graphs, scan photographs, resize drawings, and download visuals from the Internet for your presentation.

To effectively use visuals in your presentations, you'll need to ask yourself which visuals are best for your particular purpose, audience, and situation. You should also ask yourself which visuals you can create effectively.

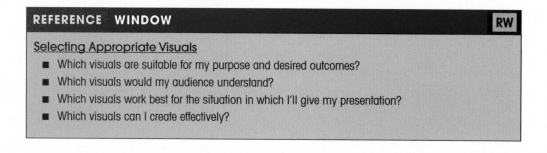

REFERENCE WINDOW   RW

Selecting Appropriate Visuals
- Which visuals are suitable for my purpose and desired outcomes?
- Which visuals would my audience understand?
- Which visuals work best for the situation in which I'll give my presentation?
- Which visuals can I create effectively?

Answering these questions to the best of your ability will increase the chances that your visuals will be effective.

Selecting Appropriate Visuals for Your Purpose

The following sections provide suggestions to help you select appropriate visuals—tables, graphs, charts, or illustrations—for your particular purpose.

Using Tables

Tables organize words and numerical data in horizontal rows and vertical columns. Tables are especially useful in informative presentations where your purpose is to provide your audience with specific information in a systematic and economical manner. Tables are also effective in:

- making facts and details accessible
- organizing data by categories
- summarizing results and recommendations
- comparing sets of data
- facilitating decisions

In your presentation at RMSC, you might want to explain the many benefits students receive as a result of volunteering in their local communities. You could use a table to summarize and emphasize the broad benefits as well as the specific benefits within each main category. See Figure 2-4.

Figure 2-4   TEXTUAL TABLE

Benefits of Academic Volunteerism	
Category	**Specific Benefits**
Develops civic values	Focus on relationships, rather than content Understand other cultures and needs Gain sense of ethical duty
Improves professional development	Develop problem-solving skills Improve rhetorical skills Practice professional skills
Inspires students	Develop personal philosophy Become aware of learning Increase involvement

Or, perhaps you want to show the number of students who completed internships in the past year. You could use a table to make those numbers more accessible to your audience. Using a table allows you to organize the number of interns according to semester, and the student's year in school. See Figure 2-5.

Figure 2-5   NUMERICAL TABLE

Number of Students Completing an Internship During the School Year 2000-2001 (by Semester)	Fall	Summer	Winter	Total
Freshman	0	2	2	4
Sophomore	1	6	3	10
Junior	11	13	13	37
Senior	15	14	15	44
Total	27	35	33	95

In both instances, using a table (figures 2-4 and 2-5) allows you to organize the information so that your audience can quickly see and understand your presentation.

Using the Table feature of your word processor, you can create professional-looking tables. Remember to follow these suggestions to make your tables more effective:

- Keep the table simple. Limit the amount of text and numerical data you use. Dense text is difficult to read, and complex numbers are difficult to understand.
- Use a descriptive title and informative headings. Use a title that explains what you're summarizing or comparing, and label rows and columns so your readers know what they're looking at.
- Remove excess horizontal and vertical lines. To simplify your table, use as few vertical and horizontal lines as possible.
- Use shading and emphasis sparingly. Shading and textual features, such as bolding, italics, and underlining, can be distracting. Don't use heavy shading, and keep textual variety to the main headings.
- Align numbers by place value.
- Keep all numbers consistent in value and number of significant digits.

Whether or not you use a table in your presentation will depend on your purpose. Although tables are good for showing exact numbers (such as, how many Juniors completed an internship during fall semester), they're not as good for showing trends (for instance, the increase or decrease over the past five years in the number of internships).

Using Graphs

Graphs show the relationship between two variables along two axes: the independent variable on the horizontal axis, and the dependent variable on the vertical axis. Like tables, graphs can show a lot of information concisely. Graphs are especially useful in informative presentations when you're showing quantities, or in persuasive presentations when you're comparing similar options using factors such as cost. Graphs are also effective for:

- comparing one quantity to another
- showing changes over time
- indicating patterns or trends

Common graphs include bar graphs and line graphs. **Bar graphs** are useful in comparing the value of one item to another over a period of time, or a range of dates or costs. In your presentation at RMSC, suppose you want to show the difference between the number of men and women completing internships with nonprofit agencies over the past 12 years. By using a bar graph, you could easily compare the differences between students. See Figure 2-6.

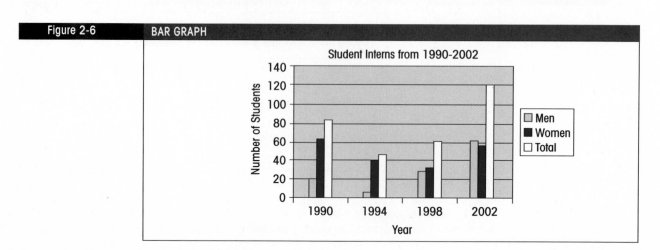

Figure 2-6   **BAR GRAPH**

Line graphs are especially effective for illustrating trends. You should use them instead of bar graphs when you have large amounts of information, and exact quantities don't require emphasis. Suppose you want to show the number of youths participating in YES!-sponsored activities during the first six months of each of the last three years (1999-2001). Using a bar chart would require 18 different bars. A more effective way to show the data would be a line graph, as shown in Figure 2-7. Your audience would immediately recognize that, while the number of youth participants has fluctuated in other years, it currently remains constant.

Figure 2-7	LINE GRAPH

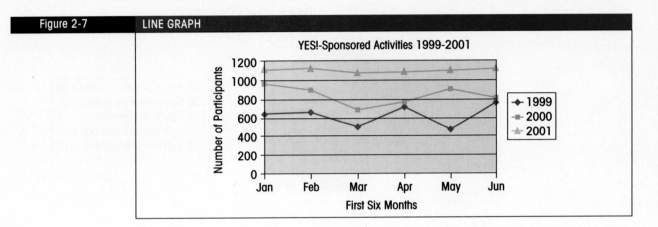

Whether or not you use a graph in your presentation will depend on your purpose. If you choose to use a graph, follow these guidelines:

- Keep graphs simple, clear, and easy to read. Limit the number of comparisons to no more than five.
- Compare values that are noticeably different. Comparing values that are similar means that all the bars will appear identical, and all the lines will overlap.
- Make each bar or line visually distinct. Use a different pattern, shade, or color for each line or bar in a group, and keep bars the same width.
- Label each line and bar. Remember that you're trying to help your listeners understand and use the information.
- Label both axes.

You can create simple bar graphs and line graphs by using the graphing feature of your spreadsheet or database program, or the chart feature of your word-processing or presentations program.

Using Charts

The terms **chart** and graph often are used interchangeably; however, they are distinct. While charts show relationships, they don't use a coordinate system like graphs. Charts are especially helpful in presentations where your goal is to help your listener understand the relationships between the parts and the whole.

Common charts include pie charts, organizational charts, and flowcharts.

Pie charts are best for showing percentages or proportions of the parts that make up a whole. Pie charts allow your listeners to compare the sections to each other, as well as to the whole. Pie charts can be created to display either the percentage relationship or the amount relationship.

Whether or not you use a pie chart in your presentation will depend on your purpose. In your presentation at RMSC, you want to explain how nonprofit organizations, such as YES!, provide assistance to the residents of the Colorado Springs area. You could do that by using a pie chart to show what percent of the agency's budget is allotted to its priority programs, such as self-sufficiency training. See Figure 2-8. Or, you could create the pie chart to show the amounts spent on each type of program.

Figure 2-8	PIE CHART

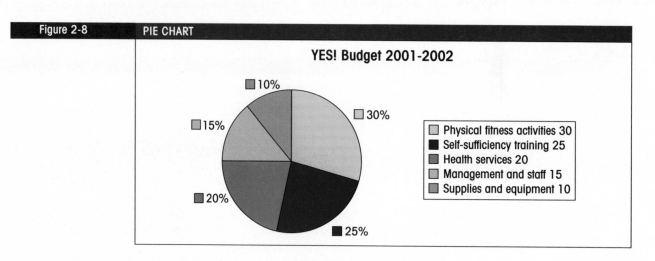

General suggestions for creating effective pie charts include

- Keep slices of the pie relatively large. Comparisons of more than eight sections are difficult to see and differentiate. If necessary, combine several small sections into a section titled, "Other."

- Use a descriptive title for the whole and label each segment. Help your audience understand what you're comparing in terms of the whole, as well as each section of the pie. Keep all labels horizontal so they can be read easily.

- Make sure the parts add up to 100 percent.

- Begin the largest section at the top of the pie. The largest section should begin at the 12 o'clock position. The other sections should get smaller as they move around the pie clockwise, except for the "Other" section, which is usually the last section.

- Use a normal flat pie chart, unless it has fewer than five slices. In other words, you should *not* display the pie chart with 3D perspective, pulled-out pie slices, or in donut format. These effects can detract from seeing the pie as a whole, and can make the chart difficult to read.

You can create simple pie charts by entering your data into a spreadsheet program and then using the graphing feature of that program, or you can use a program such as Microsoft Chart directly in Word, PowerPoint, or other applications software.

Organizational charts show the hierarchical structure of a company or other organization, illustrating the relationship between departments, for example. In your presentation at Rocky Mountain State College, you could show the structure of the YES! organization by creating an organizational chart, as shown in Figure 2-9.

Figure 2-9 | ORGANIZATIONAL CHART

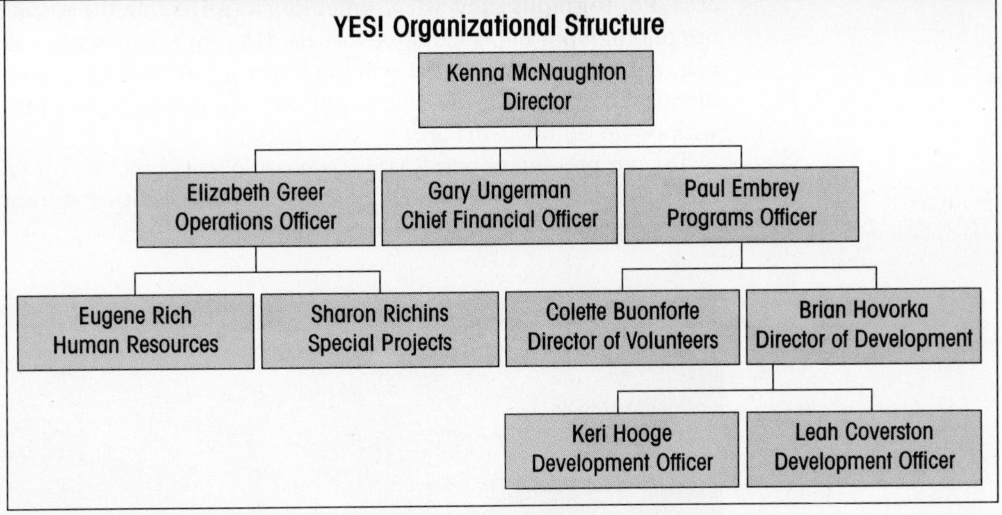

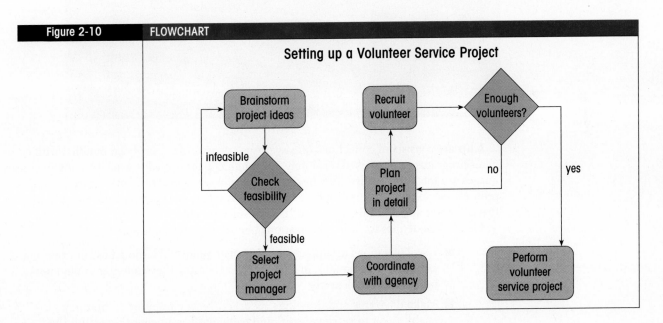

You can create organizational charts using the Organization Chart feature in Microsoft applications. There are also a number of software applications designed specifically for creating charts.

Flowcharts are useful for describing the steps in a procedure, or stages in a decision-making process. Flowcharts are especially effective in demonstrations and training presentations because they can visually supplement verbal instructions, and show the results of alternative decisions. See Figure 2-10.

Figure 2-10 | FLOWCHART

Using Illustrations

Illustrations, including diagrams, drawings, maps, photographs, and clip art, are helpful in showing relationships that aren't numerical. You can use **diagrams** and simple drawings to show how to assemble a piece of equipment, or how the parts of an item or process are related to each other.

Maps are helpful for showing spatial relationships (position and location) in a geographic area. **Photographs** show what something looks like. In the past it was difficult to obtain and use photographs in presentation visuals, but now it is relatively easy because of digital cameras and scanners. Moreover, you can improve the quality of your photographs by removing blemishes, enhancing the colors and contrast, cropping, and making other modifications with photo-editing software.

In your presentation at RMSC, you could scan a picture (or take one with a digital camera) of student interns. You could then use photo-editing software to enhance the picture, enlarge it, and use it on a poster. See Figure 2-11.

Figure 2-11	PHOTOGRAPH

Clip art consists of collections of easy-to-use images that have been bundled with computer programs or purchased separately. Although clip art is readily available, not all clip art images are the same quality. Whenever you use clip art, you should make sure the image is professional-looking and appropriate for your presentation. There are also many Web sites that offer free still and animated clips, as well as sound clips.

General guidelines for using illustrations in your presentations include:

- Use illustrations to supplement your main points. You should use illustrations, especially photographs, in a presentation because they convey meaning, not because they look pretty.

- Make diagrams and drawings accurate. New computer technology enables you to retrieve, edit, and even alter an image. Distorting the image can make it harder for your listeners to recognize and accurately interpret the illustration.

- Provide scale and focus. Crop or trim photographs to emphasize what is important and eliminate unnecessary details.

- Abide by all copyright laws. Illustrations, including photographs and clip art, retrieved from the Internet are subject to copyright laws. Make sure you understand and abide by copyright laws.
- Avoid plagiarism. If you use someone else's chart, diagram, illustration, or photograph, give proper credit.

In summary, selecting an appropriate visual for your purpose is a matter of knowing the strengths and weaknesses of each type of visual. If you want your audience to know facts and figures, a table might be sufficient; however, if you want your audience to make a particular judgment about the data, a bar graph, line graph, or pie chart might be better. If you want to show processes and procedures, diagrams are better than photographs.

The following Reference Window summarizes the strengths of each type of visual for the particular purposes you may have in your presentations. Use this summary to help you decide which visual is appropriate for a particular type of information and purpose.

REFERENCE WINDOW **RW**

Selecting Appropriate Visuals for Your Purpose

Purpose	Table	Bar graph	Line graph	Pie chart	Flowchart	Organizational chart	Drawing	Photograph	Map
Summarize costs	X	X	X	X					
Relate parts to whole	X				X	X		X	X
Illustrate trends		X	X	X					
Demonstrate cause and effect		X	X						
Compare alternatives	X	X	X	X				X	
Summarize advantages/disadvantages	X								
Provide chronology	X	X	X		X		X		
Follow procedure/work flow					X				
See parts and apparatus	X						X	X	
Explain organization	X					X			
Show spatial relationship								X	X

Selecting **Appropriate Visuals for Your Audience**

Now that you know the purpose of each type of visual, you also need to understand how to choose a visual based on your audience. In analyzing whether a visual is appropriate for a particular audience, a general guideline to follow is that audiences familiar with the topic prefer visuals they can interpret themselves, such as flowcharts, graphs, and diagrams. On the other hand, audiences unfamiliar with the topic need help interpreting the information. Visuals for these audiences should consist of basic tables, graphs, and simple diagrams.

In addition, non-expert audiences generally have a harder time interpreting numerical data than words, so try to avoid numerical visuals. On the other hand, if you can't avoid numerical data, plan to devote extra time during your presentation to explain the numerical data. Likewise, non-expert audiences unfamiliar with certain types of images need additional help interpreting those images. For example, if you show an apparatus, equipment, or machine to non-experts, you must explain in detail what they are seeing and why it's important.

Selecting **Appropriate Visuals for Your Situation**

You not only have to select different visuals for different purposes and audiences, you also have to select visuals based on your situation. Selecting visuals that are appropriate for your situation involves determining which visuals work best for the medium, equipment, and room setup where you'll give your presentation. If the room doesn't have a slide projector or overhead transparency projector, you might find it difficult to use photographs. If you're limited to using a chalkboard, white board, or notepad, you might not have time to create a complex table. In such cases, you might have to provide the complex tables or graphs in posters or handouts. Flowcharts may be effective on a flip chart in a small, well-lit room; however, flip charts aren't effective in a large room, or with large audiences. Maps also are difficult to use in presentations unless they are enlarged or projected, and then they usually need a lot of explanation for the audience to understand them.

No matter which visual you select, be sure everyone in your audience can see, and make sure the medium you use to display the visual enables your audience to understand and correctly interpret your visual.

Now that you've determined which visuals are appropriate for your presentation, you'll need to determine whether you can create them yourself or, need to have someone else create them for you.

Creating **Effective Visuals**

Even though computer programs now make it easier to create visuals, such as graphs and illustrations, you may still need to use a technical illustrator or graphic artist to create specialized diagrams and drawings. In analyzing whether to create visuals yourself or obtain the help of a professional, you should consider what your audience will expect, how much time you have to prepare your visuals, whether you have the expertise and equipment necessary to create the visuals, and whether you have the budget to hire an illustrator or artist.

REFERENCE WINDOW	**RW**

Questions for Determining Whether You Can Create Visuals Yourself
- What are the expectations for my visuals?
- How much time will I have to prepare the visuals?
- Do I have adequate knowledge or expertise to create the visuals?
- What computer equipment and other production resources do I have available for creating my own visuals?
- How much money is budgeted to hire a technical illustrator or graphic artist?

If you decide to create your own visuals, be aware of the difficulties involved. You should consider the following guidelines (in addition to the suggestions presented earlier for each type of visual):

- Keep your visuals simple. Remember that "less is more" when it comes to creating effective visuals.
- Make your visuals professional-looking. Shabby-looking or amateurish visuals will detract from your presentation and from your credibility.

■ Keep your visuals consistent. Keep titles to all of your visuals consistent in size and color so your audience can quickly recognize what your visuals are about.

■ Use color sparingly and purposefully. Use the brightest color for the most important information, or to indicate patterns. Don't add color just to make things "look good," or you may end up with something garish.

Of course, one alternative to preparing visuals yourself, or hiring someone to prepare them for you, is to purchase CDs of photographs and clip art, or download images from the Internet. But be aware of copyright laws. As a student, you fall under copyright "fair use" rules, which basically means that you can, for educational purposes only, use copyrighted material on a one-time basis without getting permission from the copyright holder. On the other hand, if you work for a not-for-profit or for-profit company, much stricter copyright laws apply. Learn the copyright laws and abide by them.

Once you've created your visuals or obtained them from some other source, you'll need to plan how to manage and present your visuals during your presentation. The following section will help you understand how to use your visuals.

Making **the Most of Your Visuals**

Effective visuals can become ineffective if they aren't presented successfully. You'll need to prepare everything beforehand, and then plan how you'll integrate your visuals into your presentation. Perhaps the easiest way to figure out how to present visuals in your presentation is to create a simple storyboard showing the points you want to discuss, and the visual you want to accompany each point.

Using a Storyboard

A **storyboard** is essentially a table or map of instructions and visuals that explains how to complete a process. Storyboards are used in the motion picture industry to map the narrative of a movie with the particular camera shots and special effects that are to accompany that narrative. You can adapt the same storyboarding technique in planning your presentation. Simply take a piece of paper and fold it in half lengthwise. On the left side of the page, briefly describe your presentation point, or write down a heading from your outline. Then on the right side of the page, list or sketch the visual or visuals that you want to accompany that point. You can also include any physical movements or gestures that you want to make, such as pointing to a particular part of a slide or overhead. Figure 2-12 shows a sample storyboard for your presentation at Rocky Mountain State College.

Figure 2-12	STORY BOARD

Benefits of Academic Volunteerism

The first category is Civic Values. Students develop their ability to center on relationships rather than content. They develop an understanding of other cultures and needs, as well as a sense of ethical duty toward society.	*Show table listing civic values.*
The second category is Professional Development. Students develop problem-solving skills, critical-thinking skills, and writing skills.	*Show photo of students performing skills.*
The third category is Personal Inspiration. Students develop a sense of who they are and of responsibility for their own actions. They become involved participants rather than just academic observers.	*Show table listing types of attributes that students develop.*

A storyboard like the one in Figure 2-12 can help you choose and use the best possible visuals for your presentation.

Effectively Presenting Visuals

In addition, you should follow these simple guidelines for effectively presenting your visuals:

- Use visuals to support your ideas, not just as attention getters or gimmicks. Most visuals work best when they supplement your ideas, rather than being tacked on at the beginning or end of your presentation. However, in a formal setting, you should begin your presentation with a slide or overhead showing your name, the title of your presentation, and your company logo.
- Display the visual as you discuss it. Use your storyboard to indicate when you want to display the visual, and then remove the visual when you're through discussing it. Don't let your visuals get ahead or behind of your verbal presentation.
- Stand to the side, not in front, of the visual. Avoid turning your back on your audience as you refer to a visual. Talk directly to your audience, rather than turning toward or talking at the visual.
- Introduce and interpret the visual. Explain to your audience what they should be looking at in the visual and point to what is important. But don't get sidetracked and spend all your time explaining the visual.
- Avoid using too many visuals. Present your material in simple, digestible amounts instead of overwhelming your audience with too much information.
- Turn off the equipment when you're finished.

Figure 2-13 provides a basic worksheet for helping you select appropriate visuals and determining whether you can create them.

| Figure 2-13 | PRESENTATION VISUALS WORKSHEET |

Presentation Visuals Worksheet

Which visuals are suitable for your purpose and desired outcomes?
- ☐ Text table
- ☐ Numerical table
- ☐ Bar graph
- ☐ Line graph
- ☐ Pie chart
- ☐ Organizational chart
- ☐ Flowchart
- ☐ Diagram
- ☐ Illustration

Which visuals would your audience expect and understand?
- ☐ Text table
- ☐ Numerical table
- ☐ Bar graph
- ☐ Line graph
- ☐ Pie chart
- ☐ Organizational chart
- ☐ Flowchart
- ☐ Diagram
- ☐ Illustration

Which visuals work best for the situation in which you ll give your presentation?
- ☐ Text table
- ☐ Numerical table
- ☐ Bar graph
- ☐ Line graph
- ☐ Pie chart
- ☐ Organizational chart
- ☐ Flowchart
- ☐ Diagram
- ☐ Illustration

Which of the visuals you checked above could you create effectively?

_____

_____

_____

_____

How much time will you have to prepare the visuals? _____

What knowledge or expertise do you have to create these visuals?

_____

_____

What computer equipment and other production resources are available for creating these visuals?

_____

_____

How much money has been budgeted to hire help in creating these visuals? _____

Now that you've determined which visuals would be appropriate for your presentation and how to integrate them into your presentation, you're prepared to plan how to deliver your presentation.

Session 2.1 QUICK CHECK

1. Define the purpose for each of the following visuals:
   a. table
   b. graph
   c. chart
   d. illustration

2. Describe a strength and weakness of each of the following visuals:
   a. table
   b. graph
   c. chart
   d. illustrations

3. If you want to show how the number of students in your major has increased in the last five years, which of the following visuals would be appropriate: (a) table, (b) bar graph, (c) line graph, (d) pie chart?

4. If you want to show what percent of your monthly budget goes to housing, which of the following visuals would be appropriate: (a) table, (b) bar graph, (c) line graph, (d) pie chart?

5. If you want to show the managerial structure of your company, which of the following visuals would be appropriate: (a) table, (b) pie chart, (c) organization chart, (d) flowchart?

6. If you want to show the procedure for getting money from an ATM, which of the following visuals would be appropriate: (a) organization chart, (b) flowchart, (c) map, (d) photograph?

7. If you want to show where the Student Senate meets, which of the following visuals would be appropriate: (a) flowchart, (b) map, (c) drawing, (d) photograph?

8. What is a storyboard and how would you use it to make your presentation more effective?

SESSION 2.2

In this session, you'll learn how to: choose an appropriate method for delivering your presentation, overcome your nervousness and improve your delivery, give team presentations, and set up for your presentation.

Choosing an Appropriate Delivery Method

The **delivery method** is your approach for the presentation—written out and read word for word, using a simple outline or notes, or off-the-cuff. Questions you should ask yourself in choosing a delivery method include those that will enable you to determine what is the most appropriate method for your purpose, audience, and situation.

REFERENCE WINDOW **RW**

<u>Questions to Ask in Determining an Appropriate Delivery Method</u>
- What delivery method is the most appropriate for my purpose?
- What delivery method will my audience expect?
- What delivery method is the most appropriate for this setting and situation?

You could present the information you prepared in several different ways. Common delivery methods include

- written or memorized delivery, reading your entire presentation or repeating it from memory.
- extemporaneous delivery, giving your presentation from brief notes or an outline.
- impromptu delivery, speaking without notes and without rehearsal.

Each type of presentation has its own advantages and disadvantages. You should select the delivery method that is appropriate for your purpose, audience, and situation. The following sections will help you determine which type of presentation is best.

Giving a Written or Memorized Presentation

Giving a written or memorized presentation involves completely writing out your presentation and then reading it word for word, or memorizing it in advance.

| Figure 2-14 | WRITTEN PRESENTATION |

Written or memorized presentations are especially effective when you are:
- unfamiliar with the topic or have a highly complex topic
- interested in using specific words for persuading or informing your audience
- addressing a large, unfamiliar, or formal audience

- speaking with a group, or under a strict time limit
- extremely nervous or anxious
- inexperienced in public speaking

Written or memorized presentations don't leave a lot to chance, so they work well in formal settings when you must stick to a topic and stay on time. They're also helpful if you think you'll forget what you prepared, or become nervous and tongue-tied as a result of your inexperience with the topic, or with giving presentations. Written or memorized presentations often are given on certain occasions, such as formal paper sessions at academic or professional conferences.

On the other hand, written or memorized presentations take a long time to prepare, and once you've memorized your presentation, it's not easy to alter it in response to changes in time limits or audience questions. Perhaps the biggest drawback to written or memorized presentations is that it's difficult to sound natural while reading your presentation, or reciting it from memory. So your listeners may lose interest.

For your presentation to the RMSC Student Senate, you're one of several speakers presenting your ideas to the entire Senate. You also have a strict time limit of 12 minutes. In this instance, you want to give a written or memorized presentation so that you can cover everything you want to say in the fewest possible words.

Giving an Extemporaneous Presentation

Extemporaneous presentations involve speaking from a few notes or an outline. Extemporaneous presentations are more flexible than written or memorized presentations, and are ideal for speaking in a more informal setting.

Figure 2-15	EXTEMPORANEOUS PRESENTATION

Extemporaneous presentations are ideal when you are:

- familiar with the topic or audience
- presenting to a medium-sized group, or in an informal setting
- giving a shorter presentation, or have a flexible time limit

- seeking audience participation or questions
- experienced in public speaking

Speaking extemporaneously works well when you're using media requiring no advance preparation, such as chalkboards, white boards, and notepads. An extemporaneous delivery also allows you to have a more natural-sounding presentation, or to adapt your presentation for audience questions or participation.

On the other hand, when you give an extemporaneous presentation, you may have a tendency to go over your time limit, leave out crucial information, or lack precision in explaining your ideas to your listeners. In addition, speaking extemporaneously can make you appear less credible if you have a tendency toward nervousness or anxiety.

Suppose that following your presentation at RMSC, you're asked to speak for 20-30 minutes before a subcommittee of the Student Senate. In that instance, you would probably want to use an extemporaneous delivery so you could speak more naturally and allow members of the subcommittee to ask questions.

Giving an Impromptu Presentation

Impromptu presentations involve speaking without notes, an outline, or memorized text. Impromptu presentations are more flexible than either written, memorized, or extemporaneous presentations; however, they're also more difficult to make effective.

Figure 2-16	IMPROMPTU PRESENTATION

Impromptu presentations work best when you're in the following situations:

- very familiar with your topic and audience
- speaking to a small, intimate group, or in an in-house setting
- asked to speak at the spur of the moment
- more interested in getting the views of your audience than in persuading them

Generally, you should be wary of impromptu presentations because you leave too much to chance. Speaking without notes may result in taking too much time, saying something that offends your audience, or appearing unorganized. If you think you might be asked to speak impromptu, jot down some notes beforehand so you'll be prepared.

Kenna McNaughton, your supervisor, will probably ask you to take 2–3 minutes during the next YES! staff meeting to discuss your presentation at Rocky Mountain State College. You'll want to write down a few notes so you'll be more focused, but you don't need to do extensive planning.

REFERENCE WINDOW				RW

Three Delivery Methods

Method	Preparation	Audience	Situation	Strengths
Written or memorized	Requires much advance preparation	Large	Formal setting; complex or unfamiliar topic; unfamiliar with audience; definite time limit; inexperienced presenter	Effective when exact wording is important; helps overcome nervousness
Extemporaneous	Some advance preparation	Medium, small	Informal setting; familiar with topic and audience; flexible time limit; experienced presenter	Allows more natural presentation; enables audience participation
Impromptu	Little advance preparation, but difficult to give	Small	Informal setting; very familiar with topic and audience; shorter time limits; experienced presenter	Allows flexibility; enables audience participation; spur of the moment

No matter which method of delivery you choose, you'll need to decide whether you want your audience to have an opportunity to ask questions. Preparing for questions from the audience is an important part of giving an effective presentation.

Preparing for Questions from the Audience

Some professional speakers suggest that you should savor the idea of questions from the audience, rather than trying to avoid them. The absence of questions, they argue, may actually indicate that your audience had no interest in what you said, or that you spoke too long. Adopting the attitude that interested listeners will have questions enables you to anticipate and prepare for the questions your audience will ask.

Figure 2-17   INTERESTED LISTENERS HAVE QUESTIONS

Things you should consider in preparing for questions include:

- Announce a specific time limit for questions and stick to it. When you want to end, simply state, "We have time for one more question."
- Realize that your audience will ask questions about the information in your presentation that is new, controversial, or unexpected.
- Listen carefully to every question. If you don't understand the question, ask to have it rephrased.
- Repeat the question to make sure everyone in the audience heard it.
- Keep your answers brief. If you need additional time, arrange for it after your presentation.
- If you can't answer a question, admit it, and move on.
- Don't be defensive about hostile questions. Treat every person's question as important and respond courteously.

In your presentation at RMSC, you anticipate that your audience will have questions, such as the following: "What other schools allow their students to receive college credit for working with nonprofits?" "How would a partnership between RMSC and YES! facilitate students receiving credit?" "How would allowing credit for internships affect the number of hours for graduation?" You begin immediately to plan how to answer such questions.

Now that you've determined which type of presentation you want to give, and you're prepared to answer questions from your audience, it's time to think about an almost universal problem—overcoming nervousness.

Overcoming **Nervousness**

Just thinking about speaking in front of other people may cause your heart to beat faster and your palms to sweat. You aren't alone. Feeling nervous about giving a presentation is a natural reaction. But you don't need to let your nervousness interfere with you giving a successful presentation. Being nervous is not all bad, because it means your adrenalin is flowing, and you'll have more energy and vitality for your presentation. In most instances, your nervousness will pass once you begin speaking.

Sometimes, however, nervousness arises from feelings of inadequacy, or from worrying about problems that could occur during a presentation. The best way to overcome these concerns is to carefully plan and prepare your presentation, and then practice it so you can relax and not worry.

Figure 2-18	PLAN, PREPARE, AND PRACTICE

Other things you can do to overcome your nervousness include:

- Focus your presentation on your listeners' needs, not on yourself. When you focus your mind on meeting the needs of your audience, you begin to forget about yourself and how the audience might respond to you.

- Think positively about your presentation. Be optimistic and enthusiastic about your opportunity to gain experience. Visualize yourself as calm and confident.

- Work with your nervousness. Realize that some nervousness is normal and will help make your presentation better. Remember, your audience isn't nearly as concerned about your nervousness as you are.

- Give yourself plenty of time before your presentation. Arrive early to avoid rushing around before your presentation. Devote a few minutes beforehand to relax and review your presentation notes.

- Talk to people beforehand. It's easier to talk to people you know than to complete strangers. If you think of your audience as friends who want you to succeed, you'll gain new confidence in presenting your ideas to them.

- When you first stand up, look at your audience and smile. Then take a few slow breaths to calm yourself before you begin to speak.
- Don't expect everything to be perfect. Have back up plans in case something goes wrong, but handle problems with grace and a sense of humor.
- Observe other presenters. Make a list of the things they do that you like, and try to implement those things into your own presentations.

In preparation for your presentation to the RMSC Student Senate, you decide to meet a few of the Senators beforehand. After meeting a few of the students who represent your class of seniors, you realize that they're concerned with many of the same questions you had, such as how to gain valuable real-world experiences. You realize that they're interested in obtaining helpful information from your presentation that will enable them to make an informed decision in the Student Senate.

Practicing **Your Presentation**

The most effective way to overcome your nervousness and deliver a smooth presentation is to practice, practice, practice. Begin by simply rehearsing the key points of your presentation in your mind. Then rehearse your presentation in front of a few close friends. Ask your friends what you can do to improve your presentation. Pay special attention to what they say about key aspects of your presentation, such as your introduction, main points, and conclusion. Then rehearse your presentation again.

| Figure 2-19 | PRACTICING GIVES YOU CONFIDENCE |

As you rehearse, use your visual aids and try to speak at the same pace you'll use when giving your presentation. Ask someone to time your presentation. By practicing your presentation until you're comfortable with every aspect of it, you'll go a long way toward reducing the apprehension that comes with feeling unprepared. Practicing your presentation will help you feel more confident as a speaker.

REFERENCE WINDOW	RW

Practicing Your Presentation

- Practice in front of a few friends and a sample of your presentation audience.
- Ask your friends to give you suggestions on how to improve your presentation.
- Time your presentation using the speaking pace you'll use during your presentation.
- Practice with your visual aids.
- Pay particular attention to your introduction, main points, and conclusion.

In an effort to prepare for your presentation to the Student Senate you ask another intern to listen to what you prepared. She says she's not clear on how working with YES! has helped you develop problem-solving skills. You make a note to add another example to support that main point.

The next sections will help you learn how to improve your delivery by establishing eye contact and using a pleasant, natural speaking voice.

Improving Your Delivery

Now matter how well you prepare your presentation, you won't be successful if your delivery is ineffective. No one enjoys a presentation when the speaker refuses to look up, or drones on endlessly in a monotone voice. The best presentations are those where the presenter appears confident and speaks naturally in a conversational manner.

As you practice your presentation, remember to project yourself as a confident and qualified speaker. Two ways that help you appear confident are establishing eye contact with your listeners and speaking in a natural voice.

Establishing Eye Contact

One of the most common mistakes beginners make is failing to establish eye contact with their audience. Speakers who keep their eyes on their notes, stare at their visuals, or look out over the heads of their audience create an emotional distance between themselves and their listeners.

A better method is to look directly at your listeners, even if you have to pause to look up. To establish eye contact, you should look at individuals, not just scan the audience. Focus on a particular member of the audience for just a second or two, then move on to someone else until you eventually get to most of the people in the audience or, if the audience is large, to most parts of the presentation room. You can usually judge how things are going by your audience's reaction, and make adjustments accordingly.

Figure 2-20   ESTABLISH EYE CONTACT

REFERENCE WINDOW   **RW**

<u>Establishing Eye Contact</u>
- Look directly at your listeners.
- Look at individuals; don't just scan the audience.
- Focus on a particular person, then move on to someone else.
- Eventually look at most of the people or most areas of the audience.

As part of your presentation at RMSC, you'll want to look directly at each member of the Student Senate. That will enable you to create a personal connection with your audience, and see how they're responding to your presentation.

Using a Pleasant, Natural Voice

Most successful presenters aren't blessed with the deep voice of a professional news broadcaster or the rich, full voice of an opera singer; however, they use a pleasant, natural voice to make their presentations more interesting.

Figure 2-21   USE YOUR NATURAL VOICE

Consider these suggestions for making your voice more pleasant and appealing:

- Use your natural speaking voice and a conversational manner. Think of talking to your audience as you would to a friend or teacher. That will allow you to use a voice that is more natural and easy to listen to.

- Vary the pitch, rate, and volume of your voice. Overcome monotony by emphasizing important words, pausing at the end of lengthy sentences, and slowing down during transitions. However, don't let the volume of your voice drop at the end of sentences.

- Stand up straight. Improving your posture allows you to project your voice by putting your full strength behind it.

- Learn to relax. Relaxing will improve the quality of your voice by keeping your muscles loose and your voice more natural.

- Practice breathing deeply, which gives you adequate air to speak properly.

Using Proper Grammar and Pronunciation

One of the best ways to be seen as a credible speaker is to use proper grammar and pronunciation. To assure you're pronouncing a word correctly, check its pronunciation in a dictionary. Some common problems in pronunciation include:

- mispronunciations caused by dropping a letter, such as "liberry" instead of library, and "satistics" instead of statistics

- mispronunciations caused by adding a letter or inserting the wrong letter, such as "acrost" instead of across, "learnt" instead of learned, or "stastistics" instead of statistics

- colloquial expressions, such as "crick" instead of creek, or "ain't" instead of isn't or aren't

- lazy pronunciation caused by dropping the final letters, such as "speakin" rather than speaking
- filler words, such as "a," "um," "like," and "ya know."

As part of your presentation to the Student Senate, you wonder how to pronounce the word "data." You look it up in your dictionary and find that the preferred pronunciation is "dāta," not "dăta."

Using **Non-verbal Communication**

Nonverbal communication is the way you convey a message without saying a word. Most nonverbal communication deals with how you use your body to communicate—how you look, stand, and move.

Checking Your Appearance and Posture

Your appearance creates your audience's first impression of you, so make sure your dress and grooming contribute to the total impression you want to convey to your audience. Dress appropriately for the situation, and in a manner that doesn't detract from your presentation.

For your presentation at the RMSC Student Senate, you should wear nicer clothing than you wear to class. This might mean dress slacks and shirt for a man, and a skirt and blouse, or dress, for a woman. For a formal presentation, you should wear business attire, such as a suit and tie for man and a suit or tailored dress for a woman.

Figure 2-22	DRESS APPROPRIATELY

An important part of how you communicate is your posture. Refrain from slouching as your audience may interpret that to mean that you don't care or you're insecure. Stand tall and keep your hands at your side, except to change overheads. Don't bend over or stretch up to speak into the microphone; adjust the microphone for your height.

Using Natural Gestures and Movement

The gestures you use will depend on your personality and your delivery method. It's important to choose gestures that are natural for you, so ask someone else whether your gestures are distracting. Informal presentations lend themselves to more gestures and movement than formal presentations where you're standing in front of a microphone on a podium. But giving a formal presentation doesn't mean you should hide behind the lectern, or behave like a robot. Even formal presentations allow for gestures that are purposeful, spontaneous, and natural.

In your presentation at the RMSC Student Senate, you plan to stand at the podium. But during a staff meeting at YES!, you would stand closer to your coworkers, and would probably be more animated.

Avoiding Annoying Mannerisms

Be aware of your unique mannerisms or recurring movements that can be annoying, such as raising your voice and eyebrows as if you are talking to children; playing with keys, a pen, or equipment; or fidgeting, rocking, and pacing. All of these mannerisms can communicate nervousness, as well as detract from your presentation.

REFERENCE WINDOW   **RW**

Your Non-verbal Communication

Eyes	Establish eye contact by looking directly at listeners and focusing on a particular person.
Voice	Use your natural speaking voice and a conversational manner.
	Vary the pitch, rate, and volume of your voice.
	Breathe deeply.
Appearance and Posture	Stand tall and keep your hands at your side.
Gestures	Use natural gestures.
Movement	Avoid recurring movements that can be annoying, and mannerisms, such as rocking and pacing.

After you practice your presentation to the RMSC Student Senate in front of a friend, she points out that you kept clicking the clip on your pen. You make a note to leave your pen in your backpack during your presentation.

Giving Team or Collaborative Presentations

Giving your presentation as part of a group or team is a common occurrence. Since much of the work in business and industry is collaborative, it's only natural that presentations often are given as a team. The benefits of team presentations include:

- providing more people with valuable experience. Collaborative presentations involve more people and give each member of a team experience in communicating ideas.

- providing more workers with exposure and the rewards of a task accomplished.

■ allowing for a greater range of expertise and ideas.

■ enabling more discussion.

■ presenting greater variety in presentation skills and delivery styles.

| Figure 2-23 | GIVING TEAM PRESENTATIONS |

A successful team presentation depends on your group's ability to plan thoroughly and practice together. The following suggestions are meant to help you have a successful group presentation:

■ Plan for the transitions between speakers.

■ Observe time constraints.

■ Show respect for everyone and for his or her ideas.

■ Involve the whole team in your planning.

■ Be sensitive to personality and cultural differences.

Figure 2-24 provides a basic worksheet for practicing and delivering your presentation.

Figure 2-24   PRESENTATION DELIVERY WORKSHEET

Presentation Delivery Worksheet

What delivery method is the most appropriate for your purpose, audience, and situation?
- ☐ Written or memorized delivery chronology
- ☐ Extemporaneous delivery
- ☐ Impromptu delivery

What questions will your audience probably ask?

_____
_____
_____
_____

What are your audience s needs?

_____
_____
_____
_____

What do you enjoy most in a presentation? How can you implement this in your own presentation?

_____
_____
_____
_____

Team Preparation
   Transitions between speakers _____
   Time allotted for each speaker _____

Rehearsal Checkoff
- ☐ Practiced presentation in front of friends of sample audience
- ☐ Asked friends for suggestions and feedback on presentation
- ☐ Timed your presentation   How long was it? _____
- ☐ Practiced with visual aids
- ☐ Gave particular attention to introduction, main points, and conclusion

- -

Evaluation by Your Target Audience

Established eye contact with audience:	☐ excellent	☐ good	☐ needs improvement
Used natural voice	☐ excellent	☐ good	☐ needs improvement
Used conversational manner	☐ excellent	☐ good	☐ needs improvement
Varied pitch, rate, and volume of voice	☐ excellent	☐ good	☐ needs improvement
Stood up straight	☐ excellent	☐ good	☐ needs improvement
Appeared relaxed	☐ excellent	☐ good	☐ needs improvement
Used proper grammar and pronunciation	☐ excellent	☐ good	☐ needs improvement
Well dressed and groomed	☐ excellent	☐ good	☐ needs improvement
Used natural gestures and movements	☐ excellent	☐ good	☐ needs improvement
Free of annoying mannerisms	☐ excellent	☐ good	☐ needs improvement

Setting Up for Your Presentation

Even the best-planned and practiced presentation can fail if your audience can't see or hear your presentation, or they're uncomfortable. That's why it's important to include the set up for your presentation as an important element of preparation. Of course, there are some things over which you have no control. If you're giving your presentation as part of a professional conference, you can't control whether the room you're assigned is the right size for your audience. Sometimes (but certainly not always) you can't control what projection systems are available, the thermostat setting in the room, or the quality of the speaker system. But you can control many of the things that could interfere with or enhance the success of your presentation, if you consider them in advance.

You've probably attended a presentation where the speaker stepped to the microphone only to find that it wasn't turned on. Or, the speaker turned on the overhead projector to find that the bulb was burned out. Or, the speaker had to wait while the facilities staff adjusted the focus on the slide projector. Much of the embarrassment and lost time can be prevented if the speaker plans ahead and makes sure the equipment works.

Figure 2-25	SETTING UP FOR THE PRESENTATION

But even when the equipment works, it might not work the same as your equipment. One way to prevent this problem is to use your own equipment, or practice in advance with the available equipment. When you must use the available equipment but can't practice with it in advance, you should prepare for the worst and plan ahead.

Here are a few suggestions for planning ahead:

- Contact the facilities staff before your presentation to make sure they have the equipment you need. Also make sure the equipment is scheduled for the time and place of your presentation.
- Make sure your equipment is compatible with the facilities at your presentation site. For instance, what version is the software installed on the computer you'll use?

In considering the layout of the room, you'll want to make sure the chairs are arranged so that everyone in the audience can see and hear your presentation. You'll also want to make sure the microphone stand provides enough room for your notes, or that the equipment, such as the overhead projector, is close enough that you won't have to walk back and forth to your notes.

In considering the equipment, you'll want to check to make sure all the needed equipment is available and functioning properly. You'll also want to make sure you have adequate space for your equipment and access to electrical outlets. You might want to make arrangements for extra bulbs for the projector or overhead, or bring your own.

In considering the presentation materials, you'll want to make sure that you have chalk or markers for the chalkboard and white board, an easel to support your visuals, or thumbtacks you can use to mount your visuals on the wall or a poster board. You'll also want to make sure you have a glass of water in case your throat gets dry.

As you go through the Facilities Checklist, you find that everything you need is available in your presentation room at Rocky Mountain State College. You feel confident knowing that you have done everything possible on your part to prepare for your presentation. When the presentation time comes, you deliver your message with a natural, clear voice, and keep eye contact with your audience. Your audience responds favorably to your presentation, asks meaningful questions for which you are prepared, and compliments you on a job well done. Your presentation is a success in every way.

Session 2.2 QUICK CHECK

1. List and define three common presentation delivery methods.

2. Which delivery method(s) are appropriate if you must speak under a strict time limit and want to use specific wording in your presentation?

3. Which delivery method(s) are appropriate if you're asked to speak on the spur of the moment?

4. Which delivery method(s) are appropriate if you want audience participation?

5. True or False. You should avoid questions from the audience because it shows that your audience didn't pay attention to your presentation.

6. List the most important way to overcome nervousness about giving a presentation.

7. Define non-verbal communication and give one example.

8. Give an example of a filler word you should avoid in your presentation.

REVIEW ASSIGNMENTS

Tanner Granatowski is an intern for Business With a Heart, another nonprofit organization in the Colorado Springs area. Business With a Heart matches people willing to donate goods, time, or talents with those in desperate need. The non profit company also partners with local businesses to distribute goods, similar to food banks. You're asked to help Tanner prepare and give three presentations for Business With a Heart.

The first presentation will be a 20-minute presentation to members of the local Chamber of Commerce (approximately 40 people). Your purpose in this presentation is to inform the Chamber of the goals and purposes of Business With a Heart. The presentation will take place in the large banquet hall of the new Colorado Springs City Center, which is fully equipped with the latest technology.

The second presentation will be a 10-minute presentation to 10 members of the Board of Directors of The Henderson Foundation, a national foundation that gives money to non-profit organizations. Your purpose in this presentation is to persuade the Board of Directors to donate $400,000 to help Business With a Heart expand its programs. The presentation will take place in the 100-year-old foundation board room. It has electricity, but no computer projection equipment.

The third presentation will be a 40-minute presentation to five members of the staff at Business With a Heart. Your purpose in this presentation is to show staff members how to contact local business owners over the phone to find out if they are interested in donating their excess goods. The presentation will take place in a small staff room. Do the following:

1. Explain the differences and similarities between the three presentations in terms of your audience. Complete an Audience Analysis Worksheet for each presentation.

2. Explain how your purpose and the type of information you will present in each presentation will affect the visuals that you would use.

3. Explain the differences and similarities between the three presentations in terms of the presentation situation. Complete a Situation and Media Assessment Worksheet for each presentation.

4. Explain how your purpose and the type of information you will be presenting in each of these presentations will affect the visuals that you use. Complete a Presentation Visuals Worksheet for each presentation.

5. Give an example of how you would use a numerical table in one presentation.

6. Give an example of how you would use a graph in one presentation.

7. Give an example of how you would use a chart in one presentation.

8. Give an example of how you would use an illustration in one presentation

9. Explain how your purpose, audience, and situation would affect the delivery method you would use for each presentation. Complete a Presentation Delivery Worksheet for each presentation.

10. Create a storyboard showing an idea and visual for one presentation.

11. List two questions you think the audience might ask for each presentation.

12. Give an example of how your nervousness might vary for the presentations. Explain what you would do to overcome your nervousness.

13. Describe what you would wear for each presentation.

14. Using the Facilities Checklist, describe one aspect you can control and one you can't control for each presentation.

CASE PROBLEMS

Case 1. Wyoming ESCAPE Wyoming ESCAPE is a Jackson Hole-based company that plans corporate retreats, taking advantage of Wyoming's beautiful scenery and recreation. Wyoming ESCAPE provides activities to help harried workers and executives unwind and play team-enhancing games—everything from ropes courses to river raft races in the summer, and snowman building and cross-country skiing in the winter. The staff at Wyoming ESCAPE asks you to help them prepare for three presentations.

The first presentation will be a 20-minute presentation to sales personnel (approximately 15 people). Your purpose in this presentation is to inform the sales staff about the activities you provide so that they can market the retreats. The presentation will take place at company headquarters in a large conference room. The conference room does not have a computer projection system, but does have a slide projector.

The second presentation will be a 10-minute presentation to approximately 45 potential participants. Your purpose in this presentation is to persuade your audience to consider Wyoming ESCAPE for their corporate retreat, and to contact your sales staff for further details. The presentation will take place at a national human resources conference in the ballroom of a large hotel. The hotel has a computer projection system, as well as a slide projector.

The third presentation will be a 40-minute presentation to five staff members who'll conduct the activities. Your purpose in this presentation is to demonstrate how to conduct several new activities that will be used during corporate retreats. The presentation will take place in a small conference room. There is no slide projector or computer projection system in the conference room, but there is a large white board.

Do the following:

1. Complete a Purpose and Outcomes Worksheet for each presentation.

2. Explain the differences and similarities between the audiences for the three presentations, including any general demographics that you can determine. Complete an Audience Analysis Worksheet for each presentation.

3. Explain how the settings for these presentations would probably affect your audience's expectations and the appropriate level of formality.

4. Determine appropriate and inappropriate media for each presentation. Complete a Situation and Media Assessment Worksheet for each presentation.

5. Complete a Focus and Organization Worksheet to determine an appropriate organizational pattern and organize the text in your presentation accordingly.

6. Explain how your purpose, audience, and setting would affect the visuals you would use. Complete a Presentation Visuals Worksheet for each presentation.

7. Give an example of a visual you could use to show sales personnel that the number of participants has decreased in the last year.

8. Give an example of a visual you could use to convince potential participants that they would enjoy attending Wyoming ESCAPE.

9. Give an example of a visual you could use to show the staff a new game for the retreat.

10. Create a storyboard showing an idea and visual for one presentation.

11. Using a Presentation Delivery Worksheet, specify which delivery method you would use for each presentation, and list one question you think the audience might ask for each presentation. Also explain how your level of nervousness might differ for each presentation, and what you would do to overcome your nervousness.

12. Using a Facilities Checklist for each presentation, list two set up details you would want to check for each presentation.

Case 2. FamilyOrigins.com   Tamar Ruest works for FamilyOrigins.com, a company that allows family members to speak to each other free-of-charge over the Internet, share stories and photographs through personal Web pages, and obtain genealogy-related supplies over the Internet, such as government reports, printed family histories, and forms for creating a family tree. You're asked to create three presentations.

The purpose of the first presentation is to inform your listeners of the success of FamilyOrigins.com. Your presentation will be given to 50 attendees at a genealogy conference held in a large conference room in a local motel. There is no computer projection system or slide projector available at the motel, but your company has an overhead projector you could take to the conference.

The purpose of the second presentation is to persuade your audience of the need for genealogy. Your audience consists of 15 members of your family (or someone else's) attending a family reunion held at an outdoor pavilion at a local state park. There is an electrical outlet at the pavilion, but no slide projector, computer projection system, or blackboard.

The third presentation, demonstrating how to download the form to create a family tree, will be given to your classmates. You should base your media selection upon the facilities at your school and classroom.

Do the following:

1. Complete a Purpose and Outcomes Worksheet for each presentation.

2. Explain the differences and similarities between the above three groups in terms of their age, level of education, and familiarity with the subject. Complete an Audience Analysis Worksheet for each presentation.

3. Explain how the settings for these presentations would affect your audience's expectations and the appropriate level of formality. Complete a Situation and Media Assessment Worksheet for each presentation.

4. Determine appropriate and inappropriate media for each presentation.

5. Complete a Focus and Organizational Worksheet to determine an appropriate organizational pattern and organize the text in your presentation accordingly.

6. Explain how your purpose, audience, and setting for each presentation would affect the visuals you would use.

7. Complete a Presentation Visuals Worksheet for each presentation, giving an example of an appropriate visual for each presentation.

8. Create a storyboard showing an idea and visual for one presentation.

9. Using a Presentation Delivery Worksheet, identify which delivery method you would use for each presentation. List two questions you think the audience might ask for each presentation. Explain how your level of nervousness might differ for each presentation, and what you would do to overcome your nervousness.

10. Complete a Facilities Checklist for each presentation, determining two things you should check for each presentation.

Case 3. Kids Kreative Communication Kids Kreative Communication sells fairy tale and nursery rhyme software for teaching young children to read, including online coloring books and stories that use a particular child's name. You're asked to give some presentations for Kids Kreative.

The purpose of the first presentation is to demonstrate how a particular software program works. Your audience will be five elementary school teachers who will use the software at a local elementary school. Your presentation will be given in the school's computer classroom, which has a white board and a computer projection system.

The purpose of the second presentation is to interest approximately 40 elementary school principals attending a national teaching convention in the complete line of Kids Kreative software. Your presentation will be given in a hotel conference room which has an overhead projector and a slide projector.

The purpose of the third presentation is to inform 10 programmers at Kids Kreative of some of the needs of current software users. Your presentation will be given at Kids Kreative headquarters, in a small conference room which has an overhead projector and a white board.

Do the following:

1. Complete a Purpose and Outcomes Worksheet for each presentation.

2. Explain the differences and similarities between the above three groups in terms of their age, level of education, and familiarity with the subject. Complete an Audience Analysis Worksheet for each presentation.

3. Explain how the settings for these presentations would affect your audience's expectations and the appropriate level of formality. Complete a Situation and Media Assessment Worksheet for each presentation.

4. Determine appropriate and inappropriate media for each presentation.

5. Complete a Focus and Organization Worksheet to determine an appropriate organizational pattern, and organize the text in your presentation accordingly.

6. Explain how your purpose, audience, and setting for each presentation would affect the visuals you would use. Complete a Presentation Visuals Worksheet for each presentation.

7. Create a storyboard showing an idea and a visual for one presentation.

8. Using a Presentation Delivery Worksheet, specify which delivery method you would use for each presentation. List one question you think the audience might ask for each presentation. Explain how your level of nervousness might differ for each presentation, and what you would do to overcome your nervousness.

9. Complete a Facilities Checklist for each presentation, determining which items on the checklist would apply to each presentation.

Case 4. Flores High Performance Seminars Juanita Flores owns Flores High Performance Seminars, a company providing monthly seminars and training on coaching, leadership, teambuilding, and presentations. Juanita asks you to give a presentation to your class on one of these topics. Working with another member of the class, create a 5-7 minute presentation for your classmates. Do the following:

1. Decide what type of presentation you'll give.

2. Complete a Purpose and Outcomes Worksheet for your presentation.

3. Define your audience according to their general demographic features of age, gender, level of education, and familiarity with your topic. Complete an Audience Analysis Worksheet for your presentation.

4. Assess the situation for your presentation by describing the setting and size of your audience. Complete a Situation and Media Assessment Worksheet.

5. Select appropriate media for your presentation and explain why they are appropriate.

6. Complete a Focus and Organization Worksheet and organize the text in your presentation accordingly.

7. Show two ways you could focus your presentation and limit the scope of your topic.

8. Select a method for gaining your audience's attention, and write an introduction using that method.

9. Create an advance organizer or overview for your presentation.

10. Identify at least two sources for information on your topic and consult those sources.

11. Select an appropriate organizational pattern for your presentation.

12. Identify four transitional phrases that you'll use in your presentation.

13. Write a summary for your presentation recapping the key ideas.

14. Complete a Presentation Visuals Worksheet.

15. Create an appropriate visual for your presentation.

16. Using the Presentation Delivery Worksheet, decide on an appropriate presentation style. Write a list of questions you think your classmates will ask.

17. Practice your presentation in front of another group in your class, and ask them to complete the evaluation part of the Presentation Delivery Worksheet.

18. Complete a Facilities Checklist for your presentation.

19. Set up your classroom.

20. Give your presentation to your classmates.

QUICK | CHECK ANSWERS

Session 2.1

1. (a) organize information in horizontal rows and vertical columns (b) show the relationship of two variables along a horizontal and a vertical axis (c) show the relationship of variables without using a coordinate system (d) show relationships that aren't numerical

2. (a) table (strengths): effective for making facts and details accessible, organizing data by categories, summarizing results and recommendations, and comparing sets of data; table (weaknesses): not effective for showing change across time, trends, procedures, or spatial relationships. (b) graph (strengths): effective for comparing one quantity to another, showing changes over time, and indicating patterns or trends; graph (weaknesses): not effective for showing organizational hierarchy, procedures or work flow, parts and wholes, or spatial relationships. (c) chart (strengths): effective for comparing parts to the whole, explaining organizations, and showing chronology, procedures, and work flow; chart (weaknesses): not effective for showing changes over time or percentages. (d) illustration (strengths): effective for showing how things appear, the assembly and relationship of parts and processes to each other, and spatial relationships; illustration (weaknesses): not effective for summarizing data, providing chronology, or showing processes.

3. a., b., and c.

4. d.

5. c.

6. b.

7. b., c., and d.

8. technique from movie industry showing dialogue and accompanying camera shots and special effects; list idea you're discussing on left side of sheet and the accompanying visual on the right side of the sheet.

Session 2.2

1. written or memorized presentation—write out presentation and read it word for word or memorize it; extemporaneous presentation—speak from a few notes or outline; impromptu presentation—speak without notes or outline, or off-the-cuff.

2. written or memorized presentation

3. impromptu presentation

4. extemporaneous presentation, impromptu presentation

5. False; questions probably mean your audience listened and was interested in what you had to say.

6. planning, preparation, and practice

7. conveying a message without talking; appearance, posture, body movement, gestures, and mannerisms.

8. "uh," "um," "you know," "er," "a," "like"

New Perspectives on

MICROSOFT® POWERPOINT® 2000

Read This Before You Begin

To the Student

Data Disks

To complete the Level I tutorials, Review Assignments, and Case Problems in this book, you need two Data Disks. Your instructor will either provide you with Data Disks or ask you to make your own.

If you are making your own Data Disks, you will need two blank, formatted high-density disks. You will need to copy a set of folders from a file server or standalone computer or the Web onto your disks. Your instructor will tell you which computer, drive letter, and folders contain the files you need. You could also download the files by going to www.course.com, clicking Data Disk Files, and following the instructions on the screen.

The following table shows you which folders go on your disks, so that you will have enough disk space to complete all the tutorials, Review Assignments, and Case Problems:

Data Disk 1

Write this on the disk label:
Data Disk 1: Level I Tutorial 1

Put these folders on the disk:
Tutorial.01

Data Disk 2

Write this on the disk label:
Data Disk 2: Level I Tutorial 2

Put these folders on the disk:
Tutorial.02

You may need an extra blank, formatted disk to save some solutions.

When you begin each tutorial, be sure you are using the correct Data Disk. See the inside front or inside back cover of this book for more information on Data Disk files, or ask your instructor or technical support person for assistance.

Using Your Own Computer

If you are going to work through this book using your own computer, you need:

Computer System Microsoft PowerPoint 2000 and Windows 95 or higher must be installed on your computer. This book assumes a complete installation of PowerPoint 2000.

Data Disks You will not be able to complete the tutorials or exercises in this book using your own computer until you have Data Disks.

Visit Our World Wide Web Site

Additional materials designed especially for you are available on the World Wide Web. Go to http://www.course.com.

To the Instructor

The Data files are available on the Instructor's Resource Kit for this title. Follow the instructions in the Help file on the CD-ROM to install the programs to your network or standalone computer. For information on creating Data Disks, see the "To the Student" section above.

You are granted a license to copy the Data Files to any computer or computer network used by students who have purchased this book.

OBJECTIVES

In this tutorial you will:

- Start and exit PowerPoint

- Identify the components of the PowerPoint window

- Open and view an existing presentation

- Create a presentation using the AutoContent Wizard

- Edit text of the presentation in the Outline Pane and the Slide Pane

- Insert and delete slides

- Check the spelling and style in a presentation

- Use the PowerPoint Help system

- Create notes

- Save, preview, and print a presentation

USING POWERPOINT TO CREATE PRESENTATIONS

Presentation to Reach Potential Customers of Inca Imports International

CASE

Inca Imports International

Three years ago Patricia Cuevas and Angelena Cristenas began an import business called Inca Imports International. Working with suppliers in South America, particularly in Ecuador and Peru, the company imports fresh fruits and vegetables to North America during the winter and spring (which are summer and fall in South America) and sells them to small grocery stores in the Los Angeles area.

Inca Imports now has 34 employees and is a healthy and growing company. It has recently made plans to construct a distribution facility in Quito, Ecuador, and to launch a marketing campaign to position itself for further expansion. Patricia (president of Inca Imports) assigned Carl Vetterli (vice president of sales and marketing) the task of identifying potential customers and developing methods to reach them. Carl has scheduled a meeting with Patricia, Angelena (vice president of operations), Enrique Hoffmann (director of marketing), and other colleagues to review the results of his market research and to find ways of helping sales representatives increase sales.

Carl decides he wants to prepare two separate presentations for this meeting. His first presentation will include a demographic profile of Inca Imports' current customers, the results of a customer satisfaction survey, a vision statement of the company's future growth, a list of options for attracting new clients, and recommendations for a marketing strategy. Carl has already prepared this presentation, using many of PowerPoint's special features. For his second presentation, he wants a brainstorming session on how to help Inca Imports' sales representatives improve their sales effectiveness. He has not prepared this presentation, and asks you to help him create it.

SESSION 1.1

In this session, you'll learn how to start and exit PowerPoint, identify the parts of the PowerPoint window, and open and view an existing presentation. You'll also learn how to create a new presentation using the AutoContent Wizard and how to insert and modify text in both the Slide Pane and the Outline Pane.

What Is PowerPoint?

PowerPoint is a powerful presentation graphics program that provides everything you need to produce an effective presentation in the form of black-and-white or color overheads, 35 mm photographic slides, or on-screen slides. You may have already seen your instructors use PowerPoint presentations to enhance their classroom lectures.

Using PowerPoint, you can prepare each component of a presentation: individual slides, speaker notes, an outline of the presentation, and audience handouts. The presentation you'll create for Carl will include slides, notes, and handouts. Before you begin creating this presentation, however, you'll first preview Carl's existing presentation. You'll learn about some of PowerPoint's capabilities that can help make your presentations more interesting and effective.

Starting PowerPoint

You start PowerPoint in the same way that you start other Windows 98 programs—using the Start button on the taskbar.

To start PowerPoint:

1. Make sure Windows 98 is running on your computer, and that the Windows 98 desktop appears on your screen.

   TROUBLE? If you're running Windows NT Workstation on your computer or network, don't worry. Although the figures in this book were created while running Windows 98, Windows NT and Windows 98 share the same interface, and PowerPoint 2000 runs equally well under either operating system.

2. Click the **Start** button on the taskbar to display the Start menu, and then point to **Programs** to display the Programs menu.

3. Point to **Microsoft PowerPoint** on the Programs menu. See Figure 1-1.

Figure 1-1 STARTING MICROSOFT POWERPOINT

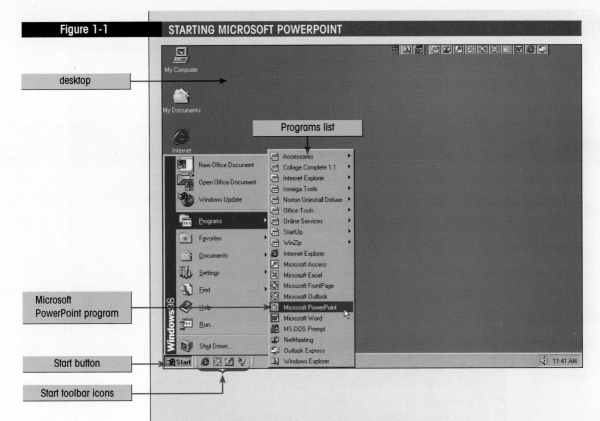

desktop

Programs list

Microsoft
PowerPoint program

Start button

Start toolbar icons

TROUBLE? If you don't see Microsoft PowerPoint on the Programs menu, ask your instructor or technical support person for help.

TROUBLE? If the Office Shortcut Bar, which appears along the top border of the desktop in Figure 1-1, looks different on your screen or does not appear at all, don't be concerned. Since the Office Shortcut Bar is not required to complete these tutorials, it has been omitted from the remaining figures in this text.

4. Click **Microsoft PowerPoint**. After a short pause PowerPoint opens, and the PowerPoint dialog box appears on the screen. If necessary, click the **Maximize** button ☐ so that the PowerPoint window fills the entire screen. See Figure 1-2.

Figure 1-2   THE POWERPOINT STARTUP DIALOG BOX

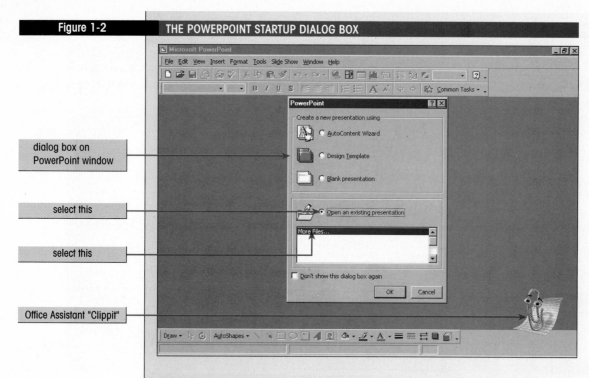

dialog box on
PowerPoint window

select this

select this

Office Assistant "Clippit"

TROUBLE? If the Office Assistant (see Figure 1-2) opens when you start PowerPoint, right-click the Office Assistant, and then click Hide to close it; you'll learn more about the Office Assistant later in this tutorial.

Now that you've started PowerPoint, you're ready to open Carl's existing presentation.

Opening an Existing PowerPoint Presentation

Before you prepare Carl's second presentation, Carl suggests that you view his first presentation as an example of PowerPoint features. He gives you a disk with a PowerPoint file so you can open and view it. You'll do that now.

To open an existing presentation:

1. Place your Data Disk in the appropriate drive.

TROUBLE? If you don't have a Data Disk, you need to get one before you can proceed. Your instructor or technical support person will either give you one or ask you to make your own by following the instructions on the "Read This Before You Begin" page preceding this tutorial. See your instructor or technical support person for more information.

2. If necessary, click the **Open an existing presentation** option button to select it.

3. Make sure **More files** is selected in the list box below the Open an existing presentation option button (as shown in Figure 1-2), and then click the **OK** button. The Open dialog box appears on the screen.

4. Click the **Look in** list arrow to display the list of disk drives on your computer, and then click on the drive that contains your Data Disk.

5. Double-click the **Tutorial.01** folder, double-click the **Tutorial** folder, click **Customer**, and then click the **Open** button to display Carl's presentation.

TROUBLE? If you see filename extensions on your screen (such as ".ppt" appended to "Customer" in the filename), do not be concerned; they will not affect the accuracy of your work.

6. If necessary, click the **Maximize** button 🔲 so the presentation window fills the screen, and then, if necessary, click the **Normal View** button 🔲 near the lower-left corner of the screen. See Figure 1-3.

Figure 1-3	THE POWERPOINT WINDOW

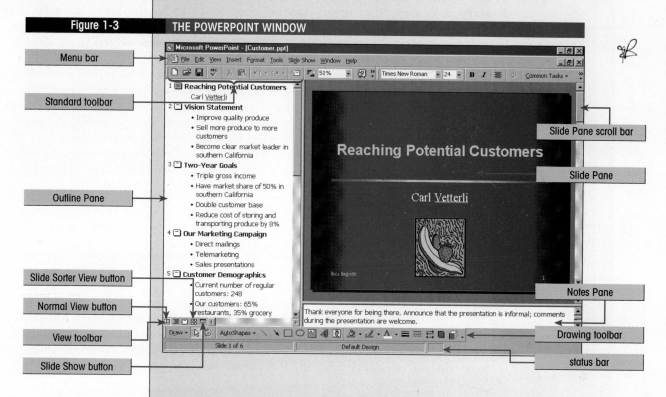

TROUBLE? If your screen doesn't show the Drawing toolbar (located near the bottom of the screen, with the word "Draw" on the left edge), click View on the main menu, point to Toolbars, and then click Drawing.

Now that you've opened Carl's presentation, you're ready to view some of the PowerPoint features. You'll begin by reviewing the PowerPoint window.

Understanding the PowerPoint Window

The PowerPoint window contains features common to all Windows programs, as well as features specific to PowerPoint, such as the options available on the toolbars.

Common Windows Elements

You'll recognize that several elements of the PowerPoint window are common to other Windows 98 programs. For example, as shown in Figure 1-3, the PowerPoint window has a title bar, menu bar, and window sizing buttons. These elements function the same way in PowerPoint as they do in other Windows programs. However, the PowerPoint window also includes items that are specific to PowerPoint, such as some of the toolbar buttons and the panes.

The Toolbars

Like many Windows programs, PowerPoint supplies several toolbars, as shown in Figure 1-3. Recall that a **toolbar** is a horizontal or vertical ribbon of icons that provides menu shortcuts. When you move the mouse pointer over one of the icons on the toolbar, the outline of the button appears, followed by a **ScreenTip**, which is a light yellow box containing the name of the button. Although many of the toolbar buttons accomplish the same tasks in PowerPoint as they do in other Windows programs, such as the Save button on the Standard toolbar, you'll also notice some differences. For example, the Drawing toolbar contains specific buttons for adding shapes, lines, and other graphic objects to the slides in your PowerPoint presentation.

Further, just above the Drawing toolbar on the left side of the screen is the View toolbar, which contains five buttons that allow you to change the way you view a slide presentation. You are currently in Normal View. Clicking the Outline View button ▦ allows you to see more of the outline and less of the slide, and clicking the Slide View button ▢ allows you to see more of the slide and less of the outline. Clicking the Slide Sorter View button ▦ changes the view to miniature images of all the slides at once and lets you reorder the slides or set special features for your slide show. Finally, to present your slide show, you click the Slide Show button ▽.

The PowerPoint Panes

In Normal View, also called Tri-Pane View, the PowerPoint window contains three panes: the Outline Pane, the Slide Pane, and the Notes Pane (see Figure 1-3). The **Outline Pane** lists an outline of your presentation, including titles and text of each slide. The **Slide Pane** shows the slide as it will look during your slide show. You can use either the Outline Pane or the Slide Pane to add or edit text, but you can only use the Slide Pane to add or edit graphics. The **Notes Pane** contains any notes that you might prepare on each slide. For example, the Notes Pane might contain points to cover or phrases to say during the presentation.

Now that you're familiar with the PowerPoint window, you're ready to view Carl's presentation.

Viewing a Presentation in Slide Show View

You want to see how Carl's presentation will appear when he shows it in Slide Show View at Inca Imports' executive meeting. You'll then have a better understanding of how Carl used PowerPoint's features to make his presentation informative and interesting.

> *To view a presentation in Slide Show View:*
>
> 1. Make sure Slide 1, "Reaching Potential Customers," appears in the Slide Pane. (If you would prefer to start the slide show on a different slide, use the Slide Pane scroll bar to move to the desired slide, and then start the slide show.)
>
> TROUBLE? If a different slide is in the Slide Pane, drag the scroll button in the vertical scroll bar (located on the right side of the Slide Pane) to the top of the scroll bar.

2. Click the **Slide Show** button on the View toolbar (just below the Outline Pane). The slide show begins by filling the entire viewing area of the screen with Slide 1 of Carl's presentation. See Figure 1-4.

| Figure 1-4 | SLIDE 1 IN SLIDE SHOW VIEW |

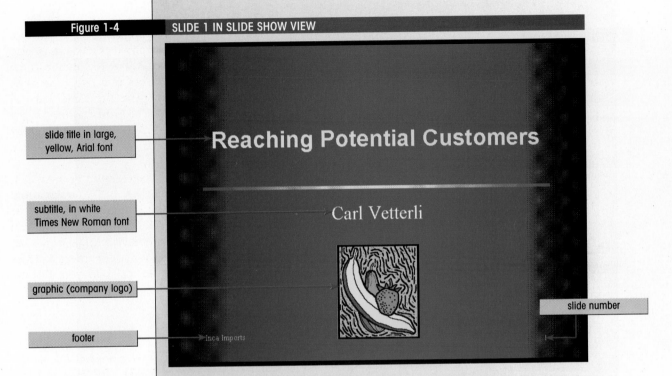

slide title in large, yellow, Arial font

subtitle, in white Times New Roman font

graphic (company logo)

slide number

footer

As you view this first slide, you can already see some of the types of objects that PowerPoint allows you to place on a slide: text in different fonts, font sizes, and font colors (to differentiate between the slide title and subtitle); graphics (the Inca Imports' logo, to identify the company clearly); footers; slide numbers; and colored background with gradient fills. A **footer** is a word or phrase that appears at the bottom of each slide in the presentation (for example, "Inca Imports" in the lower-left corner of Figure 1-4). A **gradient fill** is a type of shading in which one color blends into another, which can help make the slide more eye-catching; for example, in Figure 1-4, black blends into blue and then back into black horizontally across the screen. Take a few minutes to study these elements, and then continue to the next slide.

3. Press the **Spacebar.** The slide show goes from Slide 1 to Slide 2. See Figure 1-5. You can also press the Right Arrow key or click the left mouse button to advance to the next slide.

Additionally, PowerPoint provides a method for jumping from a slide to any other slide in the presentation during the slide show: right-click anywhere on the screen, point to Go, and then click Slide Navigator. The **slide navigator** is a dialog box that displays a list of all the slides by their title. Simply click on a title, and then click the Go To button to go to that slide. You also can right-click on the screen during a slide show, and then click other options to view other slide features.

Notice that during the transition from Slide 1 to Slide 2, the presentation did three things: (1) played the sound of chimes, (2) displayed Slide 2 by splitting Slide 1 horizontally and scrolling the top and bottom of Slide 2 onto the screen (called a **slide transition**), and (3) shot three arrows at a target on the screen with an accompanying "whoosh" sound with each arrow (called **object animation**). These PowerPoint transition and animation effects are entertaining and reinforce the major points of information on the slide.

Figure 1-5	SLIDE 2 WITH TITLE AND BULLETED LIST

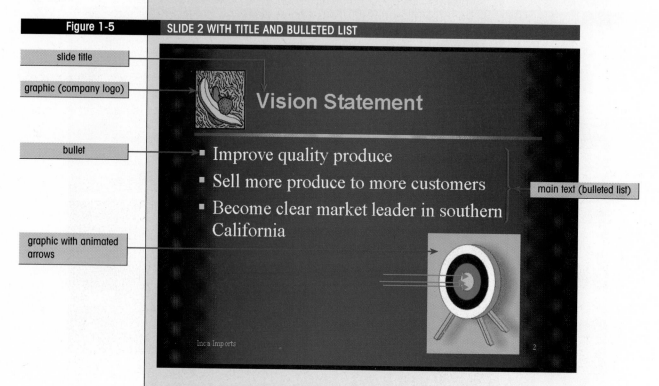

slide title

graphic (company logo)

bullet

main text (bulleted list)

graphic with animated arrows

TROUBLE? If you missed some of the action during the transition from Slide 1 to Slide 2, or if you would like to see it again, press the Left Arrow key twice to redisplay Slide 1, and then press the Spacebar to go to Slide 2 again.

TROUBLE? If you didn't hear any sound as Slide 2 appeared on the screen, your computer may not have a sound card and speakers, or the computer sound may have been turned off. If you have questions about the sound on a laboratory computer, consult your technical support person.

Notice in Figure 1-5 that Slide 2 displays Inca Imports' logo, a title in a large yellow font, and a bulleted list, with yellow, square bullets and white text. A **bulleted list** is a list of paragraphs with a special character (dot, circle, box, star, or other character) to the left of each paragraph. A **bulleted item** is one paragraph in a bulleted list. Using bulleted lists reminds both the speaker and the audience of the slide's main points.

In addition to bulleted lists, PowerPoint also supports numbered lists. A **numbered list** is a list of paragraphs that are numbered consecutively within a main text box. To number a list automatically, select the text box, and then click the Numbering button 🔢 on the Formatting toolbar.

4. Press the **Spacebar** to proceed to Slide 3. During the transition from Slide 2 to Slide 3, you again hear the sound and see the slide scroll onto the screen from the center. You also notice that the slide doesn't display a bulleted list. On this

slide, you'll display the bulleted items, as well as a chart, one at a time. This allows the speaker to keep the audience focused only on the item currently being discussed.

5. Press the **Spacebar** to display the chart "Projected Gross Income" onto Slide 3. You can easily create attractive and effective charts and graphs using PowerPoint. Now you're ready to display the first bulleted item on the slide.

6. Press the **Spacebar** to display the first bulleted paragraph, "Triple gross income."

7. Press the **Spacebar** again to display the next bulleted paragraph. Notice that as each new bulleted item appears in a white font with a yellow bullet, the previous item dims to a gray font and bullet. Again, this helps keep the audience focused.

8. Press the **Spacebar** twice more to display the final two items in the bulleted list in Slide 3. See Figure 1-6.

| Figure 1-6 | SLIDE 3 IN SLIDE SHOW VIEW |

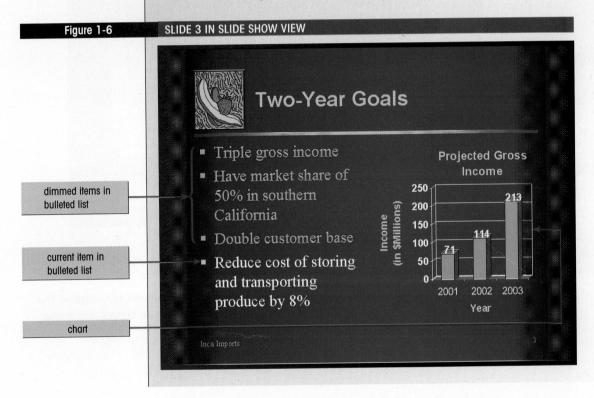

In these first three slides, you saw many PowerPoint features that help make Carl's presentation informative and enjoyable. Next, you'll proceed to the other slides in Carl's presentation, where you'll see additional PowerPoint features.

To finish viewing the slide show:

1. Press the **Spacebar** to display Slide 4. Remember, you can see the slide number in the lower-right corner of the screen. This slide contains a clip-art image of a telephone. A **clip-art image** is a picture, often a drawing or cartoon, that you can get from the PowerPoint ClipArt Gallery. Using clip art visually emphasizes the main point of the slide.

2. Press the **Spacebar** to display the first bulleted item. This time the presentation makes a "laser" sound as the item appears on the screen.

3. Press the **Spacebar** as many times as necessary to see the rest of Slide 4, to move on to Slide 5 and view and read its contents, and then to display Slide 6. See Figure 1-7. As Slide 6 appears on the screen, instead of hearing chimes, you hear a drum roll. Using different sound effects can help keep your audience alert and entertained.

Figure 1-7	SLIDE WITH SOUND CLIP

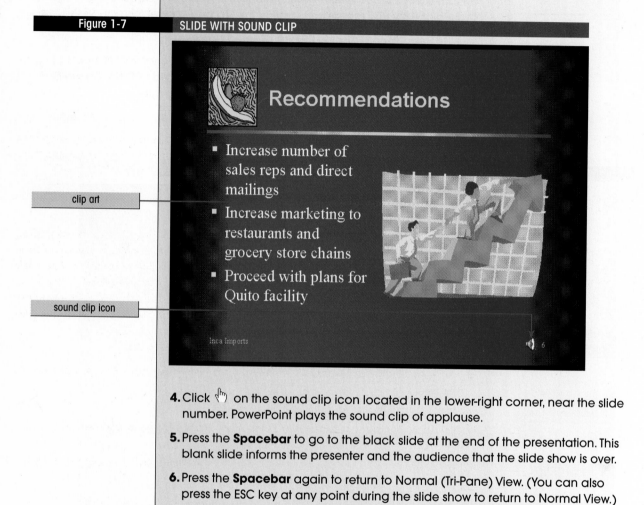

clip art

sound clip icon

4. Click 🖑 on the sound clip icon located in the lower-right corner, near the slide number. PowerPoint plays the sound clip of applause.

5. Press the **Spacebar** to go to the black slide at the end of the presentation. This blank slide informs the presenter and the audience that the slide show is over.

6. Press the **Spacebar** again to return to Normal (Tri-Pane) View. (You can also press the ESC key at any point during the slide show to return to Normal View.)

As you can see from this slide show, PowerPoint has many powerful features. You'll learn how to include many of these features in your own presentations as you work through these tutorials. Now that you've finished viewing Carl's presentation, you're ready to close it.

Closing a Presentation and Exiting PowerPoint

Once you've completed viewing a presentation, you can close it and exit PowerPoint. If you've created or edited a presentation, you should always save it first; you'll learn how later in this tutorial.

To close a presentation and exit PowerPoint:

1. Click the **Close** button ☒ on the right side of the menu bar. The presentation window closes but leaves the PowerPoint window on the screen.

   TROUBLE? If you clicked the PowerPoint Close button in the extreme upper-right corner of the screen, the entire PowerPoint window closed. If this happened, just omit the next step.

2. Click the **Close** button ☒ in the upper-right corner of the screen to exit PowerPoint. You should now be viewing your computer desktop on your screen (unless other programs are running).

You're now ready to create Carl's presentation for brainstorming on methods to help Inca Imports' sales representatives. Before you begin, however, you should plan the presentation.

Planning a Presentation

Planning a presentation before you create it improves the quality of your presentation, makes your presentation more effective and enjoyable, and, in the long run, saves you time and effort. As you plan your presentation, you should answer several questions: What is my purpose or objective for this presentation? What type of presentation is needed? Who is the audience? What information does that audience need? What is the physical location of my presentation? What is the best format for presenting the information contained in this presentation, given the location of the presentation?

In planning your presentation, you identify the following elements:

- **Purpose of the presentation**: To identify means of helping sales reps improve their sales
- **Type of presentation**: Brainstorming session
- **Audience for the presentation**: Patricia, Angelena, Enrique, and other key staff members in a weekly executive meeting
- **Audience needs**: To develop an environment conducive to developing new ideas
- **Location of the presentation**: Small boardroom
- **Format**: Oral presentation; electronic slide show of six to eight slides

Having carefully planned your presentation, you'll now use the PowerPoint AutoContent Wizard to create it.

Using the AutoContent Wizard

PowerPoint helps you quickly create effective presentations by using **Wizards**, which you'll recall ask you a series of questions about your tasks and then help you perform them. The **AutoContent Wizard** lets you choose a presentation category such as "Recommending a Strategy," "Generic," or "Brainstorming Session." After you've selected the type of presentation you want, the AutoContent Wizard creates a general outline for you to follow.

When you create a new presentation without using the AutoContent Wizard, you can start from an existing design template or existing PowerPoint presentation, or you can start with a blank presentation. A **design template** is a file that contains the colors and format of the background and the type style of the titles, accents, and other text. To create a new presentation from a design template, click File on the main menu, click New, and then select the desired template. To start with a blank presentation, simply click the New button on the Standard toolbar. Once you start creating a presentation with or without a design template, you can change to any other PowerPoint design template.

Because the presentation you'll create, a brainstorming session, is predefined, you'll use the AutoContent Wizard. The AutoContent Wizard will automatically create a title slide and standard outline, which you then can edit to fit Carl's needs.

To create a presentation with the AutoContent Wizard:

1. Start PowerPoint, click the **AutoContent Wizard** option button in the PowerPoint startup dialog box, and then click the **OK** button. The first of several AutoContent Wizard dialog boxes appears. See Figure 1-8.

Figure 1-8	OPENING DIALOG BOX OF AUTOCONTENT WIZARD

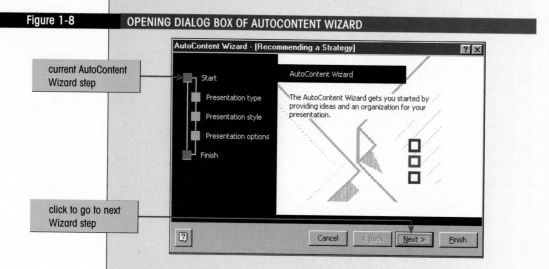

current AutoContent Wizard step

click to go to next Wizard step

TROUBLE? If the PowerPoint startup dialog box doesn't appear on your screen, click File, and then click New. When the New Presentation dialog box opens, click the General tab, click the AutoContent Wizard button, and then click the OK button.

TROUBLE? If the Office Assistant opens, click the No, don't provide help now option button.

2. Read the information in the AutoContent Wizard dialog box, and then click the **Next** button to display the next dialog box of the AutoContent Wizard.

This dialog box allows you to select the type of presentation; you want to select the presentation on brainstorming.

3. In the list of types of presentation, click **Brainstorming Session**. See Figure 1-9.

Figure 1-9 | SELECTING TYPE OF PRESENTATION IN AUTOCONTENT WIZARD DIALOG BOX

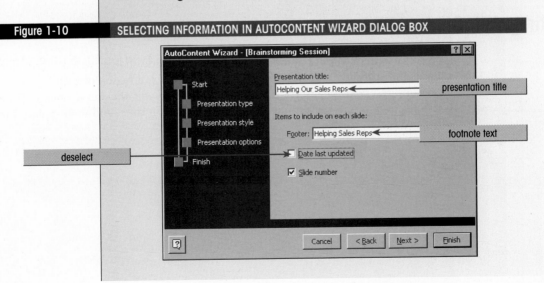

click to see list of desired presentation types

click to select this presentation type

TROUBLE? If you don't see Brainstorming Session in the AutoContent Wizard dialog box, click the General button, and then click Brainstorming Session.

TROUBLE? If a Microsoft PowerPoint dialog box appears with the message that PowerPoint can't find the template used in this document, insert the Office 2000 CD into your CD drive, and then click the Yes button. The desired template will then become installed on your computer. If you don't have an Office 2000 CD, consult your instructor or technical support person.

4. Click the **Next** button to display the dialog box with the question, "What type of output will you use?"

5. If necessary, click the **On-screen presentation** option button to select it, and then click the **Next** button. In this dialog box, you'll specify the title and footer (if any) of the presentation.

6. Click I in the Presentation title text box and type **Helping Our Sales Reps**, click I in the Footer text box and type **Helping Sales Reps**, and then click the **Date last updated** check box to deselect it. Leave the Slide Number box checked. The dialog box should now look like Figure 1-10.

Figure 1-10 | SELECTING INFORMATION IN AUTOCONTENT WIZARD DIALOG BOX

presentation title

footnote text

deselect

7. Click the **Next** button. The final AutoContent Wizard dialog box appears, letting you know that you've completed the AutoContent Wizard.

8. Click the **Finish** button. PowerPoint now displays the AutoContent outline in the Outline Pane and the title slide (Slide 1) in the Slide Pane. See Figure 1-11.

Figure 1-11	OUTLINE AND SLIDE AFTER COMPLETING THE AUTOCONTENT WIZARD

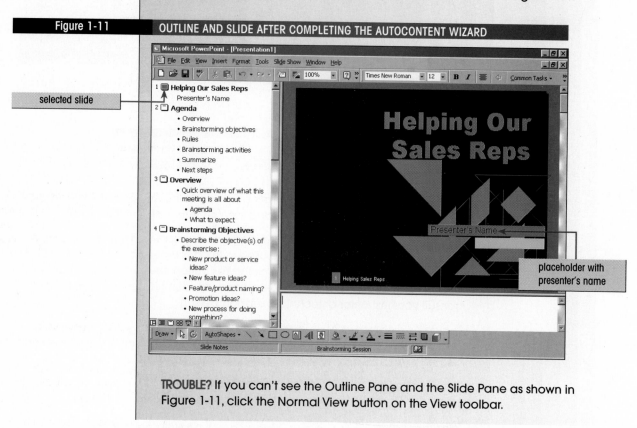

TROUBLE? If you can't see the Outline Pane and the Slide Pane as shown in Figure 1-11, click the Normal View button on the View toolbar.

Now that you've used the AutoContent Wizard, you're ready to edit its default outline to fit Carl's specific presentation needs.

Editing **AutoContent Slides**

The AutoContent Wizard automatically creates the title slide as well as other slides, with suggested text located in placeholders. A **placeholder** is a region of a slide or a location in an outline reserved for inserting text or graphics. To edit the AutoContent outline to fit Carl's needs, you must select the placeholders one at a time, and then replace them with other text.

REFERENCE   WINDOW   **RW**

Creating Effective Text Presentations

- Think of your text presentation as a visual map of your oral presentation. Show your organization by using overviews, making headings larger than subheadings, including bulleted lists to highlight key points, and numbering steps to show sequence.
- Follow the 6 x 6 rule: Use six or fewer items per screen, and use phrases of six or fewer words. Omit unnecessary articles, pronouns, and adjectives.
- Keep phrases parallel.
- Make sure your text is appropriate for your purpose and audience.

You'll now begin to edit and replace the text to fit Carl's presentation. The first text you'll change is the presenter's name placeholder (which currently has your name or that of the person who owns the computer) with the actual presenter's name, Carl Vetterli. (If the scheduled presenter changes after creating the presentation, recall that you can use the Find command to locate Carl Vetterli's name and then replace it accordingly. Click Edit on the menu bar, click Replace, enter the text that you want replaced in the Find what text box, enter the replacement text in the Replace with text box, and then click either Replace or Replace All.)

To edit and replace text in a slide:

1. In the Outline Pane, drag I across the text of the presenter's name (currently your name or the computer owner's name) to select it. When the text becomes selected, it appears as white text on a black background.

2. Type **Carl Vetterli**, and then click anywhere else on the slide. As soon as you start to type, the placeholder disappears, and the typed text appears in its place.

   Notice that PowerPoint marks "Vetterli" with a red wavy underline to indicate that the word may be misspelled. This is a result of PowerPoint's **Spell Checker**, a feature that automatically marks any word not found in the PowerPoint dictionary. In this case, "Vetterli" is correctly spelled, but sometimes you might make typographical errors. If this happens, *right*-click on the red wavy underlined word to display a list of suggested spellings and then click the correct word, or simply edit the misspelled word. Instead of correcting the spelling, you'll tell PowerPoint to ignore the word "Vetterli" and not mark it as misspelled on this or any other slides.

3. Right-click I on the word **Vetterli** to display the shortcut menu, and then click **Ignore All**. See Figure 1-12.

Figure 1-15   MOVING A SLIDE IN THE OUTLINE PANE

line to mark new position

mouse pointer

selected slide being moved

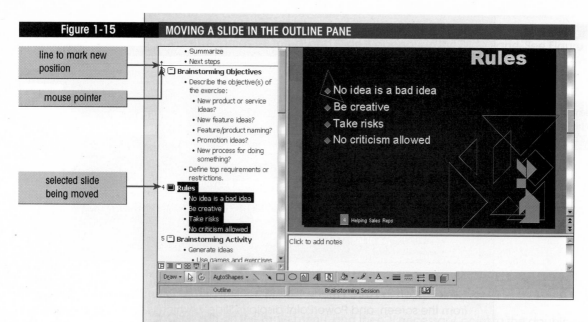

Now you'll have to change the order of the items on the agenda slide.

3. If necessary, scroll the Outline Pane so you can see all the text of Slide 2, and then click ⊕ on the bullet to the left of "Brainstorming objectives" within the Outline Pane.

4. Drag the bulleted item down below "Rules" so that the Outline Pane and the Slide Pane appear as in Figure 1-16. (Note that you can also move text in the Slide Pane by selecting the text box, clicking ⊕ on a bulleted item, and dragging it to a new location within that slide.)

Figure 1-16   MOVING A BULLETED ITEM

selected and moved bulleted item in Outline Pane

switched items in Slide Pane

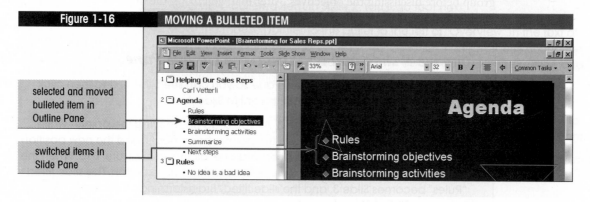

As you can see, any time you want to move text from within a slide or from one slide to another, you can simply drag the text within the Outline Pane.

Carl is pleased with these changes, but decides that further editing is needed. He asks you to customize Slide 4, "Brainstorming Objectives," to fit the objectives of helping Inca Imports' sales representatives. You'll first replace and delete the current text, and then you'll promote some of the bulleted items.

Promoting and Demoting Outline Text

To **promote** an item means to increase the outline level of an item, for example, to change a bulleted item into a slide title. To **demote** an item means to decrease the outline level, for example, to change a slide title into a bulleted item within another slide. For Slide 4, your first task is to edit the current text.

To edit Slide 4:

1. Go to Slide 4 by clicking within the Slide 4 text in the Outline Pane or by dragging the scroll button in the Slide Pane.

2. Using the Outline Pane, delete the last bulleted item, "Define top requirements or restrictions."

   You could have made these deletions in the Slide Pane just as well. In the next step, you'll use the Slide Pane, just to see how you can use either pane for deleting or modifying text.

3. Make sure Slide 4 appears in the Slide Pane.

4. In the Slide Pane, drag ⌶ over the first sub-bulleted item, **New product or service ideas**, making sure you don't select the question mark, because you want to leave the question mark on the screen. See Figure 1-17.

   Notice that when you click within the bulleted list, or select text within the bulleted list, the text box containing the list becomes selected. A **text box** is a rectangular object that contains text. When it is selected, a box with hashed lines appears around it.

Figure 1-17	SELECTING TEXT TO BE REPLACED

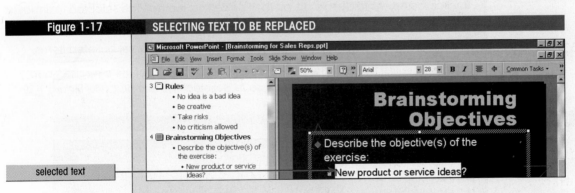

5. Type **What are sales reps doing right**, select the next phrase, **New feature ideas** (but not the question mark), type **What are they doing wrong**, select the next phrase, **Feature/Product naming** (but not the question mark), type **What could they be doing better**, select the next phrase, **Promotion ideas** (but not the question mark), and then type **How can we reward them more for doing things better**.

6. Delete the entire final sub-bulleted item, "New process for doing something?" Your slide should now appear as in Figure 1-18.

Figure 1-18   MODIFIED BULLETED LIST

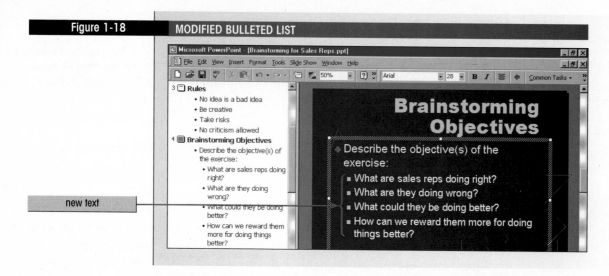

Because these are important questions to consider, Carl asks you to promote all the second-level bulleted (or sub-bulleted) items (those with the yellow square bullets) to top-level bulleted items (those with blue diamond-shaped bullets).

To promote bulleted items:

1. Click ✛ on the yellow bullet to the left of "What are they doing right?" in the Slide Pane to select the text. (Note that you also could have clicked the bullet in the Outline Pane.)

2. Click the **Promote** button ⬅ on the Formatting toolbar. The selected text moves to the left and increases in font size, and the bullet becomes a blue diamond.

3. Repeat this method to promote the other three second-level bulleted items.

4. Delete the first bulleted item, "Describe the objective(s) of the exercise", and then click in a blank area of the slide to deselect the text box. See Figure 1-19.

Figure 1-19   COMPLETED SLIDE 4

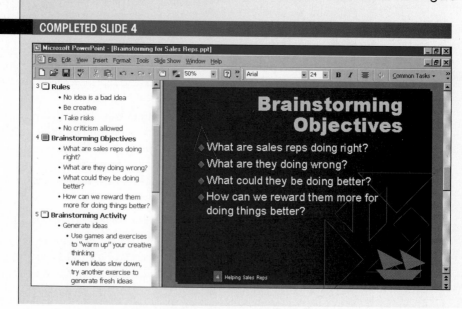

You realize that you've worked for about 15 minutes since the last time you saved the presentation. You'll save your work now.

5. Click the **Save** button 🖫 on the Standard toolbar to save the PowerPoint file. Because the presentation has been saved previously, PowerPoint automatically saves it using the current (default) filename.

You've now completed editing Slide 4. Next, you'll customize the presentation by promoting a bulleted item in the current Slide 5 so that it becomes a new slide.

To promote a bulleted item to a slide:

1. In the Outline Pane, scroll down so you can see all the text of Slide 5, and then click on the bullet to the left of the first bulleted item, "Generate ideas," to select this bulleted item and all its sub-bulleted items. (In the Slide Pane you can't promote a bulleted item to a slide, or sub-bulleted items into bulleted items in one step.)

2. Click ⬅ so that the bulleted item becomes Slide 6. See Figure 1-20.

| Figure 1-20 | NEW SLIDE 6 CREATED BY PROMOTING A BULLETED ITEM |

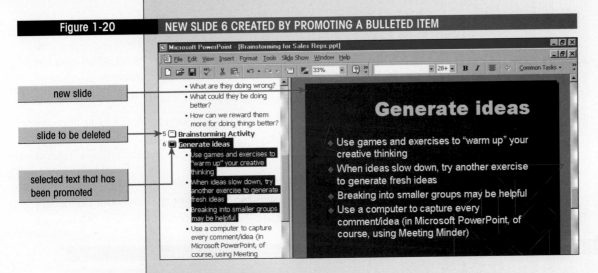

TROUBLE? If PowerPoint displays a light bulb at the top of the screen, ignore it for now. It marks a problem with consistency or style in this slide and will be explained when the Style Checker is discussed.

Next, you'll delete the now unnecessary Slide 5 and then edit the newly created slide on generating ideas.

3. Delete Slide 5 using either method shown previously.

TROUBLE? If PowerPoint displays a warning that this will delete a slide and its notes page along with any graphics, click the OK button to perform the deletion.

4. Edit the new Slide 5 so that the outline and the slide appear as in Figure 1-21. Begin by changing the slide title from **Generate ideas** to **Generating ideas**, and then make the other indicated changes in the main text. Notice that as you add and delete text, the size of the font might increase or decrease so that all the text fits within the text box.

Figure 1-21   EDITED SLIDE 5

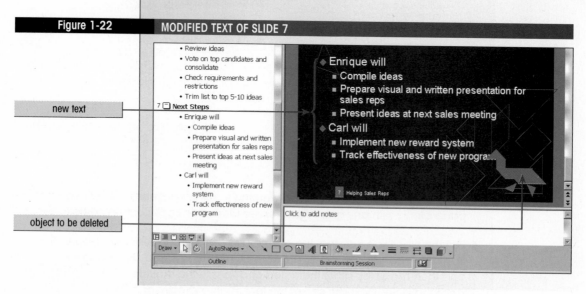

TROUBLE? If, as you add bulleted items, the Office Assistant appears and tells you that PowerPoint will resize the font to fit within the text box, click the Office Assistant OK button.

TROUBLE? If you type a word that PowerPoint marks with a red wavy underline to indicate a misspelling, right-click on the marked word, and then click the correctly spelled word from the list of suggestions. If the correctly spelled word isn't among the list of suggestions, edit the word by deleting and adding letters in the appropriate places.

Because you've changed Slide 5, you'll need to edit Slide 2 ("Agenda") accordingly.

5. Edit Slide 2, "Agenda," so that the third bulleted item is "Generating ideas," not "Brainstorming activities."

6. Your last change is to edit Slide 7, "Next Steps." Edit Slide 7 so that it appears like Figure 1-22. Remember to use the Promote button ◀ and Demote button ▶ as necessary.

Figure 1-22   MODIFIED TEXT OF SLIDE 7

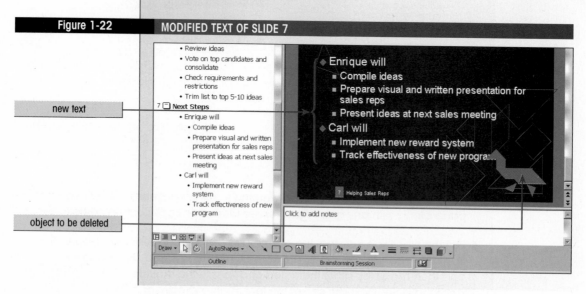

As you can see, because a graphic (a green "duck") partially covers the word "program" of the last bulleted item of the slide, you'll need to remove this graphic.

7. Click ✛ on the graphic that you want to remove. The graphic becomes selected, as shown by the small squares surrounding it.

8. Press the **Delete** key to delete the graphic. Now you can read the entire text without difficulty.

9. Save the presentation using the default filename, "Brainstorming for Sales Reps."

This completes your first draft of the presentation for Carl. He looks over your work and is pleased with what he sees. However, he decides another slide is necessary, and asks you to create and add it to the presentation.

Adding a New Slide and Choosing a Layout

Carl would like the presentation to end with a slide that recognizes the outstanding service of the four members of the marketing team. You'll add the slide now.

To add a slide:

1. If necessary, go to the last slide (Slide 7) of the presentation. When you want to add a slide into a presentation, move to the slide after which you want the new one to appear.

2. Click the **New Slide** button 🖹 on the Standard toolbar. PowerPoint displays the New Slide dialog box. See Figure 1-23.

| Figure 1-23 | NEW SLIDE DIALOG BOX |

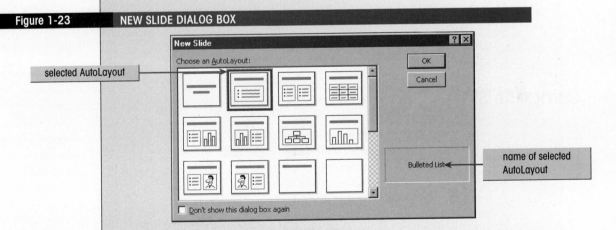

selected AutoLayout

name of selected AutoLayout

Before adding a new slide, you must decide where you want the placeholders for titles, text, and graphics to go. PowerPoint lets you select a variety of **AutoLayout** slides, which are preformatted slides with placeholders already in them, as well as one with a blank layout. Carl wants the new slide to be a bulleted list.

3. If necessary, scroll up in the Choose an AutoLayout list box, and then click the **Bulleted List** layout (top row, second column), as shown in Figure 1-23.

4. Click the **OK** button. PowerPoint inserts a new slide containing a title place-holder and main text placeholder for the bulleted list.

5. Click the title placeholder (where the slide says "Click to add title"), and then type **Our Marketing Team**.

6. Click the main text placeholder, and then type the four bulleted items (names of the marketing team members) shown in Figure 1-24.

Figure 1-24   **COMPLETED NEW SLIDE 8**

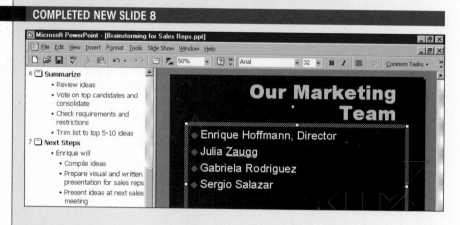

7. Click anywhere outside the text areas to deselect the text box.

You have now added a new slide, with a new layout, which completes the presentation. Note that you can also add (insert) slides into the current presentation from an existing presentation by clicking Insert on the main menu and then clicking Slides from Files. PowerPoint then lets you select the file that contains the other presentation, view the slides of that presentation, and insert the desired slides. Finally, you can also insert new text and slides by using the Office Clipboard.

Your next task is to use the Style Checker to check for consistency and style within your presentation.

Using the Style Checker

The **Style Checker** automatically checks your presentation for consistency and style, and marks problems on a slide with a light bulb. For the Style Checker to be active, the Office Assistant usually must appear on the screen. (PowerPoint also allows you to change the Style Checker options to meet the specific needs of your presentation.) For example, the Style Checker notes a potential problem on Slide 5.

To fix the problem marked by the Style Checker:

1. If the Office Assistant doesn't appear on your screen, click **Help** on the menu bar, and then click **Show Office Assistant**.

2. Go to Slide 5, which has the title "Generating ideas." A light bulb appears near the title of the slide because the capitalization is wrong. Often you won't know the style problem, but you can determine it by clicking the light bulb.

3. Click the light bulb at the top of the screen. The Office Assistant displays the problem. See Figure 1-25. The Style Checker will automatically fix the problem if you click on the blue first option in the Office Assistant dialog box.

| Figure 1-25 | CAPITALIZATION ERROR MARKED BY STYLE CHECKER |

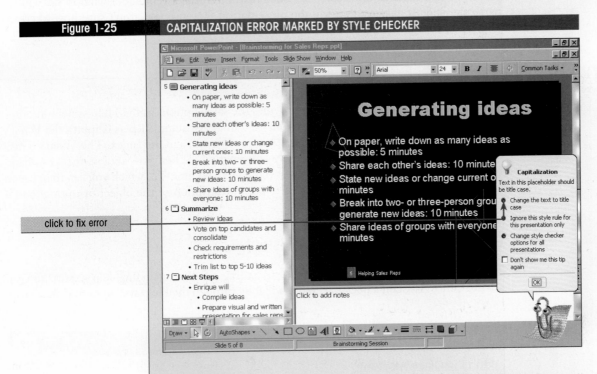

4. Click the **Change the text to title case** option button. The title "Generating ideas" automatically becomes "Generating Ideas."

5. Go to Slide 8. A light bulb appears near the top of the bulleted list.

6. Click the light bulb to determine the problem and to list options for fixing or ignoring the problem. In this case, the Style Checker detects that the words are all capitalized, whereas normally in a bulleted list only the first word is capitalized. In this case, you want PowerPoint to ignore the problem for this slide only, which is not one of the options listed.

7. Click the **OK** button on the Office Assistant dialog box to close it and to ignore the problem in this slide. If a capitalization problem appears on any other slide, the light bulb will again appear.

As you create your own presentations, watch for the problems marked by the Style Checker. Of course, in some cases, you might want more than six bullets on a slide, or you might want the font size of the body text to be less than 20 points. In these cases, just ignore the light bulb, or click it and then click the OK button. It will not appear on the screen when you give your slide show, or when you print your presentation.

When you show the presentation to Carl, he is satisfied with it. You're now ready to prepare the other parts of Carl's presentation: the notes (also called speaker notes) and audience handouts (which are simply a printout of the slides). **Notes** are printed pages that contain a picture of and notes about each slide. They help the speaker remember what to say while a particular slide is displayed during the presentation. Because you aren't sure how to create notes, you consult the PowerPoint Help system.

Using **Help**

The PowerPoint online Help system provides the same options as the Help system in other Windows programs—asking for Help from the Office Assistant (such as Clippit), the What's This? command, the Help Contents, the Answer Wizard, and the Index. The What's This? command provides context-sensitive help information. When you choose this command from the Help menu, the pointer changes to the Help pointer ⌖**?**, which you can then use to click any object or option on the screen to see a description of the object or option. You'll now use the Office Assistant to get help.

Getting Help with the Office Assistant

The Office Assistant is an interactive guide to finding information in the Help system. You can ask the Office Assistant a question, and it will look through the Help system to find an answer.

REFERENCE WINDOW   **RW**

Using the Office Assistant
- Click the Microsoft PowerPoint Help button on the Standard toolbar or click the Office Assistant itself if it's on the screen (or choose Microsoft PowerPoint Help from the Help menu, or press the F1 key).
- Click in the text box, type your question, and then click the Search button.
- Choose a topic from the list of topics displayed by the Office Assistant. The Help Pane appears on the screen. Click additional topics as necessary.
- To access the Help Contents, Answer Wizard, or Index, click the Show button in the Help Pane, and then click the desired tab.
- When you're finished, close the Help window and, if desired, the Office Assistant.

Don't underestimate the power of the Office Assistant. If you type a question for which the Office Assistant has no answer or gives you an answer you don't want, try to rephrase your question. With the Office Assistant and other Help features, you can learn to use almost any of PowerPoint's features.

For example, you could use the Office Assistant to get help with creating notes in PowerPoint. When you click the Microsoft PowerPoint Help button 🔳 to display the Office Assistant, you could type the question "How do I create notes?" The Office Assistant would then list options regarding notes, one of which is "Create notes." When you click that option, PowerPoint displays a Help Pane that explains how to create notes: You simply click the Notes Pane, and then type your notes for the current slide. With that information, you're ready to create notes in Carl's presentation.

Creating **Notes for Slides**

You'll create notes for three of the slides in the presentation.

To create notes:

1. Go to Slide 1, and then click in the Notes Pane where the placeholder text "Click to add notes" is located. Carl wants to remember to introduce Inca Imports' employees who have joined the meeting for this part of the presentation.

2. Type **Introduce people who have joined meeting after break**. See Figure 1-26.

Figure 1-26	NOTES ON SLIDE 1

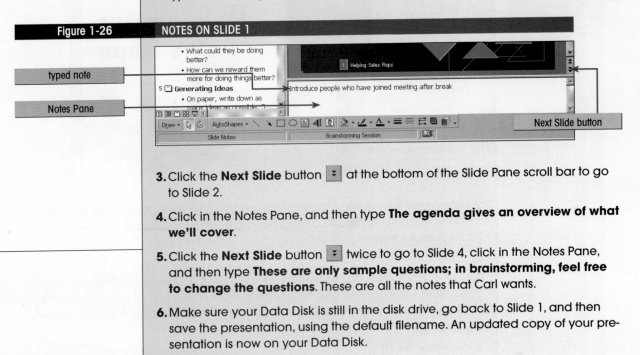

typed note

Notes Pane

Next Slide button

3. Click the **Next Slide** button at the bottom of the Slide Pane scroll bar to go to Slide 2.

4. Click in the Notes Pane, and then type **The agenda gives an overview of what we'll cover**.

5. Click the **Next Slide** button twice to go to Slide 4, click in the Notes Pane, and then type **These are only sample questions; in brainstorming, feel free to change the questions**. These are all the notes that Carl wants.

6. Make sure your Data Disk is still in the disk drive, go back to Slide 1, and then save the presentation, using the default filename. An updated copy of your presentation is now on your Data Disk.

Before Carl gives his presentation, he'll print the Notes Pages of the presentation so he'll have the notes available during his presentation. Carl also might want the notes pages to include headers and footers. Similar to a footer, a **header** is a word or phrase that appears at the top of each page in the Notes Pages. You'll practice inserting a footer in an exercise at the end of the tutorial.

You can now view the completed presentation to make sure that it is accurate, informative, and visually pleasing. Click the Slide Show View button and then proceed through the slide show.

Previewing **and Printing the Presentation**

Before you print or present a slide show, you should always do a final spell check of all the slides and speaker notes by using the PowerPoint Spell Checker feature. You'll have a chance to use the spell checker in the Review Assignments and Case Problems at the end of this tutorial.

Before printing on your black-and-white printer, you should preview the presentation to make sure the text is legible in grayscale (shades of black and white).

To preview the presentation in grayscale:

1. Make sure Slide 1 appears in the Slide Pane, and then click the **Grayscale Preview** button [image] on the Standard toolbar. If necessary, drag the colored minia-ture out of the way so you can see the text in black and white. See Figure 1-27.

| Figure 1-27 | SLIDE 1 IN GRAYSCALE |

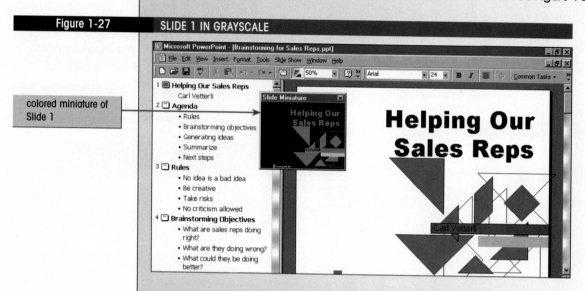

colored miniature of Slide 1

2. Look at the text on each slide to make sure it is legible. Depending on your Windows printer driver, the background graphics (geometric shapes in this case) might make some of the text hard to read, so you might want to omit the graphics from the slides.

3. Click **Format**, click **Background** to display the Background dialog box, click the **Omit background graphics from master** check box, and then click the **Apply to All** button. The slide appears as before, but without the background graphics.

4. Click **File**, and then click **Print** to open the Print dialog box. Don't click the Print button on the Standard toolbar, or PowerPoint will immediately start printing without letting you change the print settings.

PowerPoint allows you several printing options. For example, you can print the slides in color using a color printer, print in grayscale using a black-and-white printer, print handouts with 2, 3, 4, 6, or 9 slides per page, or print the notes pages (printed notes below a picture of the corresponding slide). You can also format and then print the presentation onto overhead transparency film (avail-able in most office supply stores).

5. Click the **Print what** list arrow, select **Handouts**, and then in the Handouts sec-tion, click the **Slides per page** list arrow, and then click **4**. If you're using a black-and-white printer, make sure the **Grayscale** check box is selected. See Figure 1-28.

Figure 1-28	PRINT DIALOG BOX

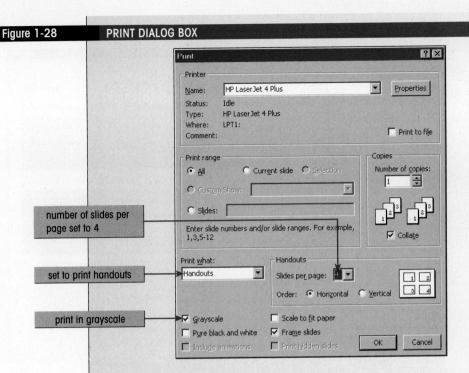

number of slides per page set to 4

set to print handouts

print in grayscale

6. Make sure all the other options are set as in Figure 1-28, and then click the **OK** button to print the handouts. Be patient. Graphics usually take a long time to print, even on a fast printer. You should have two handout pages, each containing four slides.

You're now ready to print the notes.

7. Display the Print dialog box using the method above, click the **Print what** list arrow, click **Notes Pages**, and then click the **OK** button to print the notes.

8. To see how the slides look as a group, first click the **Grayscale View** button to return to color view, and then click the **Slide Sorter View** button 🔲 on the View toolbar. Compare your handouts with the eight slides shown in Figure 1-29.

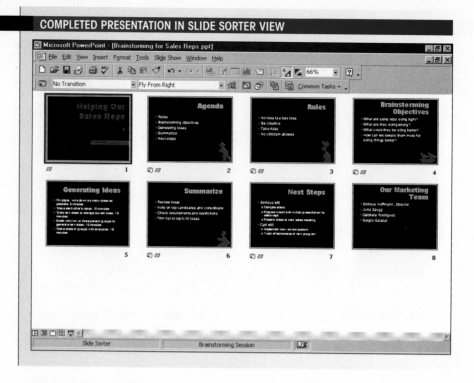

Figure 1-29   COMPLETED PRESENTATION IN SLIDE SORTER VIEW

In addition to delivering a presentation by an on-screen slide show or by printed pages, you can also send a presentation via e-mail or publish the presentation to the Web. To send a presentation via e-mail, click File on the main menu, point to Send To, and then click Mail Recipient (as Attachment) (which allows you to send the current slide as the e-mail message body), or Mail Recipient (which allows you to send the presentation as an attachment to an e-mail message). The first time you try to send the presentation via e-mail, PowerPoint will help you set up an e-mail account with your Internet Service Provider.

To publish a presentation to the Web, click File on the main menu, and then click Save as Web Page. You can then save the file in HTML format or publish it directly to a Web server.

Another option is to insert a hyperlink in your presentation that will connect to a file or Web page. To do this, click Insert on the main menu, click Hyperlink, and then complete the information in the Insert Hyperlink dialog box.

Now that you have created, edited, saved, and printed Carl's presentation, you can exit PowerPoint, but without saving the most recent changes, because you want the color slides to contain the background graphics that you just deleted.

To exit PowerPoint:

1. Click ☒ in the upper-right corner of the PowerPoint window. Because you have made changes since the last time you saved the presentation, PowerPoint displays a dialog box with the message "Do you want to save the changes you made to Brainstorming for Sales Reps?"

2. Click the **No** button to exit PowerPoint without saving the current version of the presentation.

You have created a presentation using the AutoContent Wizard, edited it according to Carl's wishes, and created and printed notes and handouts. Carl thanks you for your help; he believes that your work will enable him to make an effective presentation.

Session 1.2 QUICK CHECK

1. Explain how to do the following in the Outline Pane:

   a. move text up
   b. delete a slide
   c. change placeholder text
   d. edit text

2. What does it mean to promote a bulleted item in the Outline Pane? To demote a bulleted item?

3. Explain a benefit of using the Outline Pane rather than the Slide Pane and a benefit of using the Slide Pane rather than the Outline Pane.

4. Explain how to add a slide to a presentation.

5. What is the Style Checker? What is an example of a consistency or style problem that it might mark?

6. How does the Office Assistant provide help?

7. What are notes? How do you create them?

8. Why is it beneficial to preview a presentation before printing it?

REVIEW ASSIGNMENTS

After Carl presents his market research and brainstorming presentations to his colleagues, Enrique Hoffman (Director of Marketing) accepts the assignment to prepare a presentation to the sales representatives on how to improve sales. Enrique asks you to finalize his slides by doing the following:

1. Start PowerPoint and make sure your Data Disk is in the disk drive.

Explore

2. Click the Open an existing file option button, open the file **Sales** in the Review folder of Tutorial.01 on your Data Disk, and then save the file as **New Marketing Campaign**. (*Hint*: To save a file with a different filename, click File and then click Save As.)

3. In the Outline Pane, delete unnecessary words, such as "a," "an," and "the," from each main text slide, to conform to the 6 × 6 rule.

4. In Slide 2, move the phrase "by telephone" so it immediately follows the phrase "Follow up" in the same item of the main text.

5. Move the second item in Slide 3, "Will develop slide presentation," down, so that it becomes the third (last) item in the main text.

6. In Slide 4, the third item of the main text is "Step #2. Establishing Contact with Potential Customers." Promote that item to become a slide title (new Slide 5).

7. In the new Slide 6, demote the second, third, and fourth bulleted items so they appear indented beneath the first item, "Organize data for our market advantage."

8. Edit the main text of Slide 8 so the phrase "Must hire" becomes simply "Hire."

Explore   9. In Slide Sorter View, move the entire Slide 9 ("Key Issues") up to become Slide 8, so that "Becoming More Effective" is the last slide. (*Hint*: Switch to Slide Sorter View, and then click and drag Slide 9 to the left until a gray line appears to the left of Slide 8.)

10. Add the following notes to the slides indicated. Slide 1: "For presentation to entire sales force." Slide 2: "Ask for suggestions of other goals." Slide 3: "Make assignments for who will do each of these tasks." Slide 8: "Ask what other key issues need to be addressed." Slide 9: "Assure sales staff that they are appreciated and are doing a great job. We just want to find ways to help them enjoy more success."

Explore   11. Add to the Notes and Handouts the header "Improving Sales" and the footer "Inca Imports." (*Hint*: Click View on the main menu, click Header and Footer, click the Notes and Handouts tab, click the Header check box, type the header in the appropriate input box, click the footer check box, type the footer in the appropriate input box, and then click the Apply to All button.)

Explore   12. Apply the Box Out transition effect to all the slides. (*Hint*: A transition effect is a method of moving one slide off the screen and bringing another slide onto the screen during a slide show. To apply the Box Out transition effect, go to Slide Sorter View, press Ctrl+A to select all the slides, click the Slide Transition Effects list arrow on the Formatting toolbar, and then click Box Out.)

13. Spell check the presentation by clicking Tools, and then clicking Spelling. Remember that if PowerPoint stops at a word that is spelled correctly but that it doesn't recognize, click the Ignore or Ignore All button.

14. Use the Style Checker.

15. View the entire presentation in Slide Show View.

Explore   16. View the presentation again in Slide Show View, only this time, begin with slide 5 and end with slide 8. (*Hint*: To begin with slide 5, go to slide 5 in the Slide Pane, and then start the slide show. To end with slide 8, move to slide 8, move to that slide in Slide Show View, and then press the Esc key.)

Explore   17. Again view the presentation in Slide Show View, except this time begin with slide 1, and then use the slide navigator to jump to slide 7, and view from slide 7 to the end. (*Hint*: To use the slide navigator, right-click anywhere on the screen, point to Go, and click Slide Navigator.)

18. Use the Save command to save the presentation to your Data Disk, using the default filename.

19. Use the Office Assistant to find out how to print the outline of the presentation, and then do so.

20. Print the notes of the presentation.

21. Close the file.

CASE PROBLEMS

Case 1. MailMinder, Inc. Tiana Wnuk works for MailMinder, Inc., a new franchise company that specializes in mail management and mail-order fulfillment service. MailMinder franchises contract with businesses to do their advanced inventory management, custom assembly, bulk mail services, and customer database management. Tiana's job is to provide training for new managers of MailMinder's fledgling franchises. She asks you to help her finalize a presentation, which she'll use to show the many services of MailMinder headquarters to franchise managers, by doing the following:

1. Open the file **Mailmndr** in the Cases folder of Tutorial.01 on your Data Disk, and save the file as **MailMinder Services**.

2. In Slide 1, change the presenter's name from "Tiana Wnuk" to your name.

Explore

3. Go to Slide 2. In the first bulleted item, use cut and paste to move the phrase "from 1998 to 2001" from the end of the bulleted paragraph to the beginning. Also, change "from" to "From" and "Gross" to "gross."

4. Also in Slide 2, demote the four bulleted items below "What accounts for the growth?" to make subparagraphs that answer this question.

5. In Slide 3, right-click on "MailMinder" and then click Ignore All so that PowerPoint won't mark the word as misspelled. Repeat this for "MailMinder's."

6. Right-click the misspelled "assistence," and then click the correct spelling.

7. Go to Slide 4. (Ignore for now the misspelled words in this and subsequent slides—you'll correct them all later.) Move the first bulleted item so that it becomes the second bulleted item, and then move the third bulleted item, "Setting up mail management systems with new clients," to the end of the bulleted list.

8. Go to Slide 5. Below the first main bulleted item, "Regional consultants," add a second and third sub-bulleted item, "Employee training," and "Help in generating quotations for potential clients." Move the last bulleted item, "Custom software," to become the first bulleted item.

9. Go to Slide 6. Promote the fourth bulleted item, "MailMinder's Other Asssistance Programs," to become the title of a new Slide 7.

10. Spell check the presentation, and then use the Style Checker.

11. View all the slides of the presentation in Slide Show View.

12. Preview the slides in Grayscale View. If some of the text is illegible, delete the background graphics.

13. Print handouts of all the slides (four slides per page) in black-and-white grayscale.

14. Save the file, using its default filename.

15. Close the file.

Case 2. Juica Juice Dawson Gappmeyer is seeking $180,000 in venture capital for his startup company, Juica Juice. Dawson hopes to expand his business, currently a one-store fast-food establishment in San Francisco, into a franchise. The store sells a wide variety of blended fruit juices, with standard and exotic flavors, along with other low-calorie and low-fat snack foods. Dawson has created a presentation to give to executives at the A. B. O'Dair & Company investment firm, and asks you to finalize the presentation by doing the following:

1. Open the file **Juica** in the Tutorial.01 Cases folder on your Data Disk and save the file as **Juica Juice Capital**.

Explore

2. Use the What's This? Help feature to learn how to increase the size of the title of Slide 1 from 44 to 54 points, and then do so. (*Hint*: Click Help on the menu bar, click What's This?, and then click the pointer on the Increase Font Size button on the Formatting toolbar.)

3. Right-click Juica and then select Ignore All so that PowerPoint won't mark this word as a misspelling.

4. Go to Slide 2. (Ignore the spelling errors on this and subsequent slides. You'll correct them all at once, later on.) Move the third bulleted item, "Capitalize on popularity. . .," to become the first bulleted item on this slide, and then add a bulleted item to the end of the list: "Expand to other locations."

5. Go to Slide 3. Edit as necessary to change "Exotic and standard" to "Standard and exotic."

6. Go to Slide 4. Demote the last three bulleted items so they appear as sub-bullets below "Other snacks."

7. Go to Slide 5. Following the 6 × 6 rule, simplify this slide by removing all the unnecessary words: "a," "an," "our," and "the." Further simplify by changing "by fourth year in operation" to "within 3 years" and delete the second ("This means you'll own . . .") and last ("Expansion to other . . .") bulleted items.

8. Go to Slide 6. Select the second main bulleted item, "Technical knowledge," along with its sub-bulleted items, by clicking the bullet to its left, and then move the selected text to become the first bulleted item on the slide.

9. Insert a new Slide 7 by clicking the New Slide button, and then selecting the Bulleted List AutoLayout. Type the title "Our Food Scientists." In the main text box, type the bulleted item "Dr. Sally M. Thursby," press the Enter key, and then press the Tab key. This causes the bulleted item to be demoted automatically. Type "Ph.D. in Food Science and Nutrition from Cornell University" and "13 years in developing commercial foods" as sub-bulleted items, and then press the Enter key. Now press the Shift + Tab keys to promote the next item. Type the bulleted item "Dr. Cecilia Goodman" and the two sub-bulleted items "Ph. D. in Food Science from Florida State University" and "8 years' experience in food industry."

10. Spell check the presentation, and then use the Style Checker.

Explore 11. Move Slide 5 to the end of the presentation. Switch to Slide Sorter View, click on Slide 5, press and hold the left mouse button, and then drag Slide 5 to the right of the last slide. When a line appears to the right of Slide 8, release the mouse button.

12. Return to Normal View, and then use the Slide Pane scroll bar to go to slide 1.

Explore 13. Change the design template from "Blueprint" (as shown in the center of the status bar at the bottom of the PowerPoint window) to "Nature." Use the Office Assistant to find the description of a design template and how to change it.

14. Save the file, using the default filename.

15. Preview the slides in grayscale to make sure they are all legible. If any text isn't legible, delete the background graphics from the slide.

16. Print the slides as handouts (four slides per page).

17. Close the file.

Case 3. PLI, Inc. Albert Bocanegra works for PLI, Inc., a national personal liability insurance company. Albert asks you to help him to prepare a presentation on the value of personal liability insurance, for the PLI sales representatives to use when they contact potential customers. Do the following:

1. Use the AutoContent Wizard to create an outline of the presentation. (If the startup PowerPoint dialog box isn't on the screen, click File, click New, click AutoContent Wizard, and then click the OK button.) Select "Selling a Product or Service" as the type of presentation from the Sales/Marketing group of presentation types, select On-screen presentation as the type of output, make the Presentation title "Personal Liability Insurance," make the footer "PLI, Inc.," and include the slide number on each slide, but not the date last updated. After finishing the AutoContent Wizard, make sure you're at Slide 1 in Normal View.

2. Click in the subtitle placeholder and then type "Why You? Why Now?"

3. Go to Slide 2. Change "Objective" to "Overview." Replace the current bulleted items (the placeholders) with these bulleted items:

■ Your liabilities in today's society

■ What can you be held liable for?

■ Financial effects of being sued

■ What is an umbrella liability insurance policy?

■ What does personal liability insurance cover?

■ How you can get this insurance for pennies a day?

Explore ▶

4. Albert now informs you that he has created slides for each of these objectives, so you won't need the remainder of the slides in the current presentation. Delete Slides 3 through 8. (*Hint*: You can delete a range of slides all at once by clicking the slide icon in the Outline Pane on the first slide, and, while holding down the Shift key, clicking the slide icon on the last slide to be deleted, and then deleting all the slides at once just as you would delete one slide.)

Explore ▶

5. Following Slide 2, insert all the slides from the file Insure located in the Tutorial.01 Cases folder on your Data Disk. (*Hint*: To insert slides, click Insert on the main menu, click Slides from Files, click the Browse button to find the desired presentation file, click the Display button to show the slides in that presentation, click the Insert All button, and then click the Close button.)

6. Save the presentation to your Data Disk, using the filename **Personal Liability Insurance**.

7. Go to Slide 3. Move the second bulleted item along with all its sub-bulleted items up above the first bulleted item.

8. Switch Slides 4 and 5, so that Slide 5 is "Financial Effects of Being Sued."

9. In Slide 5, move the last bulleted item, "You can owe thousands . . .," to make it the first bulleted item.

10. Go to Slide 6. Cut the first three bulleted items (which all begin with "Covers") so that the slide is left with only five bulleted items. Be sure to cut and not delete, because you'll paste the items into a new slide.

11. Use the New Slide button to insert a new slide after Slide 6. Select the Bulleted List AutoLayout.

12. On the new Slide 7, insert the title "Who Is Covered?"

13. Click in the main text placeholder, and then paste the text from the Clipboard.

14. Go to Slide 8. Demote the five bulleted items below "Protects against, for example." Note that you can demote the items together by selecting them all and then clicking the Demote button.

15. Spell check the presentation, and then use the Style Checker.

16. Save the presentation, using the default filename.

17. Preview the slides in grayscale, and then print them as handouts (three slides per page).

18. Close the file.

Case 4. *Orienting Freshmen on College Social Life* The chair of your college department has
asked you to participate in an orientation for new freshmen. The chair has asked you to
prepare and give a 20-minute presentation on the social life at your school. In other words,
you need to give an overview on one area of "products and services" available to the
incoming students. Prepare an on-screen presentation with the following features:

Explore

1. Use the AutoContent Wizard to begin developing an outline based on "Project/Services
   Overview" from the Sales/Marketing type of presentation. Make the presentation title
   "Social Opportunities at ..." (with the name or abbreviation of your school, college, or
   university). Include a footer, "Social Life," the date last updated, and the slide number
   on each slide.

2. Use the Office Assistant to find out how to apply a different design template to a presentation, and then apply the "Blends" design.

3. Go to Slide 1, select and delete the large text box with the author's name, and then
   select and delete the placeholder for "Your Logo Here." (*Hint*: In both cases, click anywhere in the text box, click the edge of the box so that the entire object is selected, and
   then press the Delete key.) Insert the subtitle "Having Fun While Learning."

4. In Slide 2, create five or six bulleted items of the type of social activities that occur at
   your school. For example, you could include sororities and fraternities, clubs, service
   organizations, religious groups, and sporting events.

5. In Slide 3, delete "Features &," and leave only "Benefits" in the title. Delete the bulleted item placeholders and include a list of benefits of getting involved in the college
   social life. (If you can't think of any benefits, you're studying too hard.)

6. Delete all the remaining slides, from Slides 4 on. (*Hint*: You can delete a range of slides
   all at once by clicking the slide icon in the Outline Pane on the first slide to be deleted,
   and, while holding down the Shift key, clicking the slide icon on the last slide to be
   deleted, and then deleting all the slides at once just as you would delete one slide.)

7. Add a slide for each of the five or six items on your Slide 2. On each of these slides, list
   pertinent information, such as purpose or objectives of a social organization, examples
   of activities, time and place of selected events, or how to join an organization. Make
   sure each slide has three to six bulleted items.

8. Add a new final slide, "Summary," in which you summarize key points of your presentation.

9. Spell check the presentation, and then use the Style Checker.

10. Preview the presentation in Slide Show View.

11. Save the presentation as **Social Life at** on your Data Disk.

12. Use the Office Assistant to find out how to print the outline of your presentation, and then do so.

13. Save your presentation in HTML format on your Data Disk, in preparation for publication on the Web.

14. Close the file.

INTERNET ASSIGNMENTS

The purpose of the Internet Assignments is to challenge you to find information on the Internet that you can use to create effective documents. The actual assignments are updated and maintained on the Course Technology Web site. Log onto the Internet and use your Web browser to go to the Student Online Companion to accompany this text at **www.course.com/NewPerspectives/office2000**. Click the PowerPoint link, and then click the link for Tutorial 1.

QUICK | CHECK ANSWERS

Session 1.1

1. PowerPoint provides everything you need to produce a presentation that consists of black-and-white or color overheads, 35 mm slides, or on-screen slides. The presentation component can consist of individual slides, speaker notes, an outline of the presentation, and audience handouts.

2. The Outline Pane lists an outline of your presentation, including titles and text of each slide. The Slide Pane shows the slide as it will look during your slide show. The Notes Pane contains any notes that you might prepare on each slide.

3. a. gradient fill: a type of shading in which one color blends into another

   b. footer: a word or phrase that appears at the bottom of each slide in the presentation

   c. placeholder: a region of a slide or a location in an outline reserved for inserting text or graphics

   d. bulleted list: a list of paragraphs with a special character (dot, circle, box, star, or other character) to the left of each paragraph

4. Planning improves the quality of your presentation, makes your presentation more effective and enjoyable, and saves you time and effort. You should answer several questions: What is my purpose or objective? What type of presentation is needed? What is the physical location of my presentation? What is the best format for presenting the information?

5. The AutoContent Wizard lets you choose a presentation category and then creates a general outline of the presentation for you.

6. Use six or fewer items per screen, and use phrases of six or fewer words.

7. a word that is not located in the PowerPoint dictionary, usually a misspelled word

8. so that you won't lose all your work if, for example, a power failure suddenly shuts down your computer

Session 1.2

1. a. Click on a slide or bullet icon, and drag the selected item up.

   b. Click Edit on the main menu, and then click Delete Slide.

   c. Select the text, and then type new text.

   d. Drag the I-beam pointer to select the text, and then delete or retype it.

2. Promote means to increase the level of an outline item; demote means to decrease the level of an outline item.

3. In the Outline Pane you can see the text of several slides at once, which makes it easier to work with text. In the Slide Pane you can see the design and layout of the slide.

4. Click the New Slide button on the Standard toolbar, select the desired layout from the New Slide dialog box, and then click the OK button.

5. The Style Checker automatically checks your presentation for consistency and style. For example, it will check for consistency in punctuation.

6. The Office Assistant provides help by looking through the Help system to find an answer to your question.

7. Notes are printed pages that contain a picture of and notes about each slide. Create them by typing text into the Notes Pane.

8. to make sure that the slides are satisfactory and that the presentation is legible in grayscale if you use a monochrome printer

OBJECTIVES

In this tutorial you will:

- Resize, move, and align text boxes and graphics boxes

- Add a design template and modify the design

- Change the layouts of existing slides

- Insert and resize pictures and clip-art images

- Insert a table into a slide

- Draw and manipulate a simple graphic using AutoShapes

CREATING
AND MODIFYING TEXT AND GRAPHIC OBJECTS

Preparing a Sales Presentation

CASE

Inca Imports International

Using information gathered about Inca Imports' customers, Enrique Hoffmann, director of marketing, and his staff have identified other businesses in the southern California area that fit the profile of potential new customers. Enrique and his staff will focus their marketing efforts on these retail customers, who would benefit from having a wide range of fresh produce, year-round availability, and responsive customer service. Enrique and his staff are ready to prepare a presentation for these prospective clients. They have already created an outline of the presentation in Microsoft Word.

In this tutorial, you'll import Enrique's outline into a PowerPoint presentation, and then enhance the presentation by adding graphics to some of the slides. A **graphic** is a picture, clip art, photograph, shape, design, graph, or chart that you can add to a slide. A graphic is an example of an **object**, which is an element of a slide. A slide element can be a graphic, textbox, border, or background.

SESSION 2.1

In this session, you'll learn how to format a presentation and to insert pictures and clip-art images.

Planning the Presentation

Before creating his outline, Enrique and his staff planned the presentation as follows:

- **Purpose of the presentation:** To convince potential customers to buy Inca Imports' products and services
- **Type of presentation:** A 30-minute sales presentation
- **Audience:** Retail buyers and other business representatives
- **Location of presentation:** A conference room at the offices of Inca Imports
- **Audience needs:** To recognize their need for Inca Imports' products and services and to understand how Inca Imports differs from other produce suppliers
- **Format:** One speaker presenting an electronic slide show consisting of five to seven slides

After planning the presentation, Enrique quickly created an outline using Word. He now asks you to convert this outline into a presentation and make it more interesting and effective by changing the formatting and adding graphics.

Importing a Word Outline

Your first task is to start PowerPoint, create a blank presentation, and import Enrique's brief outline into the presentation. When you import a Word outline, PowerPoint converts all text formatted using the Word Heading 1 style into PowerPoint slide titles, and then converts all text formatted using the Heading 2 style into PowerPoint bulleted items that follow the slide titles.

REFERENCE WINDOW	RW

Importing a Word Outline
- Go to the slide after which you want to insert new slides from a Word outline.
- Click Insert on the main menu, and then click Slides from Outline.
- Locate the Word file on the disk where the Word outline was saved, select it, and then click the Insert button. PowerPoint converts all Heading 1 styles to slide titles and all Heading 2 styles to bulleted items.

After you import the Word outline, you'll have to change the slide layout. A **slide layout** is a predefined arrangement of placeholders on the slide for inserting the slide title, text, graphics, or other objects.

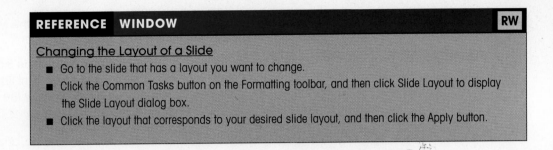

REFERENCE   WINDOW   **RW**

<u>Changing the Layout of a Slide</u>
- Go to the slide that has a layout you want to change.
- Click the Common Tasks button on the Formatting toolbar, and then click Slide Layout to display the Slide Layout dialog box.
- Click the layout that corresponds to your desired slide layout, and then click the Apply button.

Now you're ready to import the outline and change the slide layout.

To import a Word outline:

1. Start PowerPoint so that the PowerPoint startup dialog box appears on the screen.

2. Click the **Blank presentation** option button, and then click **OK**. The New Slide dialog box opens.

3. With the Title Slide selected, click **OK**. You'll now insert new slides using a Word outline. The new slides will begin after the current slide.

4. Click **Insert** on the main menu, and then click **Slides from Outline**.

5. Make sure your Data Disk is in the appropriate disk drive, open the Tutorial.02 folder on your Data Disk, open the Tutorial folder, click **Incasale** in the Names list box, and then click the **Insert** button. Slide 2 of the presentation appears in Slide Pane of the PowerPoint window. If necessary, click the **Normal View** (Tri-Pane) button ▣. See Figure 2-1.

Figure 2-1	SLIDE 1 OF THE PRESENTATION

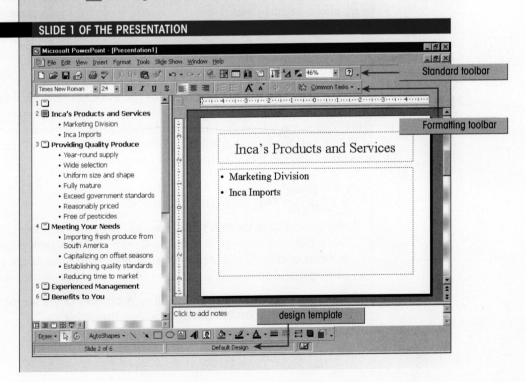

TROUBLE? If the presentation window isn't maximized, click the Maximize button in the upper-right corner of the PowerPoint window.

TROUBLE? If the Formatting toolbar appears to the right of the Standard toolbar, move the pointer to the vertical line just to the left of the Font list box, and then drag the bar down and to the left until it's positioned below the Formatting toolbar, as shown in Figure 2-1.

You now need to convert the current slide 2 into a title slide, and then delete slide 1.

6. Click **Common Tasks** on the Formatting toolbar, click **Slide Layout**, click the **Title Slide** icon in the upper-left corner of the dialog box, and then click the **Apply** button. The slide becomes a title slide.

7. Go back to slide 1, click **Edit** on the main menu, and then click **Delete Slide**.

You're now ready to save the presentation.

8. Click the **Save** button 🖫, and then save the presentation in the **Tutorial** folder of the Tutorial.02 folder using the filename **Inca Sales Presentation**.

You now have a PowerPoint file with the basic text for Enrique's presentation. To make the presentation interesting and effective, your next step is to format it.

Formatting the Presentation

Plain white slides with normal text (such as black Times New Roman) often fail to hold the audience's attention. In today's business world, more interesting color schemes, fonts, and other effects are expected. You'll begin enhancing Enrique's presentation by changing the design template.

Changing the Design Template

A **design template** is a file that contains the color scheme, attributes, and format for the titles, main text, and other text, and for the background in the presentation. Enrique's current presentation was created using the Default Design template, as shown on the status bar in Figure 2-1. Enrique would like a color scheme with a dark blue background that has a color gradient. You'll change the design template now.

To change the design template:

1. Double-click the **design template indicator** on the status bar, which currently says "Default Design." (Or, click the **Common Tasks** button on the Formatting toolbar, and then click **Apply Design Template**.) The Apply Design Template dialog box opens.

2. Click the template file **Lock And Key**. A preview of the template appears in the preview window on the dialog box. See Figure 2-2.

Figure 2-2   **LOCK AND KEY DESIGN TEMPLATE**

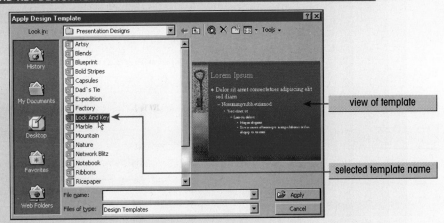

3. Click the **Apply** button. The design template of Inca Sales Presentation changes from Default Design to Lock and Key.

As you can see, the title slide (Slide 1 of the presentation) has a dark blue background with a color gradient and has a background graphic of an old lock on the left side of the slide.

Modifying the Slide Master

Instead of using the current background graphic of the Lock and Key design template, Enrique prefers an Inca Imports' graphic. He also wants you to modify some other elements of the design template. You'll begin by removing the background graphics from the slide masters. A **master** is a slide that contains the text and other objects that appear on all the slides of the same type. Masters, however, never appear when you show or print a presentation. PowerPoint presentations usually have two types of masters: the **Title Master**, which contains the objects that appear on the title slide (most presentations have only one title slide, but some have more than one), and the **Slide Master**, which contains the objects that appear on all the slides except the title slide. You'll now modify the two types of masters.

To modify the title and slide master:

1. Click **View** on the main menu, point to **Master**, and then click **Title Master**. See Figure 2-3.

Figure 2-3 | TITLE MASTER VIEW

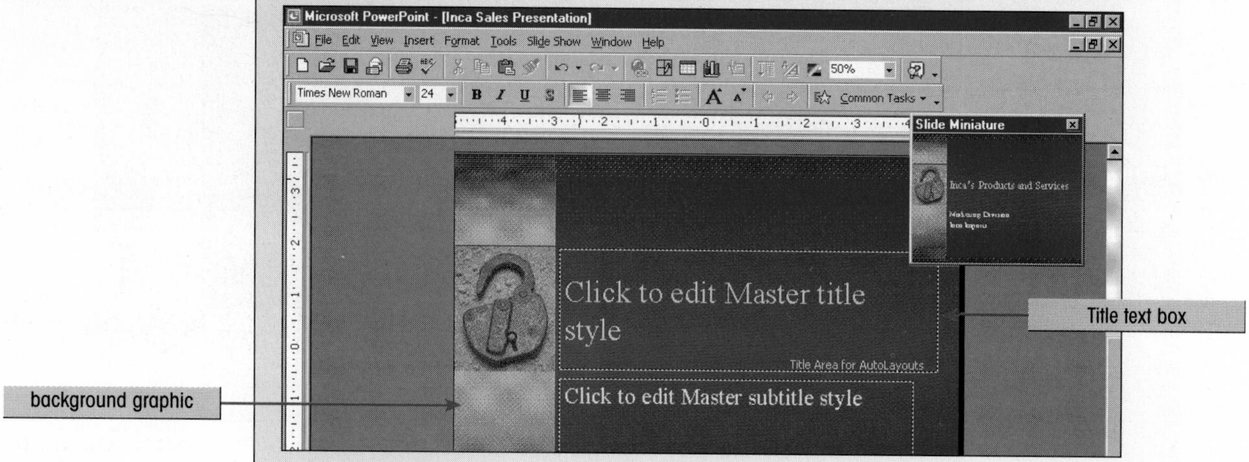

background graphic

Title text box

As you can see, the title master contains the background graphics and text placeholders for the title slide. You'll now delete the background graphics.

2. Click the graphic containing the antique lock located on the left side of the slide to select it.

3. Press the **Delete** key to delete the graphic.

Next, you'll change the Master title style. You'll first replace the current title font (Times New Roman) with a different font (Arial). When you make this change on the Title or Slide Master, the change takes effect on all the slides in the presentation. You could use the same procedure, however, to change the font on just one slide by making the change in the Slide Pane in Normal View. Further, you can use the Format Painter to make these changes. The **Format Painter** copies the formatting from one object and applies it to another. (You'll have a chance to use the Format Painter in Case Problem 2.)

4. Click on the dotted-line edge of the placeholder labeled "Click to edit Master title style." The box surrounding the placeholder becomes a thick, gray line with resize handles. A **resize handle** is a small square that, when dragged with the pointer, changes the size of the box.

5. Click the **Font** list arrow on the Formatting toolbar, and then click **Arial** to change the title font to Arial.

6. Click the **Bold** button **B** to make the title bold.

You're now ready to modify the Slide Master.

7. Go to the Slide Master by clicking the **Previous Slide** button on the vertical scroll bar in the Slide Pane.

8. Delete the background graphic of the antique key, and then change the font of the Master title style to Arial bold. See Figure 2-4.

Figure 2-4	SLIDE MASTER AFTER MODIFICATIONS

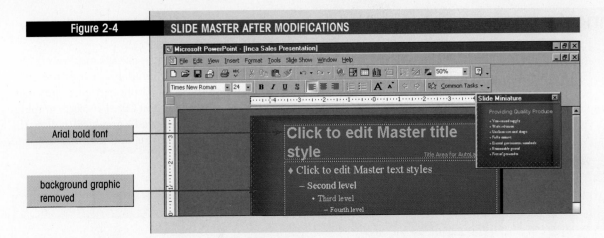

With the graphics removed from the Slide Master, you decide to make the two text boxes on the slide larger and place them closer to the left edge of the slide.

Resizing Text Boxes

You'll resize the two text boxes on the Slide Master by dragging the left center resize handle on each box.

To resize the text boxes:

1. Make sure the title text box of the Slide Master is selected. The resize handles appear.

2. Drag the left center resize handle to the left, as shown in Figure 2-3.

Figure 2-5	RESIZING THE TITLE TEXT BOX

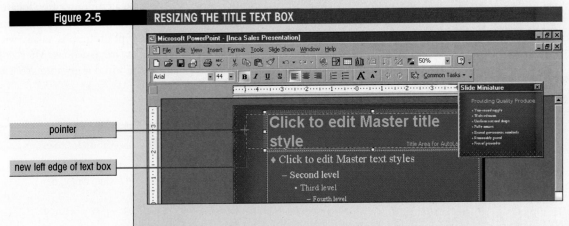

3. Resize the other text box the same way, so that the left edges of the two text boxes are aligned.

You've now made the desired changes to the design template by removing the background graphic and by changing the title font for all the slides in the presentation.

4. Return to Normal (Tri-Pane) View by clicking the **Normal View** button ▣.

Next you'll add a graphic to the title slide.

Using Graphics

Graphics add information, clarification, emphasis, variety, and even pizzazz to a PowerPoint presentation. PowerPoint enables you to include many types of graphics in your presentation: graphics created using another Windows program, scanned photographs, drawings, cartoons, and other picture files located on a CD or other disk. You can also create graphics using the Drawing tools in PowerPoint itself. Finally, you can add graphical bullets (by clicking Format, clicking Bullets and Numbering, clicking Picture, and then locating and selecting the desired graphic).

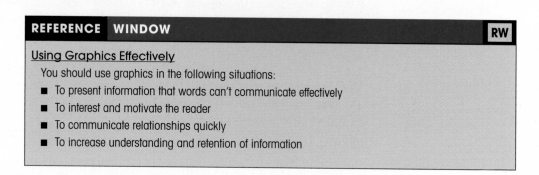

REFERENCE WINDOW   RW

Using Graphics Effectively
You should use graphics in the following situations:
- To present information that words can't communicate effectively
- To interest and motivate the reader
- To communicate relationships quickly
- To increase understanding and retention of information

You'll now add the company's logo on the left side of the title slide. A **logo** is a visual identification for a company, and including it on the title slide will help visually remind the audience of Inca Imports.

Inserting and Resizing a Picture

To use a picture in a PowerPoint presentation, the picture must be a computer file, located on an electronic medium such as a CD or hard disk. Picture files are generated by such methods as taking photographs with a digital camera, scanning photographs taken with conventional cameras, or drawing pictures using graphics software (such as Microsoft Paint). To get a computer file of the Inca Imports' logo, Enrique hired a graphic artist to create the file using graphics software.

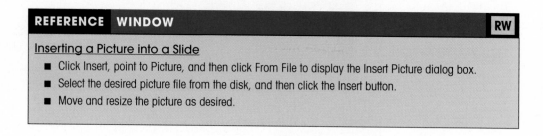

REFERENCE WINDOW   RW

Inserting a Picture into a Slide
- Click Insert, point to Picture, and then click From File to display the Insert Picture dialog box.
- Select the desired picture file from the disk, and then click the Insert button.
- Move and resize the picture as desired.

You'll now insert Inca Imports' logo to the left of the text boxes.

To insert a picture into a slide and resize the picture:

1. Make sure the Slide Pane is the active pane in the PowerPoint window. To activate any of the three panes, you can click anywhere in that pane. Recall that you can tell which pane is selected by looking at the left side of the status bar. In this case, the status bar should read "Slide 1 of 5."

2. With Slide 1 showing in the Slide Pane in Normal View, click **Insert**, point to **Picture**, and then click **From File**. The Insert Picture dialog box opens on the screen.

3. If necessary, change the **Look in** list box to the Tutorial.02 folder on your Data Disk, click **Incalogo** (or Incalogo.bmp) in the list box to select the Inca Imports' logo, and then click the **Insert** button. The picture appears in the middle of the slide, and the Picture toolbar opens as a floating box on the screen. The Picture toolbar will remain on the screen only as long as the picture is selected.

As you can see, the Inca Imports' logo needs to be moved and resized. You can move a graphic by simply dragging it to a new location. You can resize a graphic by dragging one of its resize handles. You can also resize graphics by using the Format Picture dialog box, which allows you to change the picture to a specific size or to a scale relative to the original size. To maintain the **aspect ratio** (the relative width and height of an object), you need to drag a corner resize handle. If you drag an edge resize button, you'll make the object either taller, shorter, wider, or narrower.

You'll now decrease the logo size by scaling, and then move the logo on the title slide.

To resize and move a picture:

1. Make sure the Inca Imports' logo is still selected; that is, you can see the resize handles around the edge of the graphics.

   TROUBLE? If the picture isn't selected, click it. The resize handles appear around the graphic, and PowerPoint displays the Picture toolbar. If the Picture toolbar isn't on the screen, click View on the main menu, point to Toolbars, and then click Picture.

2. Click the **Format Picture** button 🖼 on the Picture toolbar. The Format Picture dialog box opens.

3. Click the **Size** tab, and then make sure the **Lock aspect ratio** check box is checked. This ensures that you don't stretch the picture out of shape.

4. In the Scale section of the dialog box, change the **Height** from 100% to **60%**, and then press the **Tab** key. Because the aspect ratio was locked, the Width scale automatically changed to 60% also.

5. Click **OK**. The Inca logo is now smaller, with its horizontal and vertical dimensions each 60% of their original measurements.

6. Move the logo to the left of the slide title "Inca's Products and Services," as shown in Figure 2-6. You don't have to be exact in the location, because you'll refine the position later.

Figure 2-6	SLIDE AFTER INSERTING, RESIZING, AND MOVING PICTURE

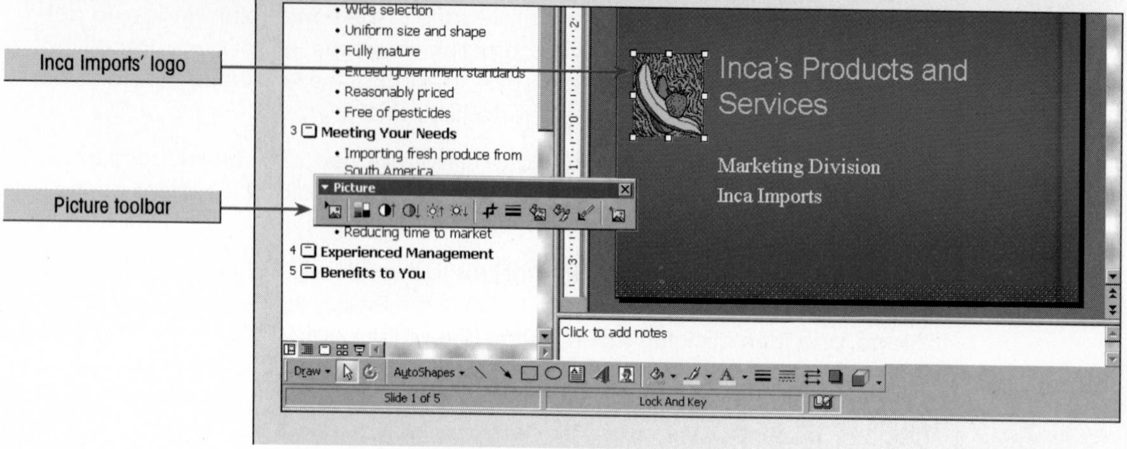

Inca Imports' logo

Picture toolbar

With the Inca Imports' logo at the approximate location you want it on the screen, you're ready to align it more precisely with the title text on the slide.

Aligning Objects

You can align objects precisely by using PowerPoint's alignment command. In PowerPoint, to **align** objects (text boxes, graphics, or other elements on the slide) means to adjust their positions so that one of their edges or their centers is at the exact same horizontal or vertical position. PowerPoint provides a command to align objects automatically along their left edges, vertical centers, right edges, tops, horizontal centers (middles), or bottoms.

You now decide that you want to align horizontal centers (middles) of the logo and the title text box.

To align objects:

1. If the Inca Imports' logo isn't selected, click it to select it, press and hold down the **Shift** key (which allows you to make multiple selections), click anywhere in the text box containing the title ("Inca's Products and Services"), and then release the **Shift** key. Both objects should now appear with resize handles to indicate that they are selected.

2. Click the **Draw** list arrow on the Drawing toolbar, point to **Align or Distribute**, and then click **Align Middle**. The text boxes are aligned along their horizontal centers.

3. Click in any blank area of the slide to deselect the objects. See Figure 2-7.

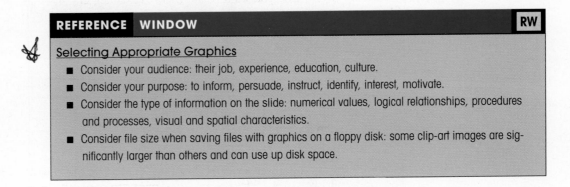

Figure 2-7

ALIGNING OBJECTS

logo and text box middle-aligned

4. Save the presentation using the default filename.

You've completed editing Slide 1. You're now ready to insert the next graphic, a clip-art image, into Slide 3 of Enrique's presentation.

Inserting and Editing Clip Art

Slide 3, "Meeting Your Needs," has four items of information. Enrique wants to include some clip art to add interest to this slide. (In PowerPoint **clip art** refers specifically to images in the Microsoft Clip Gallery.) He decides that an image of a plane flying around the globe would underscore the message of the bulleted items on the slide.

REFERENCE WINDOW   **RW**

Selecting Appropriate Graphics

- Consider your audience: their job, experience, education, culture.
- Consider your purpose: to inform, persuade, instruct, identify, interest, motivate.
- Consider the type of information on the slide: numerical values, logical relationships, procedures and processes, visual and spatial characteristics.
- Consider file size when saving files with graphics on a floppy disk: some clip-art images are significantly larger than others and can use up disk space.

To add clip art to a slide, you can use one of PowerPoint's predefined slide layouts (Text & Clip Art or Clip Art & Text), or you can insert it as you would a picture. For Slide 3, you'll first change the existing slide layout before adding clip art to it.

To change the layout of the slide and add clip art:

1. Go to Slide 3.

TROUBLE? If a light bulb appears on Slide 3, ignore it. The light bulb is from the Style Checker, which appears because "South America" is capitalized in the text. You want these words to remain capitalized.

2. Display the Slide Layout dialog box by clicking the **Common Tasks** button on the Formatting toolbar and clicking **Slide Layout**, click the layout with the description **Text & Clip Art** (third row, first column), and then click the **Apply** button to change the layout of the slide. See Figure 2-8. Notice that PowerPoint automatically reduced the size of text in the bulleted list (from 32-point to 28-point text) so that it would fit properly within the reduced text box.

Figure 2-8	SLIDE WITH NEW LAYOUT

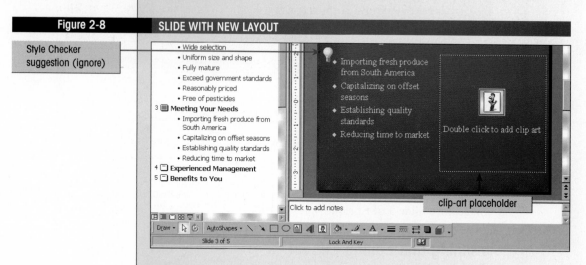

Style Checker suggestion (ignore)

clip-art placeholder

3. Double-click the clip-art placeholder. PowerPoint displays the Microsoft Clip Gallery dialog box. If necessary, click the **Pictures** tab. See Figure 2-9.

Figure 2-9	MICROSOFT CLIP GALLERY DIALOG BOX

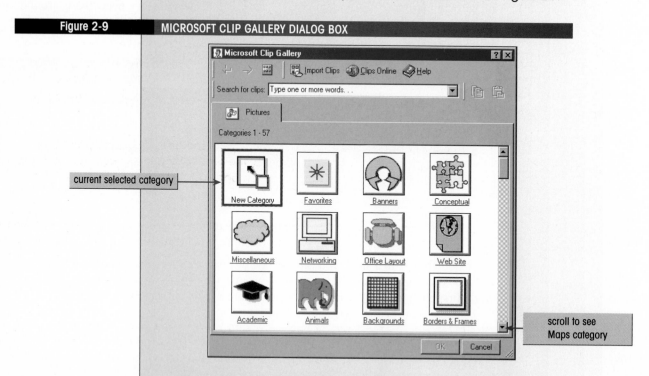

current selected category

scroll to see Maps category

TROUBLE? If the Microsoft Clip Gallery dialog box doesn't appear, consult your instructor or technical support person.

4. Scroll the Categories list box as necessary, and then click **Maps** to select that category.

TROUBLE? If you don't see a list of categories for the clip-art library, or if the clip art is missing altogether, consult your instructor or technical support person. If you do have clip art from which to choose, but you don't have the Maps category, choose any clip art you prefer to complete these steps.

5. Within the Maps category, click **air travel**, the image of an airplane flying around a world globe, to display a list of option buttons. See Figure 2-10.

| Figure 2-10 | CLIP GALLERY WITH NEW IMAGE SELECTED |

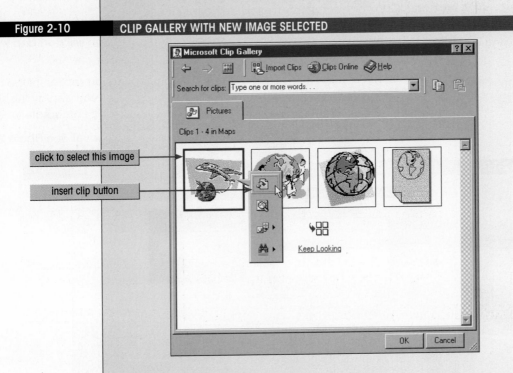

6. Click the **Insert clip** button. The clip art is inserted into the slide, and the Picture toolbar once again appears on the screen.

TROUBLE? If the colors on part of the slide become distorted, don't worry. They will automatically disappear when PowerPoint redraws the screen. For example, you could go to the next slide and then back again to redraw the slide.

You could now modify this clip-art image by changing its size, grouping or ungrouping its components, changing some of its colors, or applying animation effects to it. Enrique wants you to apply an animation effect.

Animating an Object

An **animation** effect is a special visual or sound effect of an object. You can, for example, animate an object so that in Slide Show View the object flies onto the screen. For Enrique's presentation, you'll animate the clip art so that it "swivels" when it first appears during a slide show.

To animate the clip-art image:

1. With Slide 3 on the screen in Normal View, click **Slide Show** on the main menu, and then click **Custom Animation**. The Custom Animation dialog box opens.

2. Click the **Order & Timing** tab, and then click the **Object 3** check box in the box labeled **Check to animate slide objects**. The object in the preview slide on the dialog box, as well as the object on the slide in the Slide Pane, become selected. Also notice that on the bottom part of the dialog box, Object 3 appears as the only item in the Animation order box.

TROUBLE? If you click the wrong object, such as Title 1 or Title 2, just click the check box again, and then click the correct check box.

To animate the object, you need to specify when animation will start and what type of effect you want.

3. Click the **Automatically** option button in the Start animation section of the dialog box. Leave the time, in seconds, set to zero. As soon as you display this slide in Slide Show View, the animation begins automatically and immediately.

4. Click the **Effects Tab**, and then set the Entry animation to **Swivel**. See Figure 2-11.

Figure 2-11	CUSTOM ANIMATION DIALOG BOX

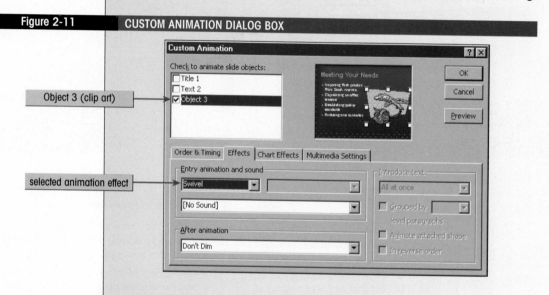

5. Click the **Preview** button to preview how the clip-art image moves around the slide before it settles into its final position.

6. Click **OK**.

7. Save the presentation using the current filename.

You can also animate other objects in addition to clipart. You'll have a chance to animate text in the end-of-tutorial assignments.

You've edited the first half of Enrique's presentation. In Session 2.2 you'll finalize the slides by creating a table and adding a graphic.

Session 2.1 QUICK CHECK

1. List four situations in which you can use graphics effectively.

2. Explain the meaning of the following terms:
   a. text box
   b. graphic
   c. object
   d. logo
   e. animation effect
   f. resize handle

3. Describe how to do the following:
   a. select a text box so that resize handles appear
   b. scale a graphic to change its size
   c. move an object on a slide
   d. change the alignment of two objects so their left edges are aligned

4. What is the Title Master? The Slide Master?

5. What is the Microsoft Clip Gallery?

6. List three criteria for selecting an appropriate type of graphic.

SESSION 2.2

In this session you'll learn how to create a table and how to draw and manipulate graphic shapes.

Creating a Table in a Slide

Because Inca Imports is a fairly new company, Enrique and his staff feel that it's important for potential clients to know that Inca employees have a significant amount of experience in the import and produce business. Enrique therefore asks you to create a table on Slide 4 of his presentation to communicate this. A **table** is information arranged in horizontal rows and vertical columns. The area where a row and column intersect is called a **cell**. Each cell contains one piece of information and is identified by a column and row label. For example, the cell in the upper-left corner of a table is cell A1 (column A, row 1), the cell to the right of that is B1, the cell below A1 is A2, and so forth. A table's structure is indicated by **borders**, which are lines that outline the rows and columns.

The table you'll create will have three columns, one for the name of the executive, one for the person's title, and one for the person's years of experience in the field (including current and past employment). The table will have six rows: one row for labels and five rows to provide information about the five executives of Inca Imports.

REFERENCE WINDOW	RW

Inserting a Table
- Change the slide layout of the desired slide to Table.
- Double-click the table placeholder.
- Specify the desired table size, that is, the numbers of columns and rows.
- Modify the borders as desired.
- Add information to the cells. Use the Tab key to move from one cell to the next, and the Ctrl+Tab keys to move to previous cells.
- Click in a blank area of the slide to exit table mode.

You'll create the table now.

To create a table:

1. If you took a break after the last session, make sure PowerPoint is running and the file **Inca Sales Presentation** is open in Normal View.

2. Go to Slide 4, open the Slide Layout dialog box, click the **Table** layout (first row, fourth column), and then click the **Apply** button.

3. Double-click the **table** placeholder. The Insert Table dialog box opens.

4. Set the number of columns to **3** and the number of rows to **6**, and then click **OK**. PowerPoint inserts the blank table into the slide and displays the Tables and Borders toolbar. See Figure 2-12.

Figure 2-12	SLIDE WITH BLANK TABLE

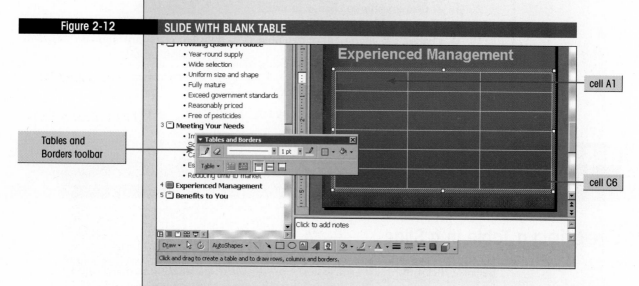

TROUBLE? If the Tables and Borders toolbar doesn't appear on the screen, click View on the main menu, point to Toolbars, and then click Tables and Borders.

With the blank table in the slide, you're ready to change the border below the top rows so that it separates the label on the top row from the information in the other rows.

To draw a border:

1. Make sure the **Draw Table** pointer ⬚ is selected. If necessary, click the **Draw Table** button ⬚ on the Tables and Borders toolbar.

2. On the Tables and Borders toolbar, click the **Border Width** list arrow, and then click **3 pt** to change the border line width to three points.

3. Click the **Border Color** button ⬚ on the Tables and Borders toolbar, and then click the light orange tile (fourth from the left). Now when you draw a border, it will be a 3-point orange line.

4. Drag ⬚ from the border below cell A1 to cell C1, along the border between the first and second row. When you release the mouse button, the thick orange line appears.

In addition to changing the vertical and horizontal border lines, you can also add and change diagonal lines within cells of a table. Click the Table button on the Tables and Borders toolbar, click Borders and Fill, click the Borders tab, and then click one or both of the Diagonal Line buttons (if you click both buttons, PowerPoint displays a large "X" through the cell).

Now you're ready to fill the blank cells with information.

To add information to the table:

1. Click the **Draw Table** button 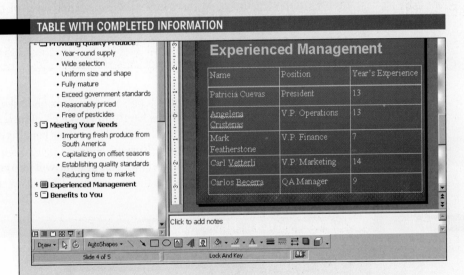 on the Tables and Borders toolbar to deselect it. The pointer should be ⟍ while it's in a blank area of the slide in the Slide Pane, or I when it's in a cell.

2. Click I in cell A1 and type **Name**, press the **Tab** key to move to cell B1 (top center cell), type **Position**, press the **Tab** key to move to cell C1 (top right cell), and then type **Years' Experience**. This completes the table labels.

3. Press the **Tab** key to move to cell A2, type **Patricia Cuevas**, tab to cell B2, type **President**, tab to cell C2, and then type **13**.

4. Complete the information in the other cells, as shown in Figure 2-13, and then click in a blank area of the slide to deselect the table.

| Figure 2-13 | TABLE WITH COMPLETED INFORMATION |

The table looks fine to Enrique, except that he wants the numbers in the third column centered rather that aligned along the left edge. You'll change the alignment now.

To change table alignment:

1. Drag I from directly to the left of the "13" in cell C2 to the right of the "9" in cell C6. All but the top cell in that column become selected. See Figure 2-14.

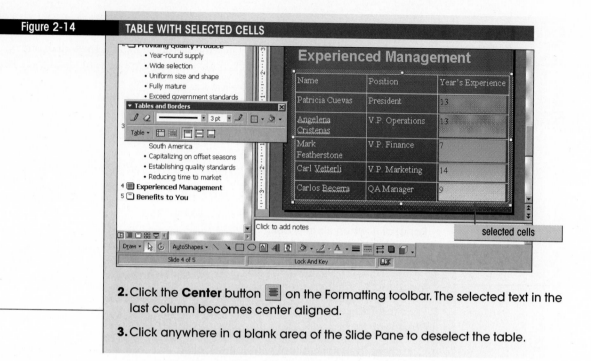

Figure 2-14   TABLE WITH SELECTED CELLS

selected cells

2. Click the **Center** button ▤ on the Formatting toolbar. The selected text in the last column becomes center aligned.

3. Click anywhere in a blank area of the Slide Pane to deselect the table.

You've completed the table that shows the experience level of the top management at Inca Imports. Your next task is to create a shape on Slide 5.

Creating and Manipulating a Shape

For the last graphic to be included in his presentation, Enrique asks you to add an inverted isosceles triangle with text to Slide 5. His hand-drawn sketch of how he wants the graphic to appear is shown in Figure 2-15. The text lists the three major benefits of the company, and will be placed along each side of the triangle. Enrique chose an isosceles triangle to point out that each of the three benefits is equally important. This graphic will be a strong visual reminder to Enrique's audience that Inca Imports has those advantages over its competition.

Figure 2-15   HAND-DRAWN SKETCH OF FIGURE FOR SLIDE 5

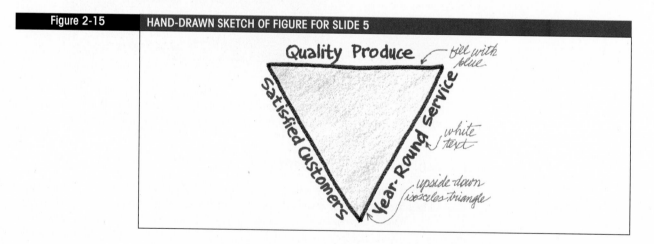

To create the triangle, you'll use PowerPoint's AutoShapes feature, which includes several categories of shapes that you can insert: lines, connectors, basic shapes (for example, rectangles and triangles), block arrows, flowcharts, stars and banners, callouts, and action buttons.

To insert a shape in a slide, using AutoShapes:

1. Go to Slide 5, change the slide layout to **Title Only**, click the **AutoShapes** list arrow on the Drawing toolbar, and then point to **Basic Shapes**. PowerPoint displays the Basic Shapes palette. See Figure 2-16.

Figure 2-16	BASIC SHAPES PALETTE

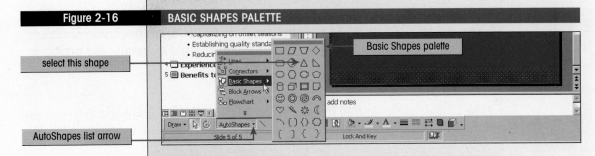

select this shape

AutoShapes list arrow

2. Click the **Isosceles Triangle** button △ on the Basic Shapes palette. The pointer will now change to ╀ when you move it into the Slide Pane.

3. Position ╀ approximately one inch below the "t" in "to" (in the title of the slide), press and hold down the **Shift** key, and then click the mouse button and drag the pointer down and to the right. The outline of a triangle appears as you drag. (The Shift key makes the triangle equilateral, that is, with all three sides of equal length.)

4. Release the mouse button and then the Shift key when your triangle is approximately the same size and shape as the one shown in Figure 2-17. The yellow diamond above the triangle is like a resize handle except that, if you drag it, the position of the tip of the triangle changes without changing the overall size of the object box.

Figure 2-17	SLIDE WITH DRAWN TRIANGLE

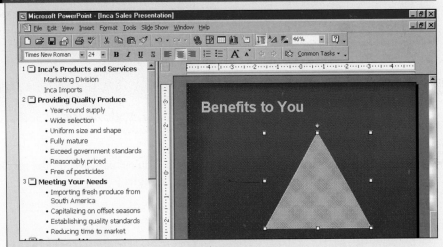

TROUBLE? If your triangle doesn't look like the one in Figure 2-17, you can move it by dragging it to a new location, resize or change its shape by dragging one or more of the resize handles, change the location of the triangle tip by dragging the yellow diamond, or you can press the Delete key to delete your triangle and then repeat Steps 1-4 to redraw it.

The default color of the drawn object is orange, which you decide is too strong. Enrique would prefer a more subtle color, like blue, to match the blues in the background.

5. With the triangle still selected, click the **Fill Color** list arrow on the Drawing toolbar. A box with color tiles appears on the screen.

6. Click the **blue tile** (the first tile from the left), which displays the ScreenTip message "Follow Background Scheme Color" to let you know this color matches the current color scheme. The fill color of the triangle automatically changes to blue.

The triangle is the desired size and color, but, looking at Enrique's sketch, you realize you need to flip (invert) the triangle so that it points down instead of up.

To flip an object:

1. With the triangle still selected, click the **Draw** list arrow `Draw▾` on the Drawing toolbar, point to **Rotate or Flip**, and then click the **Flip Vertical** button ◁.

2. Click in a blank region of the slide to deselect the triangle. Your triangle should be positioned, colored, sized, and oriented like the one shown in Figure 2-18.

Figure 2-18　　　**SLIDE WITH COMPLETED GRAPHICS OBJECT**

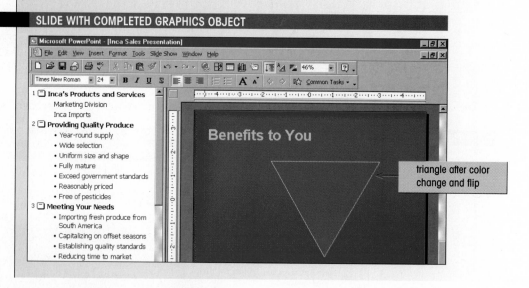

The shape is now in its final form. You're ready to add the text naming the three benefits of Inca Imports on each side of the triangle.

Adding Text

Adding text in PowerPoint is easy: you simply use the Text Box button 🖺 on the Drawing toolbar. For Enrique's presentation, you want to add text to the outside of the triangle, but in other cases you may want to add text to the inside of an AutoShape graphic. To do the latter, select the Text Box tool, click on the inside of the shape, type the text, and then turn on the word wrap text in AutoShape feature. PowerPoint then automatically formats the text so it stays within the selected AutoShape.

You'll now add three text boxes around the AutoShape triangle you just created.

To add a text box to the slide:

1. Click the **Text Box** button 📧 on the Drawing toolbar. The pointer changes to ↓.

2. Move the pointer so it is just above the upper edge of the triangle and below the "o" in "You," and then click there. (The position doesn't have to be exact.) PowerPoint creates a small empty text box, with the insertion point inside.

3. Type **Quality Produce**.

4. Drag the edge of the text box until it is positioned just above and centered on the upper edge of the triangle, as shown in Figure 2-19.

| Figure 2-19 | FIRST TEXT BOX ON TRIANGLE |

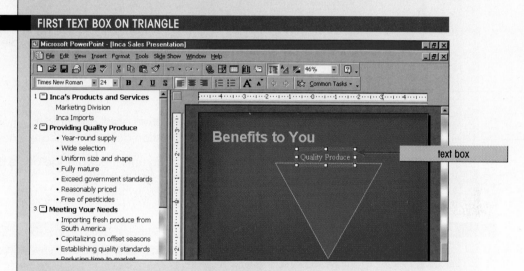

5. Click 📧, click ↓ to the right of the triangle, and then type **Year-Round Service**.

6. Create a third text box to the left of the triangle with the text **Satisfied Customers**. Click ↘ in a blank area of the slide to deselect the text box. Your slide should now look like Figure 2-20.

| Figure 2-20 | TRIANGLE WITH THREE TEXT BOXES |

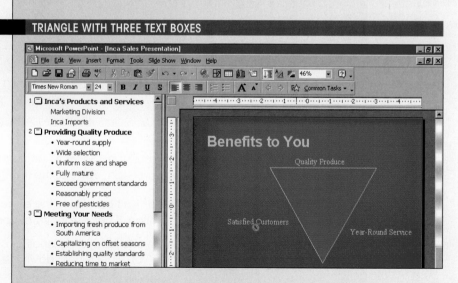

TROUBLE? If the text boxes you added to the sides of the triangle are not in the same position as the text in the figure, don't worry. You'll move the text boxes in the next set of steps.

Next, you'll rotate the text boxes to make them parallel to the sides of the triangle.

Rotating a Text Box

The method for rotating text is similar to the one for rotating graphics (or rotating any other object): you use the Free Rotate button on the Drawing toolbar.

To rotate and move the text boxes:

1. Select the text box that contains "Year-Round Service" by clicking anywhere within the text box. The resize handles appear around the box.

2. Click the **Free Rotate** button 🔄 on the Drawing toolbar. The pointer changes to ⟲, and the corners of the selected box display rotate handles (small green circles) instead of resize handles.

3. Position ⟲ over one of the rotate handles (it doesn't matter which one). The arrow in the pointer disappears.

4. Press and hold the **Shift** key, and then press and hold the mouse button. Holding down the Shift key makes the rotation occur in 15-degree increments.

5. Drag the handle counterclockwise until the top edge of the box is parallel to the lower-right edge of the triangle. See Figure 2-21. Then release the mouse button.

Figure 2-21	ROTATING AN OBJECT

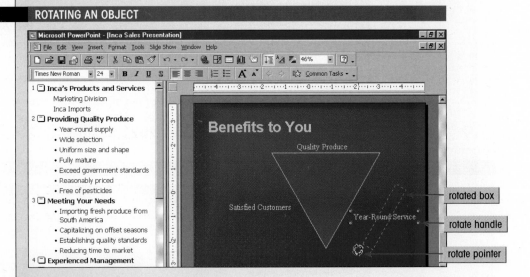

6. Move the pointer over the text "Year-Round Service," and then drag it until its box is against and centered on the lower-right edge of the triangle.

   TROUBLE? If the edge of the text box isn't parallel to the edge of the triangle, you can repeat Steps 2-5 to fix the rotation. If necessary, try not pressing the Shift key.

   TROUBLE? If the text box jumps from one location to another as you drag it, so that you can't position it exactly where you want it, hold down the Alt key as you drag the box. (The Alt key temporarily disables the Snap to Grid feature, which allows objects to move only to invisible gridlines, not to positions between the gridlines.)

7. Click the text box that contains "Satisfied Customers," repeat Steps 3-6, but this time rotate the box counterclockwise until it is parallel to the lower-left edge of the triangle, and then position the text box so it is close to and centered on the left edge of the triangle. Deselect the text box. Your slide should look like Figure 2-22.

Figure 2-22	SLIDE WITH COMPLETED GRAPHIC

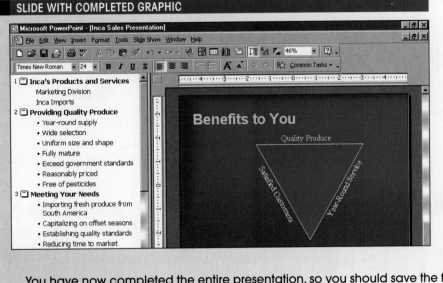

You have now completed the entire presentation, so you should save the final version to the disk.

8. With your Data Disk still in the disk drive, click the **Save** button 🖫. PowerPoint saves the file, using its current filename.

As a final check Enrique asks you to view the presentation.

Using the Pointer Pen to Mark Slides During a Slide Show

You should always run the PowerPoint Style Checker and Spell Checker, as well as view a completed slide show, before you print it. Furthermore, because Enrique has only a monochrome printer, he reminds you to make sure that all the slides will be legible in grayscale (shades of gray) before printing the presentation. Enrique has already responded to the Style Checker recommendations.

To spell check and view the completed presentation as a slide show:

1. Click **Tools** on the main menu, and then click **Spelling**. PowerPoint checks the spelling in your presentation. If you have introduced any misspellings, correct them now. Click the ignore button when the spell checker encounters names like "Becerra."

2. Save the completed presentation.

3. Drag the Slide Pane scroll box to the top of the vertical scroll bar, so that Slide 1 will appear first when you begin the slide show.

4. Click the **Slide Show** button 🖵 on the View toolbar to begin the slide show.

Having started the slide show, you're ready to use the pointer pen to mark slides.

To mark slides using the pointer pen:

1. Go to Slide 2.

2. Right-click anywhere on the screen. A menu opens.

3. Point to **Pointer Options** on the menu, point to **Pen Color**, and then click **Red** to set the pen color to red. This command automatically converts the normal pointer �---> to a pen ☇. Now, wherever you drag the pointer pen you will draw a line. The pen marks are only temporary; after you leave that slide, the marks are no longer visible when you return to that slide.

4. Move the pointer below the "R" in "Reasonably" in the next-to-the-last bulleted item.

5. Press and hold down the **Shift** key (this forces the pen to draw a straight line), and then drag the pointer from left to right to underline the word, as shown in Figure 2-23.

Figure 2-23	MARKING SLIDE WITH POINTER PEN

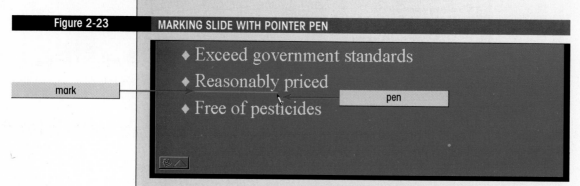

6. Try making other marks, such as circling the word "Quality" in the slide title, but without holding down the Shift key. When you're done, press the **Esc** key to turn off the pen. The pointer returns to �.

7. Continue viewing the remainder of the slides in the slide show.

You're satisfied with all the slides. Your next task is to preview the slides in black and white. You can easily preview all the slides at once by switching to Slide Sorter View.

8. Click the **Slide Sorter View** button ▦ to see all five slides at once. To enlarge the slide miniatures, click the **Zoom** list arrow, located on the right side of the Formatting toolbar, and then click **100%**. See Figure 2-24.

Figure 2-24   **COMPLETED PRESENTATION**

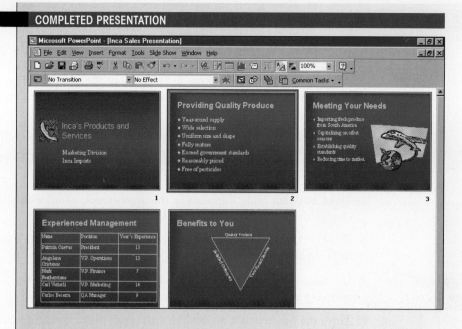

9. While still in Slide Sorter View, click the **Grayscale Preview** button on the Formatting toolbar. The slides change from color to shades of gray.

As you can see, all the slides are legible in black and white. You're ready to print the presentation and then exit PowerPoint.

To print the presentation and exit PowerPoint:

1. Click **File**, click **Print**, select **Handouts**, and then set the **Slides per page** to **6**.

2. Make sure the **Grayscale** check box is selected, and then click the **OK** button.

3. After printing is completed, click the **Close** button in the PowerPoint window.

Enrique is pleased with the slides. He thinks the graphics you've added to the presentation (logo, clip art, table, and triangle) will increase potential customers' understanding of and interest in Inca Imports.

Session 2.2 QUICK CHECK

1. What is a table in PowerPoint?

2. How would you add a table to a slide?

3. Where is cell A1 in a table?

4. How would you use AutoShapes to draw a shape, such as a rectangle or a circle?

5. How would you change the fill color of a shape?

6. How would you invert a triangle so that it points down instead of up?

7. How would you rotate an object (a text box or a graphics image)?

8. How would you draw a straight line on a slide during a slide show?

REVIEW ASSIGNMENTS

After Enrique presented his slides to potential customers, he decided it would be helpful for his colleagues at Inca Imports to know about the success of these recent marketing efforts. He asks you to help him finalize this presentation by adding graphics. Complete the following for Enrique:

1. If necessary, start PowerPoint and make sure your Data Disk is in the appropriate disk drive.

2. Open the **Report** file in the Tutorial.02 Review folder on your Data Disk, and then save it to your Data Disk as **Marketing Report**.

3. Make sure that Slide 1 appears in the presentation window in Slide View, and then change the design template from Bold Stripes to Blends.

4. Display the Title Master on the screen, delete the background graphics, and then return to Normal View.

Explore   5. Decrease the size of each of the two text boxes so that they fit just around the text contained in each box. (*Hint:* Use a corner resize handle.)

6. Move the title text box so that the right edge of the title text is about one-quarter inch from the right edge of the slide, and then align the left edges of the two text boxes.

7. Insert the picture file **Apple** from your Data Disk into Slide 1, and then move the picture to the left of the title text.

Explore   8. Position the graphic so that the shadow of the leaf appears below the "Mar" in "Marketing" and above the word "Data." So that you can see all the text, send the graphic *behind* the text by selecting the graphic, clicking the Draw button on the Drawing toolbar, pointing to Order, and then clicking Send to Back.

9. If necessary, move the graphic up or down so that the shadow appears between the title and subtitle of the slide but none of it covers any of the text.

10. In Slide 3 change the layout to Clip Art & Text, so that the clip art is on the left and the text is on the right.

Explore   11. In the placeholder for the clip art in Slide 3, add the image of a light bulb. To find the light bulb, open the Microsoft Clip Gallery, type "light bulb" in the Search for clips text box, and then press the Enter key. Select the picture with the single light bulb with colored lines around it.

12. On Slide 4, create a table with three columns and five rows.

13. Draw a 3-point-thick line along the border between rows 1 and 2. This underlines the labels that you'll type into row 1.

14. Draw another line 3-point-thick along the border below row 5 (the last row) of the table.

Explore ▷ 15. Erase (remove) all the other border lines, except the very top line, while maintaining the entire table structure. In other words, remove the four vertical border lines and the horizontal border lines below rows 2, 3, and 4. (*Hint:* Don't use the Eraser tool; it combines cells by erasing borders between them. Instead, use the Draw Table tool with the Border Style set to "No Border.") When you're done, your table should have only three horizontal border lines—above row 1, below row 1, and below row 5 at the bottom of the table.

16. In cell A1 type "Year," in cell B1 type "Sales (in $Millions)", and then in cell C1 type "Profits (in $Millions)". This completes row 1, the labels row.

17. Fill in the data as follows. In the three cells of row 2, type (without the quotation marks) "1999," "60.6," and "4.2." In the cells of row 3 (A3, B3, and C3), type "2000," "64.1," and "4.3." In the cells of row 4, type "2001," "71.2," and "4.8." And in the cells of row 5, type "2002," "115.7," and "5.2."

Explore ▷ 18. Select all the values in cells B2 to C5 (that is, the sales and profits figures), and then set the alignment to right. (*Hint:* After you select the cells, click the Align Right button on the Formatting toolbar.)

19. Change the labels in cells B1 and C1 to right alignment.

Explore ▷ 20. Add a new Slide 5. Choose "Title Only" as the slide layout, and then title the slide "Marketing Process." Add text and AutoShapes to create a slide that looks like Figure 2-25. You may have to move, resize, and align text and graphics boxes. (*Hint:* Use AutoShapes and the 3-D button on the Drawing toolbar to draw one of the arrows, and then use the Copy and Paste buttons on the Standard toolbar the others. To vertically align the centers of objects (text boxes and graphics boxes), use the Draw, Align or Distribute, Align Center command sequence).

Figure 2-25

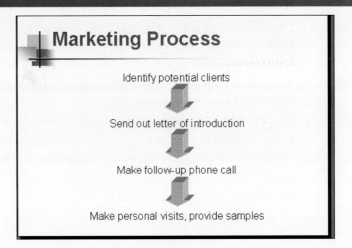

21. Spell check the presentation, and then click on any light bulb icons that appear on a slide to warn you of potential style problems. Deal with each style problem by accepting or rejecting the suggested change.

22. View the entire presentation in Slide Show View and in Grayscale View.

23. Save the file with your changes, and then print a copy of the slides (three slides per page) of the presentation. Print them using the Grayscale option if you don't have a color printer.

24. Close the file.

CASE PROBLEMS

Case 1. 4 My Body Nutrients Samuel Beacon owns a thriving company in Bethesda, Maryland. His company, 4 My Body Nutrients, manufactures and markets nutritional supplements, including vitamins, energy bars and powders, sports drinks, and muscle builders. The company markets these products to national and regional drug stores, nutrition outlets, and fitness gyms. Samuel is preparing a presentation about his company for clients and potential investors. Complete the following for Samuel:

1. Open the presentation file **4Body** in the Tutorial.02 Cases folder on your Data Disk, and then save it as **4 My Body**.

2. To Slide 1, add the company logo, **Bodylogo**, from the Cases folder on your Data Disk. Reduce the size and move the logo so that it fits near the lower-right corner of the slide but doesn't cover the slide subtitle.

3. Reduce the width of the subtitle text box so that "Nutritional Supplements" is on the first line in the text box and "for Active Adults" is on the second line.

Explore 4. Change the font in the slide title from 44-point italics to 66-point bold (not italics). (*Hint:* To change the font, use the Formatting toolbar. If you need help, consult the Office Assistant.)

Explore 5. Align the centers of the title and subtitle text boxes. (*Hint:* Use Align Center on the Align and Distribute menu.)

6. Go to Slide 2 and change its slide layout to "Text and Clip Art." To the clip-art placeholder in Slide 2, add the image of currency, which you can find by typing "currency" into the Search for clips text box and then pressing the Enter key.

7. Go to Slide 3 and change its slide layout to "Clip Art and Text." To the clip-art place-holder in Slide 3, add the image of two men climbing a red step graph, which is found in the Business group of images. (*Note:* If the Office Assistant asks if you want to change the font size, click the OK button. If PowerPoint doesn't change the font of the bulleted list from 32 point to 28 point, do it manually. If you're not sure how, ask the Office Assistant for help.)

8. Go to Slide 4 and add a clip-art image of your choice. Make sure the image relates to the information on the slide. For example, you might choose an image of a world globe. Don't use an image that you've used elsewhere in this tutorial.

9. Go to Slide 5. Change the slide layout to "Title Only."

10. Select and then delete the text box that contains the four bulleted items "Fresh," "Pure," "Effective," and "Potent."

Explore ▶ 11. Draw a 2.75-inch by 2.75-inch square in the blank region of the slide below the title. (*Hint:* Draw the square any size, and then right-click on the object and select Format AutoShape from the menu. On the Format AutoShape dialog box, click the Size tab, and then change the Height to 2.75 and the Width to 2.75.)

12. Change the fill color of the square to a light tan, the leftmost tile on the list of background scheme colors that appear when you click the Fill Color button on the Drawing toolbar.

13. On each side of the square place a text box, so that each side has one of the following words: "Fresh," "Pure," "Effective," and "Potent." Keep the normal orientation of the word on the top and bottom of the square, but rotate the words on each of the two sides of the box so they are parallel to the sides.

14. Select all four of the text boxes, change the font size to 32 point, and then use Align Center to make sure the center of the top and bottom text boxes and of the colored square are aligned. Use Align Middle to make sure the text boxes on each side of the square are aligned.

15. Insert the image of the company logo, **Bodylogo** (found on your Data Disk), into the Slide Master.

16. Scale the logo to 50% of its original size, maintaining the aspect ratio, and move the logo to the left of the placeholder so its right edge appears along the left edge of the title placeholder and just above the brown bar below the title placeholder. This logo will now appear on every slide except the title slide (Slide 1).

17. Go to Slide Sorter View by clicking the Slide Sorter View button on the View toolbar. Set the Zoom to 100%. (If you're not sure how to change the Zoom, consult the Office Assistant.) Your presentation should now look something like Figure 2-26. If your presentation is significantly different, return to Normal View (or Master Slide View) and make the necessary changes.

Figure 2-26

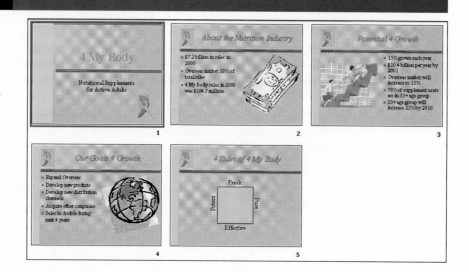

18. Run the spell checker. Check any suggested style problems by clicking on any light bulb that appears and either accepting or rejecting the suggested change.

19. Use Slide Show View to view all the slides of the presentation, and then save the file.

20. Print the slides of the presentation in grayscale as handouts with six slides per page, so that all five slides appear on one printed page.

21. Close the file.

Case 2. The Heather on South Mountain Markeleta Tausinga is a real estate agent for Chatsworth Development Company. Markeleta is preparing a presentation on a new condominium development in Aurora, Colorado, called The Heather on South Mountain. She took several pictures of South Mountain and the model home interiors in the development. She then scanned (digitized) the pictures into disk files. Markeleta asks you to finalize her presentation by inserting the pictures in the appropriate slides, as well as making other improvements. Complete the following for Markeleta:

1. Open the **Heather** file in the Tutorial.02 Cases folder on your Data Disk, and then save it as **Heather Condos**. If you get an error message that your Data Disk is full, save the file to a new, blank formatted disk.

2. While viewing Slide 1 in Normal View, insert the logo file **Heather** (located in the Cases folder of Tutorial.02 on your Data Disk), and then center it above the title on Slide 1.

3. Go to Slide 2, change the slide layout to Text & Clip Art, and then insert the image of the sun wearing sunglasses. (*Hint:* To find the clip-art image, type "summer" into the Search for clips input box, and then press the Enter key.)

4. Decrease the size of the clip-art image on Slide 2 so that it doesn't overlap the graphic at the bottom of the screen, and then increase the width of the text box so that most of the bulleted items fit on one line. (The first and last items will still require two lines.)

Explore

5. On the clip-art image on Slide 2, change the blue swirl behind the sun from blue to green. (*Hint:* Ungroup the image by clicking Draw on the Drawing toolbar, clicking Ungroup, and then clicking Yes, you want to convert it to a Microsoft Office drawing object; deselect the image; select only the blue swirl background; and then click the Fill Color button on the Drawing toolbar. If the fill color isn't green, click the Fill Color list arrow, click the green tile, and then change the fill color of the blue swirl.)

6. While still on Slide 2, use the Outline Pane to promote the last bulleted item, "Magnificent mountain vistas," to a slide title, and then modify the title so that it's capitalized correctly.

7. Change the slide layout for Slide 3 to Title Only. Insert the digitized photograph file **SouthMnt**. This is a photograph of South Mountain that has been scanned and formatted.

8. Rescale the picture to 120% of its original size, and move it so that it's centered between the left and right edges of the slide and between the title and the graphic (green leaves) at the bottom of the slide. (*Hint:* You can manipulate photographic images the same way you do other graphic files.)

Explore

9. While still viewing Slide 3, center the title text within the title box. (*Hint:* Select the text box and then click the Center button on the Formatting toolbar.) Now the complete title and the picture are centered on the slide.

10. Go to Slide 4, so that you can add a new Slide 5 using the Title Only layout.

11. On Slide 5, click the title placeholder and type the title, "Custom Interiors."

12. Insert two scanned home interior photographs, **Bedroom** and **Dining**.

Explore

13. Make the two images exactly the same height (2.75 inches)—(so they both fit easily on the slide), and then position them so that the dining room is on the left and the bedroom is on the right. Leave a margin around the pictures so the slide doesn't look cluttered. (*Hint:* Use the Size tab on the Format Picture dialog box.)

14. Below each picture, add a text box with the text "Model Dining Area" and "Model Bedroom," respectively.

Explore

15. Change the font of these text boxes to 24-point Arial, without text shadow. Use the Format Painter to change the font of the second text box. (*Hint:* If the text first appears with text shadow, click the Text Shadow button on the Formatting toolbar.)

16. Use the Align or Distribute command to center the text beneath each photograph accurately.

17. Go to Slide 7, change the slide layout to Text & Clip Art, and then insert a clip-art image of a telephone (or the cartoon with part of a telephone). Resize the clip-art image as necessary, so that it doesn't overlap the graphic at the bottom of the screen.

Explore   *Case 4. Presentation on a Favorite Activity* Prepare a presentation dealing with one of your favorite activities, such as popular music, a sport, or a hobby (e.g., photography, rollerblading, social clubs). Design it as if you're giving a class presentation to familiarize your fellow students with your activity. In creating your presentation, do the following:

1. Select an appropriate design template.

2. Create an interesting title slide, such as "Picture Perfect" or "Football Fever," using your name as the subtitle. Animate the title text appropriately by opening the Custom Animation dialog box.

3. Include at least five slides. Slide topics might be "How to Get Started," "Needed Equipment," "Where to Buy Supplies," "Clubs and Organizations," "Books and Magazines," "Improving Your Skills," or "Do's and Don'ts."

4. Include at least one object from the "Stars and Banners" category of AutoShapes, adding text within that shape. For example, you could insert a banner, increase its size, and write your hobby title in it.

5. Include clip art or other graphic images on at least three slides.

6. Create a table with information (real or fictitious) about your activity. For example, you might create a table of supplies needed and their costs.

7. Spell check your presentation, and then check for any style problems.

8. Save your presentation in the Tutorial.02 Cases folder, using the filename **My Activity**. If you get an error message that your Data Disk is full, save the file to a new, blank (formatted) disk.

9. Print your presentation slides, with three or four slides per page, making sure the slides are legible in black and white if you have a monochrome printer.

10. Close the file.

INTERNET ASSIGNMENTS

The purpose of the Internet Assignments is to challenge you to find information on the Internet that you can use to create effective documents. The actual assignments are updated and maintained on the Course Technology Web site. Log on to the Internet and use your Web browser to go to the Student Online Companion to accompany this text at **www.course.com/NewPerspectives/office2000**. Click the PowerPoint link, and then click the link for Tutorial 2.

QUICK CHECK ANSWERS

Session 2.1

1. (a) To present information that words can't communicate effectively; (b) to interest and motivate the reader; (c) to communicate relationships quickly; and (c) to increase understanding and retention

2. **a.** Text box: region of the slide that contains text
   b. Graphic: a picture, clip art, graph, chart, photograph, etc.
   c. Object: any item (text box, clip art, graph, organization chart, picture) on a slide that you can move, resize, rotate, or otherwise manipulate
   d. Logo: a visual identification for a company
   e. Animation effect: a special visual or sound effect of an object
   f. Resize handle: small square on the box around a graphic; when you drag a resize handle with the pointer, the size of the object changes

3. **a.** Click anywhere within the text
   b. Select the object, make sure the Picture toolbar is visible, click the Format Picture button on the Picture toolbar, click the Size tab on the Format Picture dialog box, and change the scale to the desired value.
   c. Select the object, and then place the pointer anywhere within the object (if the object is a text box, place the pointer on the edge of the text box), but not on a resize handle, and drag the object to the new location.
   d. Select both objects, click the Draw list arrow on the Drawing toolbar, point to Align or Distribute, and then click Align Left.

4. The Title Master is a slide that contains the objects that appear on the title slide of the presentation. The Slide Master is a slide that contains the objects that appear on all the slides except the title slide.

5. A collection of clip-art files (as well as sound clips and movie clips)

6. Consider (a) your audience (job, experience, education, culture), (b) your purpose (to inform, instruct, identify, motivate), and (c) the type of information on the slide (numerical values, logical relationships, procedures and processes, visual and spatial characteristics).

Session 2.2

1. A table is information arranged in horizontal rows and vertical columns.

2. Change the slide layout to Table; double-click the table placeholder; set the desired number of columns and rows; insert information in the cells; modify the format of the table as desired.

3. In the upper-left corner of the table

4. Click the AutoShapes list arrow on the Drawing toolbar, point to the appropriate tool (such as Basic Shapes), click the desired shape, move the pointer into the Slide Pane, and drag the pointer to draw the object.

5. Select the shape object, click the Fill Color list arrow on the Drawing toolbar, and then click the desired color tile

6. Select the triangle, click the Draw button on the Drawing toolbar, point to Rotate or Flip, and click Flip Vertical.

7. Select the object, click the Free Rotate button on the Drawing toolbar, position the pointer over one of the rotate handles, press and hold down the Shift key, and then press and hold the mouse button while you drag the pointer to rotate the object the desired amount.

8. Right-click anywhere on the slide in Slide Show View, point to Pointer Options, click Pen to display the pen, and hold down the Shift key while dragging the pen pointer.

New Perspectives on

MICROSOFT®
POWERPOINT®
2000

Read This Before You Begin

To the Student

Data Disks

To complete the Level I and Level II tutorials, Review Assignments, and Case Problems in this book, you need four Data Disks. Your instructor will either provide you with Data Disks or ask you to make your own.

If you are making your own Data Disks, you will need four blank, formatted high-density disks. You will need to copy a set of folders from a file server or standalone computer or the Web onto your disks. Your instructor will tell you which computer, drive letter, and folders contain the files you need. You could also download the files by going to www.course.com, clicking Data Disk Files, and following the instructions on the screen.

The following table shows you which folders go on your disks, so that you will have enough disk space to complete all the tutorials, Review Assignments, and Case Problems:

Data Disk 1
Write this on the disk label:
Data Disk 1: Level I Tutorial 1
Put these folders on the disk:
Tutorial.01

Data Disk 2
Write this on the disk label:
Data Disk 2: Level I Tutorial 2
Put these folders on the disk:
Tutorial.02

Data Disk 3
Write this on the disk label:
Data Disk 3: Level II Tutorial 3
Put these folders on the disk:
Tutorial.03

Data Disk 4
Write this on the disk label:
Data Disk 4: Level II Tutorial 4
Put these folders on the disk:
Tutorial.04

You may need an extra blank, formatted disk to save some solutions.

When you begin each tutorial, be sure you are using the correct Data Disk. See the inside front or inside back cover of this book for more information on Data Disk files, or ask your instructor or technical support person for assistance.

Using Your Own Computer

If you are going to work through this book using your own computer, you need:

Computer System Microsoft PowerPoint 2000 and Windows 95 or higher must be installed on your computer. This book assumes a complete installation of PowerPoint 2000.

Data Disks You will not be able to complete the tutorials or exercises in this book using your own computer until you have Data Disks.

Visit Our World Wide Web Site

Additional materials designed especially for you are available on the World Wide Web. Go to http://www.course.com.

To the Instructor

The Data files are available on the Instructor's Resource Kit for this title. Follow the instructions in the Help file on the CD-ROM to install the programs to your network or standalone computer. For information on creating Data Disks, see the "To the Student" section above.

You are granted a license to copy the Data Files to any computer or computer network used by students who have purchased this book.

OBJECTIVES

In this tutorial you will:

- Insert slides from another presentation

- Create and save a custom design template

- Apply graphics, sounds, transitions, and animation effects

- Create a graph and an organization chart

- Prepare 35mm slides and overheads

- Prepare a presentation to run on another computer

LABS

Multimedia

PREPARING AND PRESENTING A SLIDE SHOW

Annual Report of Inca Imports International

CASE

Inca Imports International

A year after receiving a loan from Commercial Financial Bank of Southern California to expand Inca Imports International's business, Patricia Cuevas (president) needs to present her first annual report on the company's progress. She will make two presentations: one to the company's board of directors and one to the company's stockholders. Patricia decides that she can create one slide show for both audiences. In her presentation, Patricia also plans to include previously created slides detailing Inca Imports' successful marketing campaign. Patricia asks you to help her prepare the presentation.

SESSION 3.1

In this session, you'll learn how to add slides from another presentation and create a custom template. Using the Slide Master, you'll change the slide color scheme, create a custom background, modify fonts, and then save the results as a template file for use in other presentations. You'll then add a scanned picture to the title slide in the presentation. Finally, you'll add an animated GIF picture and a sound clip to your presentation.

Planning the Presentation

Before you begin to create her slide show, Patricia discusses with you the purpose of and audience for both her presentations:

- **Purpose of the presentation**: To present an overview of the progress that Inca Imports has made during the past year
- **Type of presentation**: General presentation
- **Audience for the presentation**: Inca Imports' board of directors; Inca Imports' stockholders at their annual meeting
- **Audience needs**: A quick overview of Inca Imports' performance over the past year
- **Location of the presentation**: Small boardroom for the board of directors; large conference room at the meeting site for the stockholders
- **Format**: On-screen slide show for the board of directors; 35mm slide show for the stockholders; both presentations to consist of five to seven slides

Inserting Slides from Another Presentation

Because Patricia's presentation will combine previously created slides with new slides, you'll begin by opening a blank presentation (instead of using the AutoContent Wizard) and creating a title slide. You'll then insert the slides on Inca Imports' marketing campaign that Enrique Hoffmann, director of marketing, has already developed.

To open a blank presentation:

1. Start PowerPoint, click the **Blank presentation** option button in the PowerPoint startup dialog box, and then click the **OK** button. The New Slide dialog box opens with the AutoLayout selections.

   TROUBLE? If you've already started PowerPoint, close all the presentations and then click the New button on the Standard toolbar.

2. If necessary, click the **Title Slide** layout to select it, and then click the **OK** button. The placeholders for a title slide appear on the screen in Slide View.

   TROUBLE? If the presentation window isn't maximized, click the Maximize button on the presentation window. If the Office Assistant is on the screen, hide it.

3. Click the title placeholder, and then type **Annual Report**.

4. Click the subtitle placeholder, type **Inca Imports International**, press the **Enter** key, and then type **December 2000**.

5. Click anywhere outside any text boxes to deselect them.

6. Save the presentation to the Tutorial.03 Tutorial folder on your Data Disk, using the filename **Annual Report**. Your screen should look like Figure 3-1.

Figure 3-1	TITLE SLIDE OF BLANK PRESENTATION

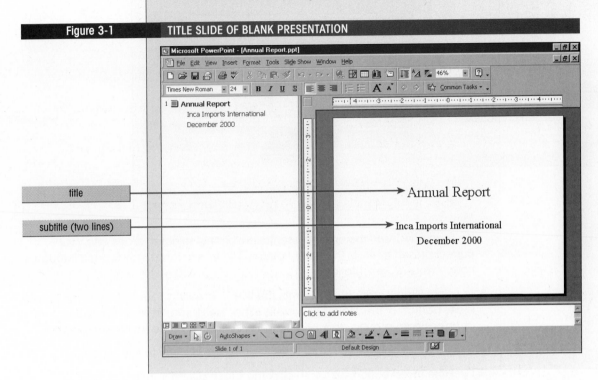

Now that you've created the title slide of the annual report presentation, you're ready to insert the previously created marketing campaign slides. In effect, you're creating a new presentation from an old one. You'll insert selected slides from Enrique's presentation now.

To insert slides from another presentation:

1. Make sure the title slide of the annual report presentation is still in the Slide Pane, click **Insert** on the menu bar, and then click **Slides from Files**. PowerPoint displays the Slide Finder dialog box. This dialog box allows you to find slides from a presentation on disk and insert any or all of the slides from that presentation.

2. If necessary, click the **Find Presentation** tab to select it, click the **Browse** button, change the **Look in** list box to **Tutorial** (in the Tutorial.03 folder on your Data Disk), click **Products** in the list of filenames, and then click the **Open** button in the Insert Slides from Files dialog box. The Slide Finder dialog box displays the slides from the existing presentation. See Figure 3-2.

Figure 3-2   SLIDE FINDER DIALOG BOX

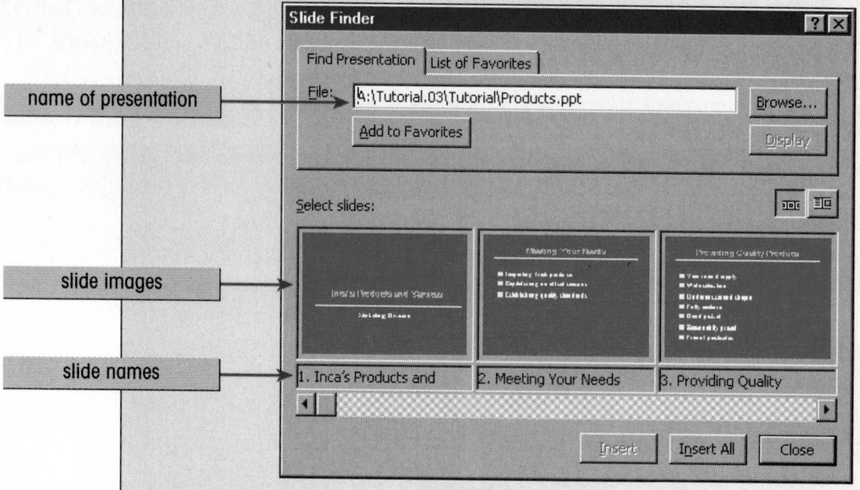

You can now insert the entire presentation, or only selected slides, into your current presentation. In this case, Patricia asks you to insert only Slides 2 through 4 from Enrique's presentation.

3. To select Slide 2, click the slide with the title "2. Meeting Your Needs" in the Select slides portion of the dialog box. Notice that the border around the slide changes from gray to dark blue to indicate that the slide has been selected.

4. Click Slides 3 and 4. You might have to scroll the display to see Slide 4.

5. Click the **Insert** button, and then click the **Close** button to return to the presentation window. Slide 4 of Enrique's presentation ("Reducing Time to Market") appears in the presentation window as Slide 4 in your new presentation.

6. Click the **Previous Slide** button ▲ to see Slide 3, and then click it again to see Slide 2.

7. Go to Slide 1, and then save the presentation using the default filename.

The three selected slides from Enrique's existing presentation are now included in your new slide show using the Default Design template, which is automatically applied whenever you open a new blank presentation. The Default Design template has a white background, black text, black round bullets, and Times New Roman font. Patricia asks you to modify this design by creating a new design template.

Creating a Design Template

Recall that a **design template** is a file that contains a color scheme; attributes and format for the titles, main text, and other text; and the background for the slides in the presentation. PowerPoint provides many predesigned templates that you can use in your own presentations, but sometimes you may want to create a custom template instead. These custom design templates can then be saved and used for other presentations.

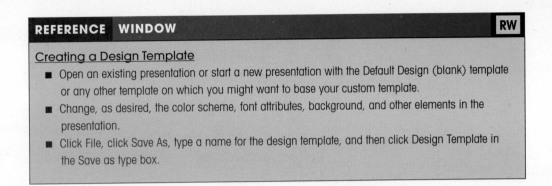

REFERENCE **WINDOW**   **RW**

Creating a Design Template
- Open an existing presentation or start a new presentation with the Default Design (blank) template or any other template on which you might want to base your custom template.
- Change, as desired, the color scheme, font attributes, background, and other elements in the presentation.
- Click File, click Save As, type a name for the design template, and then click Design Template in the Save as type box.

You'll begin to create your design template by selecting a color scheme.

Creating a Custom Color Scheme

For your design template, you can select one of the standard color schemes or create a custom color scheme. Your choice is simply a matter of taste. However, if you're unsure how colors will look together, it's safer to use a standard color scheme. For the current presentation, you'll create a custom color scheme.

To create a custom color scheme:

1. Click **Format**, and then click **Slide Color Scheme** to display the Color Scheme dialog box.

2. Click the **Custom** tab on the dialog box (see Figure 3-3). Now you can select a color for the background, the text and lines, the shadows, the title text, and so forth.

Figure 3-3	COLOR SCHEME DIALOG BOX

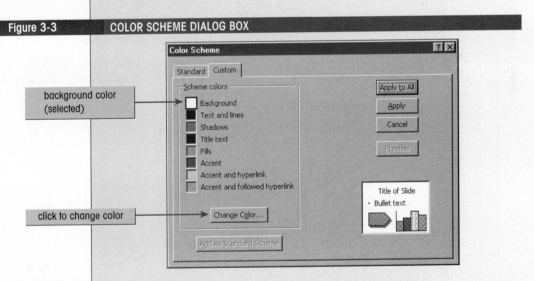

3. If necessary, click the color tile to the left of **Background** to select it, and then click the **Change Color** button. The Colors dialog box opens. Click the green hexagon, as shown in Figure 3-4, and then click the **OK** button.

Figure 3-4   **COLORS DIALOG BOX**

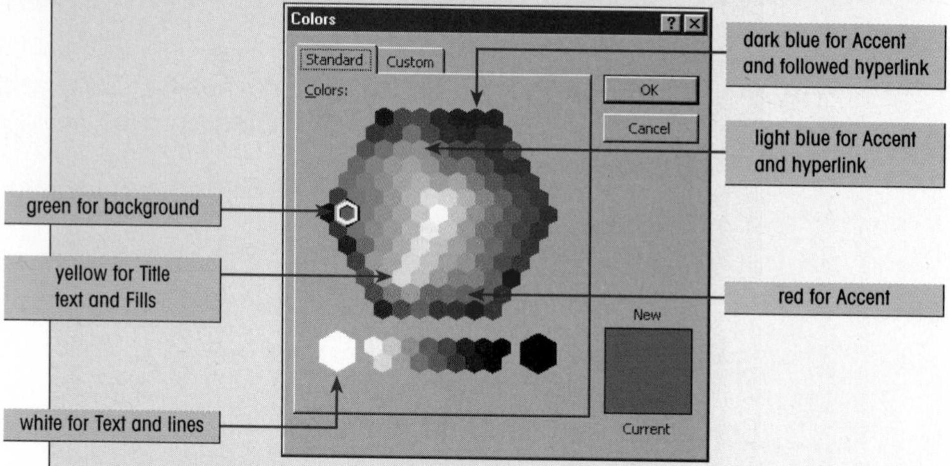

green for background

yellow for Title
text and Fills

white for Text and lines

dark blue for Accent
and followed hyperlink

light blue for Accent
and hyperlink

red for Accent

4. Click the color tile to the left of **Text and lines**, and then change its color to white, as indicated in Figure 3-4. Leave the Shadow color gray.

5. Change the **Title text** and the **Fills** colors to yellow, change the **Accent** color to red, change the **Accent and hyperlink** color to light blue, and then change the **Accent and followed hyperlink** color to a dark blue, as shown in Figure 3-4.

6. In the Color Scheme dialog box, click the **Apply to All** button, to apply this color scheme to all the slides in the presentation and to close the dialog box.

You have created a custom color scheme for this presentation and for the design template. Next you'll create a custom background.

Creating a Custom Background

The presentation currently has a solid green background, but Patricia would prefer something with more pizzazz. You can create a custom background, for example, by using a gradient fill or a textured background. Recall that a **gradient fill** is a type of shading in which one color blends into another. A **textured background** provides the appearance of a solid material such as newsprint, parchment, marble, granite, canvas, or wood. Patricia suggests that you use a gradient fill. (You'll have a chance to use a textured background in the end-of-tutorial assignments.)

To create a background with a gradient fill:

1. Click **Format**, click **Background** to display the Background dialog box, click the color list arrow located on the lower-left side of the dialog box, and then click **Fill Effects**.

2. In the Fill Effects dialog box, click the **Gradient** tab if necessary, and then click the **One Color** option button. See Figure 3-5. The one-color gradients use the current color scheme background color plus black or white, and then blend the two colors together, as shown in the dialog box. You can choose the shading style direction (for example, horizontal, vertical, or diagonal) and variants (for example, green at the top and black at the bottom or black at the top and green at the bottom).

You decide that you want the horizontal shading style with black at the top and green at the bottom.

Figure 3-5 FILL EFFECTS DIALOG BOX

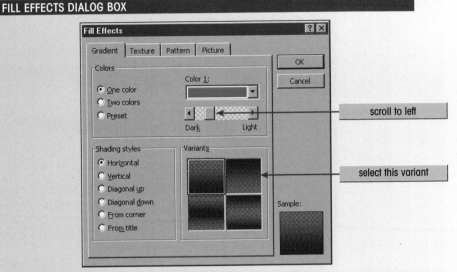

3. Click the **Variant** color tile with the gradient fill of black at the top and green at the bottom.

4. In the **Colors** section of the dialog box, drag the scroll button as far as it will go to the left, so that the complementary gradient color is as dark as possible. (To make the complementary color lighter, or even pure white, drag this scroll button to the far right.)

5. Click the **OK** button, and then in the Background dialog box, click the **Apply to All** button. See Figure 3-6.

Figure 3-6 SLIDE WITH GRADIENT FILL

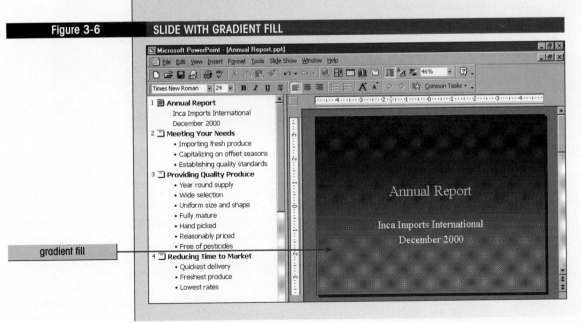

Patricia likes the color scheme and background, and now asks you to change the title font on the slides.

Modifying Fonts

Patricia wants you to change the title fonts from Times New Roman to Arial, and to change the title placeholder from center alignment to left alignment. Her purpose is to give Inca Imports' presentation a distinctive yet conservative look. You'll make these changes in the Slide Master.

To change the font in the Slide Master:

1. Click **View**, point to **Master**, and then click **Slide Master**. The Slide Master, with its text placeholders, appears in the PowerPoint window.

2. In the Slide Master, click anywhere in the title placeholder ("Click to edit Master title style"), and then change the font to **Arial**, leaving the font size at 44.

3. Click the edge of the title placeholder, and then click the **Align Left** button 🔳 on the Formatting toolbar (see Figure 3-7).

Figure 3-7   SLIDE MASTER WITH MODIFIED TEXT

left alignment selected

title text Arial and left-aligned

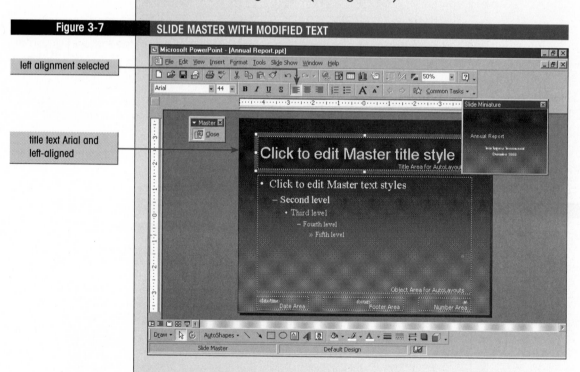

Your changes on the Slide Master also affect the title slide. However, on the title slide, you want the title to remain centered, not left-aligned. You'll now need to fix the Title Master.

4. Click the **Insert New Title Master** button 🔳 on the Standard toolbar to create a new Title Master slide.

5. Click the edge of the title placeholder to select it, and then click the **Center** button 🔳.

You have now changed the font and text alignments in the title placeholders. To further customize a presentation, you could change the bullet style (to a different character or object), but Patricia feels the default bullet style is fine. You'll practice changing the bullet style in the end-of-tutorial assignments.

This completes the creation of a new design template. You're now ready to save it.

Saving the Design Template

You want to save the current presentation as a template file so that Inca Imports' employees can use the design with other presentations.

To save a presentation as a design template:

1. Return to Normal (Tri-Pane) View and, if necessary, go to Slide 1.

2. Click **File** on the menu bar, and then click **Save As**. The Save As dialog box appears.

3. Type **Inca** in the File name text box, and then change the Save as type list box to **Design Template**. When you do this, PowerPoint automatically changes the Save in folder to Templates. However, you want to save the file to your Data Disk.

4. Locate the **Tutorial.03** folder on your Data Disk in the Save in list box, double-click **Tutorial**, and then click the **Save** button in the Save As dialog box.

Patricia will later copy the template file to the Presentations Designs folder (which usually has the path \Program Files\Microsoft Office\Templates\Presentation Designs). Inca Imports' employees can then apply the Inca design template just as they would any of the standard PowerPoint design templates.

With the design template completed, Patricia asks you to further enhance the presentation by applying graphics and sounds to it.

Applying **Graphics and Sounds**

When used well, graphics and sound effects can provide interest and motivation to your audience. Patricia now asks you to review her presentation and then add appropriate graphics and sound effects to the slides. Looking first at the title slide, you decide to add a scanned image to it.

Adding and Customizing a Scanned Image in the Title Slide

Patricia wants you to add a scanned (and edited) image of Machu Picchu, the ruins of the Lost City of the Incas, to Slide 1 (the title slide). This image serves as a second logo for Inca Imports. To add the scanned image, follow the same procedure used to insert a picture into a slide.

To add a scanned image to a slide:

1. Make sure Slide 1 appears in the Slide Pane, click **Insert** on the menu bar, point to **Picture**, and then click **From File** to open the Insert Picture dialog box.

2. If necessary, change the **Look in** folder to the Tutorial.03 Tutorial on your Data Disk, and then click the file **MachPicc**, which is a scanned picture of Machu Picchu.

3. Click the **Insert** button to insert the picture into the middle of the slide. The Picture toolbar also appears on the screen while the scanned image is selected. You'll now change the size and position of the picture.

4. Click the **Format Picture** button 📷 on the Picture toolbar to open the Format Picture dialog box, and then click the **Size** tab.

5. In the Scale section of the dialog box, make sure the **Lock aspect ratio** check box is checked, so that when you change the height, the width will also change automatically (so the picture dimensions don't become distorted), change the scale **Height** to **70%**, and then click the **OK** button.

6. Drag the picture so that it appears about halfway between the top of the slide and the top of the title text "Annual Report."

7. Click in any blank area of the slide to deselect the scanned picture (see Figure 3-8).

| Figure 3-8 | TITLE SLIDE WITH SCANNED IMAGE |

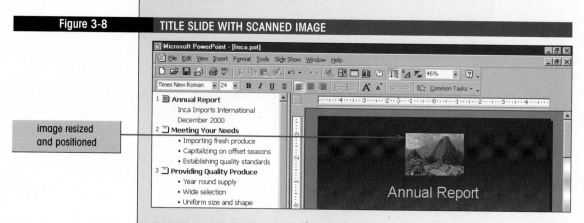

image resized and positioned

8. Save your work (this time as a presentation, not as a design template) by clicking **File** on the menu bar, clicking **Save As**, changing the file type to **Presentation**, and then changing the filename to **Annual Report**. When asked if you want to overwrite the existing file, click the **Yes** button.

With the title slide completed, you look next at Slide 2. You determine that it needs an eye-catching graphic, in this case, an animated GIF.

Adding an Animated GIF

The PowerPoint Clip Gallery provides not only static pictures but also animated GIFs, called Motion Clips. An **animated GIF** is a clip-art image that shows motion when displayed on a slide during a slide show. For Slide 2, Patricia suggests adding an animated GIF of a flying rocket, to help remind her audience that her company delivers fresh, imported produce quickly.

To add an animated GIF:

1. Go to Slide 2, "Meeting Your Needs."

2. Click **Insert** on the menu bar, point to **Movies and Sounds**, and then click **Movie from Gallery**. The Insert Movie dialog box opens, with the Motion Clips tab displayed.

3. Scroll down the clip categories, and then click **Transportation**. One or more transportation clips appear in the dialog box (see Figure 3-9).

| Figure 3-9 | INSERT MOVIE DIALOG BOX |

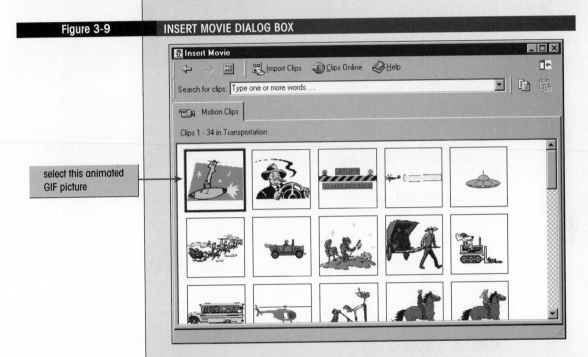

select this animated GIF picture

TROUBLE? If no motion clips appear on the dialog box and you have access to the Microsoft Office 2000 CDs, you can install the motion clips. Run Setup located on the appropriate CD, click Add or Remove Features, open the items under Office Tools (by clicking the plus sign, if necessary), set the Clip Gallery to "Run from My Computer," and then click the Update Now button. If you don't have this Office 2000 CD or if you're unsure about this procedure, consult your instructor or technical support person.

4. Click the cartoon of a man on a rocket, and then click the **Insert Clip** button 🔲. The animated GIF picture is inserted into the center of the current slide. You can't see the image on the slide yet because it's covered by the dialog box.

5. Click the **Close** button ❎ on the Insert Movie dialog box to return to Normal View.

6. Double the width (and height) by setting the **Height** scale to 200% on the **Size** tab of the Format Picture dialog box, and then move the image to the approximate position shown in Figure 3-10.

Figure 3-10   **SLIDE WITH ANIMATED GIF PICTURE**

animated GIF resized
and positioned

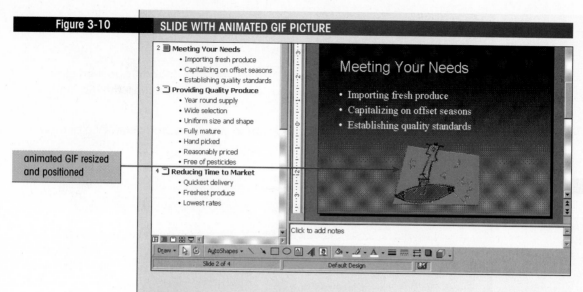

7. With Slide 2 still in the Slide Pane, test the animated GIF by clicking the **Slide Show** button [image]. As you can see, the rocket appears to be flying because of the animation of the jet flame.

8. Press the **Esc** key to exit the Slide Show and return to Normal View.

You can also add video clips to your slides. A **video clip** is an animated picture file, usually with the filename extension .avi. To add a video clip, insert it as you would a picture, locating the .avi file within the Clip Gallery, on your own disk, or on a CD.

Patricia approves your work on the title slide and Slide 2. She suggests adding sound clips to the next two slides.

Adding a Sound Clip

To use sound effects in PowerPoint, the computer system used for the presentation must have a sound card and speakers that are loud enough for your audience to hear the sounds clearly. The sound card responds to data from specific types of files. The two most popular types of files are wave (.wav) and MIDI (.mid) files. Microsoft Windows supports both types of sound files. You'll add one of each type to Patricia's presentation.

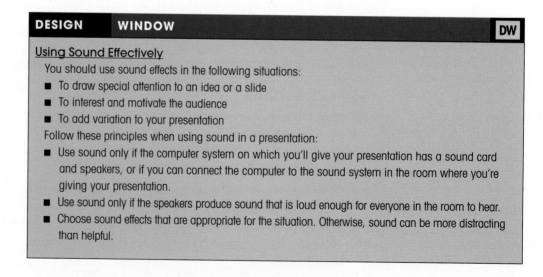

DESIGN   WINDOW   **DW**

Using Sound Effectively

You should use sound effects in the following situations:

■ To draw special attention to an idea or a slide

■ To interest and motivate the audience

■ To add variation to your presentation

Follow these principles when using sound in a presentation:

■ Use sound only if the computer system on which you'll give your presentation has a sound card and speakers, or if you can connect the computer to the sound system in the room where you're giving your presentation.

■ Use sound only if the speakers produce sound that is loud enough for everyone in the room to hear.

■ Choose sound effects that are appropriate for the situation. Otherwise, sound can be more distracting than helpful.

Patricia decides that adding a sound clip of clapping (applause) in Slide 3 would help emphasize the importance of the slide, and a sound of a fanfare in Slide 4 would help introduce this important topic. Although you could insert sound clips from the Clip Gallery, in this case you will use wave and MIDI files from a disk.

To add a wave file to Slide 3:

1. Display Slide 3, "Providing Quality Produce," in the Slide Pane.

2. Click **Insert** on the menu bar, point to **Movies and Sounds**, and then click **Sound from File**. The Insert Sound dialog box opens.

3. If necessary, change the **Look in** list box to the Tutorial.03 Tutorial folder on your Data Disk, click **Clapping** (if necessary), and then click the **OK** button.

4. When asked if you want the sound to play automatically, click the **No** button. Patricia will want to play the sound only after going through the items on the slide. PowerPoint adds the sound wave file to the presentation and displays a sound wave icon on the slide.

   TROUBLE? If an error message appears, your computer might have insufficient memory. Ask your instructor or your technical support person for assistance.

5. Drag the sound wave icon to the lower-right corner of the slide. Because the icon will appear on the screen when you give your presentation, you want the icon out of the way of any text.

6. Switch to Slide Show View so you can see how the sound icon will appear during a presentation. See Figure 3-11. Click the sound icon to hear the clapping sound.

Figure 3-11	SLIDE 3 IN SLIDE SHOW VIEW

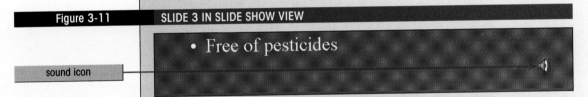

sound icon

With the sound wave icon on the screen, you can click the icon at any time during the slide show to play the sound, or you can double-click the icon in Normal View.

7. Press the **Esc** key to return to Normal View, and then double-click the sound icon to play the sound.

8. Go to Slide 4 and repeat the above steps to insert a sound clip, only this time insert the MIDI file called **Fanfare**, and then answer **Yes**, you want the sound to play automatically in the slide show. Again, drag the sound icon to the lower-right corner.

9. Test the sound in Normal View and in Slide Show View.

10. Save the presentation using the default filename.

You have prepared a design template, including creating a custom color scheme, adding a gradient background, and applying new font attributes. You have also added graphic images and sound effects to the presentation. In the next session, you'll continue to assess and enhance the remaining slides in the presentation.

Session 3.1 QUICK CHECK

1. If you wanted to insert three or four slides from another presentation into a current one, what would you do?

2. What is a design template?

3. In general terms (not keystrokes or mouse operations), how do you create a custom template?

4. What is a gradient fill?

5. What is an animated GIF picture?

6. What are three ways sound can be used effectively?

SESSION 3.2

In this session, you'll learn how to create a graph, build and modify an organization chart, and apply special effects—slide transitions and animation effects. You'll also learn how to hide a slide, save a slide as a graphic, prepare presentation materials to create 35mm slides, and prepare the presentation to run on another computer.

Creating a Chart (Graph)

On Slide 4 of the presentation, Patricia asks you to add a column chart that compares Inca Imports' time to market (that is, the time from picking to customer delivery, in hours) during the past four quarters with those of its two major competitors in southern California.

REFERENCE WINDOW   RW

Inserting a Chart

- Display the desired slide in Slide View.
- If necessary, change the slide layout to Text & Chart, Chart & Text, or Chart.
- Double-click the chart placeholder. PowerPoint displays a datasheet.
- Edit the information in the datasheet for the data that you want to plot.
- Click anywhere outside the datasheet, and then click anywhere outside the chart box.

You'll now create a chart that compares the time-to-market information. You'll begin by adding a chart to Slide 4.

To add a chart to the slide:

1. If you took a break after the last session, make sure PowerPoint is running and the file Annual Report is open in Normal View.

2. Go to Slide 4, "Reducing Time to Market."

3. Click the **Common Tasks** button on the Formatting toolbar, click **Slide Layout**, click the **Text & Chart** layout (second row, first column), and then click the **Apply** button. The text on the slide becomes formatted into a smaller text box on the left side of the slide, and a chart placeholder appears on the right side.

4. Double-click the chart placeholder. After few moments, PowerPoint inserts a sample graph and displays a **datasheet**, or a grid of cells, similar to a Microsoft Excel worksheet, in which you can add data and labels.

   TROUBLE? If the colors on the slide become distorted, don't worry. They'll return to normal once you close the datasheet window.

To create the chart for Patricia's presentation, you simply edit the information in the sample datasheet on the screen to reflect the three companies' times to market. The information on the datasheet is stored in cells, which are the boxes that are organized in rows and columns. The rows are numbered 1, 2, 3, ... and the columns are labeled A, B, C, ...

To edit the information in the datasheet:

1. Position the pointer ✛ over the cell that contains the word "East."

2. Click in the cell that contains the word "East," and then type **Inca** (short for "Inca Imports International").

3. Press the **down arrow** key to select the cell labeled "West," and then type **SCP** (which stands for "Southern California Produce," one of Inca Imports' major competitors).

4. Press the **down arrow** key to select the cell labeled "North," and then type **CCF** (which stands for "Central City Foods," Inca Imports' other major competitor). See Figure 3-12.

Figure 3-12	CREATING A GRAPH

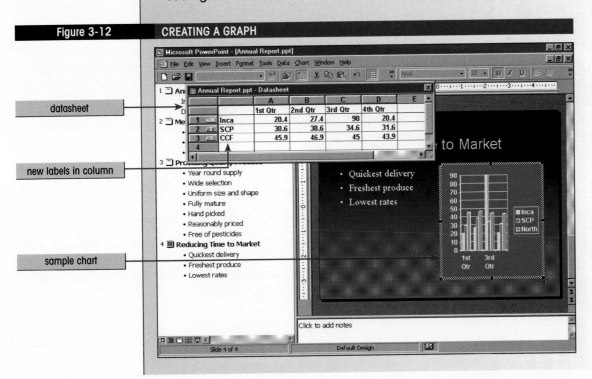

datasheet

new labels in column

sample chart

Now you're ready to change the actual numbers in the datasheet.

5. Click in cell A1, the cell at which column A and row 1 intersect, and then type **16**. This is Inca Imports' average time to market in hours during the first quarter of the year.

6. Click in cell B1, type **18**, press the **Tab** key, type **17**, press the **Tab** key, and then type **16**. This completes the data for Inca Imports.

7. Use the same procedure to replace the current data for SCP and CCF with the data shown in Figure 3-13. Carefully check your datasheet to make sure it matches Figure 3-13. Make any necessary corrections.

 Figure 3-13   COMPLETED DATASHEET

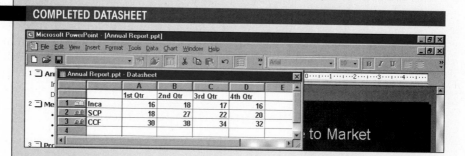

8. Click the **Close** button on the datasheet window to remove the datasheet from the screen. The completed chart appears in Slide 4.

Patricia reviews the chart and suggests that you insert a title to label the vertical axis of the chart.

To add an axis title to a chart:

1. Make sure the chart is still selected, click **Chart** on the menu bar, and then click **Chart Options** to open the Chart Options dialog box.

2. Click in the **Value (Z) axis** text box, type **Hours**, and then click the **OK** button. The label "Hours" appears to the left of the vertical axis.

3. With the Value (Z) axis title still selected, click **Format** on the menu bar, click **Selected Axis Title** to display the Format Axis Title dialog box, and then click the **Alignment** tab.

4. In the Orientation section, change the **Rotation** to **90** degrees, and then click the **OK** button to return to the chart on the slide. The word "Hours" on the vertical axis is now rotated so that it reads bottom to top.

5. Click anywhere in a blank area of the chart box to deselect "Hours."

6. Position the pointer over the left-center resize handle of the chart box, so that the pointer changes to ↔, and then drag the handle to the left until the left edge of the graph box is near the right edge of the text of the slide. See Figure 3-14.

Figure 3-14 | COMPLETED AND RESIZED GRAPH

making chart wider

axis title (rotated)

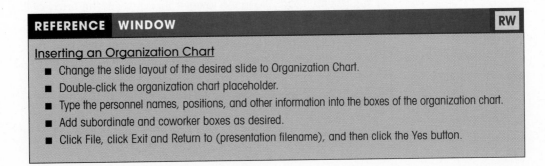

TROUBLE? If the chart box won't move to the left as indicated in Step 6, you might have selected the chart instead of the chart box. Click Edit on the menu bar, click Undo Last, and then repeat Step 6.

TROUBLE? If your chart doesn't look like the one in Figure 3-14, click the View Datasheet button on the Standard toolbar to display the datasheet. Make the necessary revisions by comparing your datasheet with Figure 3-14.

You have now completed Slide 4 of Patricia's presentation.

7. Click outside the chart area to deselect the chart, and then save your work, using the current filename.

Patricia is pleased with Slide 4. She thinks just one more slide is needed to complete her presentation: a new Slide 5, showing an organization chart of the officers of Inca Imports.

Building and Modifying an Organization Chart

Because Inca Imports is a fairly new company, Patricia feels that it's important, as part of her annual report, to include an organization chart. An **organization chart** is a diagram of boxes, connected with lines, showing the hierarchy of positions within an organization.

REFERENCE WINDOW **RW**

Inserting an Organization Chart
- Change the slide layout of the desired slide to Organization Chart.
- Double-click the organization chart placeholder.
- Type the personnel names, positions, and other information into the boxes of the organization chart.
- Add subordinate and coworker boxes as desired.
- Click File, click Exit and Return to (presentation filename), and then click the Yes button.

You'll now create the organization chart as well as make any necessary modifications to it.

To create and modify an organization chart:

1. Make sure Slide 4 is still in the Slide Pane, click the **New Slide** button to display the New Slide dialog box, select the **Organization Chart** layout (second row, third column), and then click the **OK** button. The new Slide 5 appears in the Slide Pane.

2. Click in the title placeholder, and then type **Management Organization**.

3. Double-click the org chart placeholder in Slide 5. After a short pause the Microsoft Organization Chart window appears on the screen, with the Organization Chart toolbar across the top.

   TROUBLE? If the Microsoft Organization Chart feature is not installed, PowerPoint will ask if you want to install it now. Click Yes if you have the Office 2000 or PowerPoint CD; otherwise consult your instructor or technical support person.

4. Click the **Maximize** button on the Microsoft Organization Chart window so that it fills the entire screen (see Figure 3-15). A chart with text placeholders appears in the window. This chart has two levels of organization. The first line in the box at the top of the chart is already selected, as you can tell from its different color. However, the default colors, based on the custom color scheme, are white text on a yellow background, which is almost illegible. You need to change either the box color or text color. You decide to change the text color to black.

Figure 3-15	MICROSOFT ORGANIZATION CHART WINDOW

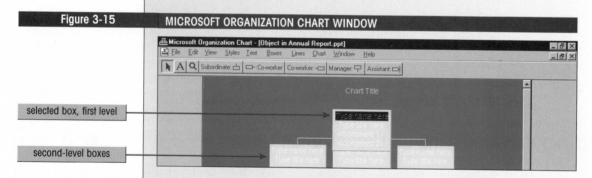

5. Press the **Ctrl + A** keys to select all the boxes, click **Text** on the menu bar, and then click **Color**. The Color dialog box opens.

6. Click the black tile in the lower-right corner of the array of tiles, and then click the **OK** button. Now all the text in all the boxes is legible.

7. Click the top line in the top organization box, and then drag across the phrase "Type name here" to select only that text. See Figure 3-16.

Figure 3-16   ORGANIZATION CHART WITH MODIFIED TEXT COLOR

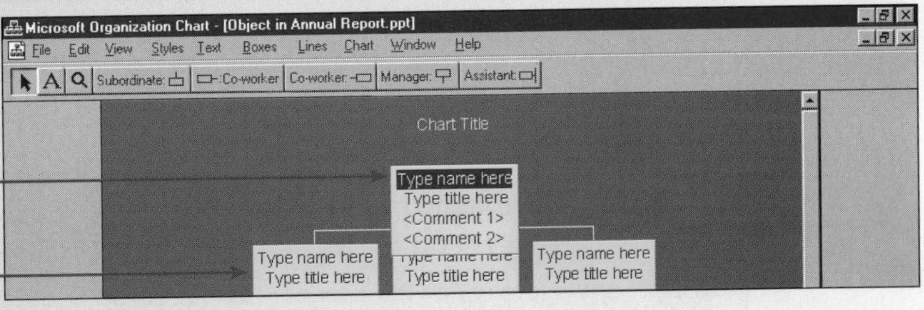

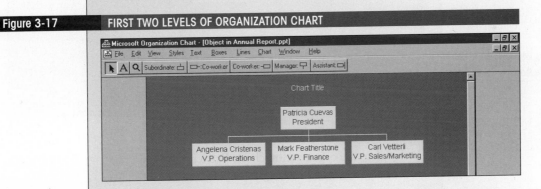

select name placeholder

black text, now legible

Now you're ready to type the names and titles into the organization chart.

To insert names and titles in the organization chart:

1. Type **Patricia Cuevas** on the first line, and then press the **Tab** key (or the **Enter** key). The placeholder text "Type title here" becomes selected.

2. Type **President**. This completes the first box. PowerPoint will automatically delete the two (extra) lines for you if you don't use them.

3. Click the second-level box on the left side. The box becomes selected, as indicated by its black background.

4. Type **Angelena Cristenas**, press the **Tab** key, and then type **V.P. Operations**. This completes the text of that text box in the organization chart.

5. Use the same procedure to complete the other two boxes of the organization chart so they contain the text shown in Figure 3-17, then click anywhere within the Microsoft Organization Chart window, but outside any text or organization box, to take the chart out of editing mode.

Figure 3-17   FIRST TWO LEVELS OF ORGANIZATION CHART

TROUBLE? If you made any typing errors, click the box containing the error, press the Tab key until the line containing the error is highlighted, and then retype that line.

You have completed the first two levels of the organization chart. Patricia also wants to list the personnel who handle produce and respond to customer delivery needs. These customer service employees work under Angelena Cristenas. You'll add the new levels of organization now.

To add subordinate levels to an organization chart:

1. Click the **Subordinate** button Subordinate: on the Organization Chart toolbar. The pointer changes to.

2. Click anywhere within the box containing "Angelena Cristenas." A new organization level appears below Angelena's box.

3. Type **Carlos Becerra**. As soon as you begin to type, the other text placeholders appear in the box.

4. Press the **Tab** key, and then type **QA Manager**. This completes the box for Carlos Becerra, QA (quality assurance) Manager.

5. Click Subordinate:, and then click the box containing "Carlos Becerra" to add a subordinate box underneath Carlos.

6. Type **Norma Lopez**, press the **Tab** key, type **Customer Service**, and then click anywhere in the Organization Chart window, but outside any text or box. Your chart should now look like Figure 3-18.

Figure 3-18   ORGANIZATION CHART AFTER ADDING SUBORDINATE BOXES

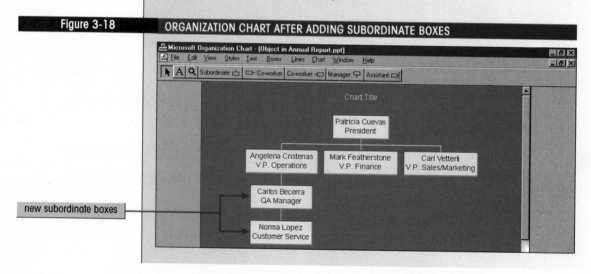

new subordinate boxes

To complete the organization chart, Patricia asks you to add a coworker to the chart.

To add a coworker to an organization chart:

1. Click the **Right Coworker** button Co-worker: on the Organization Chart toolbar. The mouse changes to. This allows you to add a coworker box to the right of an existing box.

2. Click the box containing "Norma Lopez" to add a new box to its right, type **Juanita Rojas**, press the **Tab** key, type **Manager, Quito Center**, and then click anywhere in the window, but outside any box or text, to take the chart out of editing mode.

You have completed the organization chart. To add it to Slide 5, you simply need to exit the Organization Chart window.

3. Click **File**, and then click **Exit and Return to Annual Report.ppt**. A dialog box appears on the screen asking if you want to update the object. The object in this case is the new organization chart.

4. Click the **Yes** button. The Organization Chart window closes, and the chart is inserted in Slide 5.

After looking over the organization chart, Patricia asks you to enlarge it.

5. Drag the resize handle in the upper-left corner up and to the left, until the left edge of the organization chart is near (but not against) the left edge of the slide. Drag the resize handle in the lower-right corner down and to the right until the organization chart is approximately the same size as the one shown in Figure 3-19.

Figure 3-19	COMPLETED ORGANIZATION CHART

6. Click anywhere outside the selected organization chart to deselect it.

This completes the organization chart on Slide 5, as well as all the slides in the presentation. In reviewing your work, you and Patricia decide it can be further improved by adding special effects.

Applying Special Effects

Special effects—such as fading out of one slide as another appears, animated (moving) text, and sound effects—can liven up your presentation, help hold your audience's attention, and emphasize key points. On the other hand, special effects can also distract or even annoy your audience. Your goal is to apply special effects conservatively and tastefully so that, rather than making your presentation look gawky and amateurish, they add a professional look and feel to your slide show.

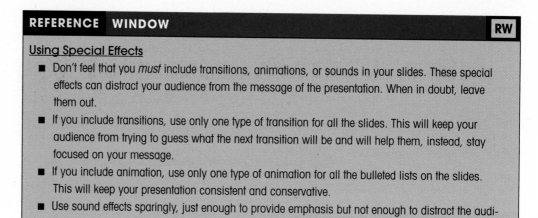

REFERENCE **WINDOW**   **RW**

Using Special Effects

- Don't feel that you *must* include transitions, animations, or sounds in your slides. These special effects can distract your audience from the message of the presentation. When in doubt, leave them out.
- If you include transitions, use only one type of transition for all the slides. This will keep your audience from trying to guess what the next transition will be and will help them, instead, stay focused on your message.
- If you include animation, use only one type of animation for all the bulleted lists on the slides. This will keep your presentation consistent and conservative.
- Use sound effects sparingly, just enough to provide emphasis but not enough to distract the audience from your message.

The first special effect that you will add is a transition effect.

Adding Slide Transitions

A **transition effect** is a method of moving one slide off the screen and bringing another slide onto the screen during a slide show. Although applying transitions is usually easier in Slide Sorter View, because you can easily select several (or all) slides at once, you can also apply a transition in the Slide Pane.

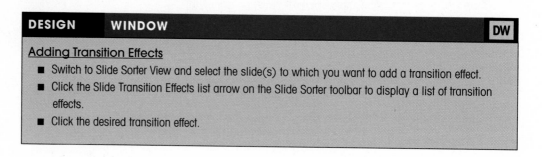

DESIGN **WINDOW**   **DW**

Adding Transition Effects

- Switch to Slide Sorter View and select the slide(s) to which you want to add a transition effect.
- Click the Slide Transition Effects list arrow on the Slide Sorter toolbar to display a list of transition effects.
- Click the desired transition effect.

You'll add a transition to all the slides in the presentation.

To add a transition effect:

1. Click ⊞ to switch to Slide Sorter View, and then change the Zoom (located on the Standard toolbar) to **100%**, so you can see the slides better.

2. Press the **Ctrl + A** keys to select all the slides. Now when you apply a slide transition, all the slides will have that transition. Currently, the Slide Sorter toolbar shows "No Transition" in the Slide Transition Effects list box (see Figure 3-20).

Figure 3-20	PRESENTATION BEFORE ADDING TRANSITIONS AND ANIMATION EFFECTS

no transitions or
animation effects

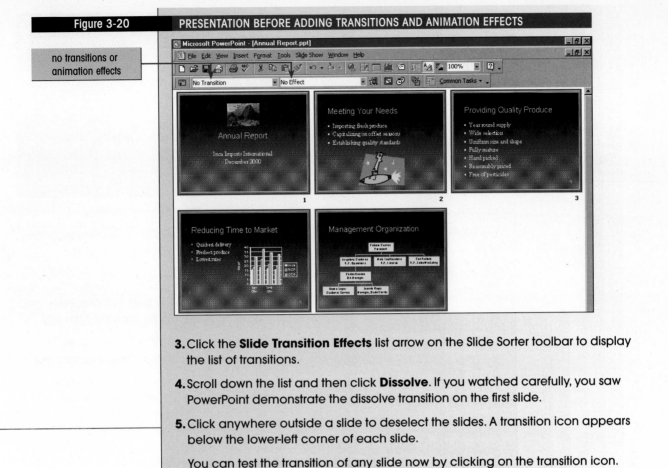

3. Click the **Slide Transition Effects** list arrow on the Slide Sorter toolbar to display the list of transitions.

4. Scroll down the list and then click **Dissolve**. If you watched carefully, you saw PowerPoint demonstrate the dissolve transition on the first slide.

5. Click anywhere outside a slide to deselect the slides. A transition icon appears below the lower-left corner of each slide.

   You can test the transition of any slide now by clicking on the transition icon.

6. Click the transition icon 🔲 below Slide 2. As you can see, PowerPoint momentarily displays Slide 1 at that location, and then performs the transition to Slide 2. Click any of the transition icons to see how the transition looks for that slide.

Having added transitions to the slides, you're ready to add more special effects: animation and sound.

Adding Animation with Sound

Animation is a special visual or sound effect applied to an object (such as graphics or bulleted text). For example, Patricia asks you to add an animation effect that allows you to progressively display individual bulleted items, one item at a time. In addition, she asks you to include sound with the animation effect. As a result, on the slides that have several bulleted items, you will add the animation effect so that when you first display the slide in your slide show, only the slide title appears, without any of the bulleted items. Then when you click the left mouse button (or press the Spacebar), the first bulleted item appears, with a "whooshing" sound. When you click the left mouse button again, the second bulleted item appears with a "whoosh," and so on. You will also tell PowerPoint to dim the previous bulleted item as a new one is added. The advantage of this type of animation effect is that you can focus your audience's attention on one item at a time, without the distractions of other items on the screen.

REFERENCE WINDOW

Adding Animation

- In Slide Sorter View, select the slide(s) to which you want to add an animation effect.
- Click the Text Preset Animation list arrow on the Slide Sorter toolbar to display a list of animation effects.
- Click the desired animation effect.
- To dim previous items in a bulleted list and add sound effects, display the desired slide in Normal View, click Slide Show on the menu bar, click Custom Animation, click the Effects tab, click the desired Animation Order item, click the After Animation list arrow, click the tile of the desired color, click the Sound list arrow, click the desired sound, and then click the OK button.

You'll now add an animation effect and sound to the bulleted lists in Patricia's presentation.

To add an animation effect and sound:

1. From Slide Sorter View, click Slide 2, press and hold down the **Shift** key, and then click Slide 4 to select the three slides that have bulleted lists. Release the **Shift** key.

2. Click the **Preset Animation** list arrow on the Slide Sorter toolbar to display the list of PowerPoint's preset, or built-in, animations. (You can also create custom animations.)

3. Click the animation effect **Fly From Right**, so that the text in each bulleted item will fly from the right edge of the slide to its position on the left edge of the slide. Notice that a slide animation icon now appears next to the transition icon below the lower-left corner of each slide with an animation effect. You can click an animation icon to preview the animation.

   You're now ready to add sound to the animation effect.

4. Click anywhere outside the selected slides to deselect them, click Slide 2 to select it, and then click 🖼 to display Slide 2 in Normal View.

5. Click **Slide Show** on the menu bar, click **Custom Animation**, click **1. Text 2** in the Animation order list box, and then click the **Effects** tab. See Figure 3-21. Notice that the Entry animation is already set to "Fly" and the direction is "From Right."

Figure 3-21	CUSTOM ANIMATION DIALOG BOX

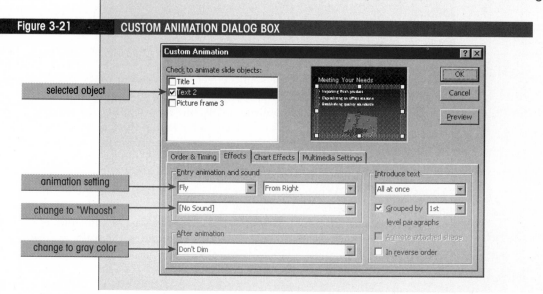

6. Click the **Sound** list arrow in the Entry animation and sound section in the dialog box, and then scroll down and click **Whoosh**. As each bulleted item flies into view during a slide show, PowerPoint will make a "whooshing" sound.

Your last task to complete the animation effect on this slide is to dim the previous bulleted items when a new one appears on the screen.

7. Click the **After animation** list arrow, and then click the gray tile (labeled "Follow Shadows Scheme Color"), the third tile from the left. As a new bulleted item appears in a slide show, the previous bulleted items will be changed to gray.

8. Click the **Preview** button in the Custom Animation dialog box to see how the animation will look and sound, and then click the **OK** button to apply these animation effects to Slide 2.

TROUBLE? If you don't hear anything, you may not have a sound card in your computer system or you may have to turn up the volume. Consult your instructor or technical support person.

9. Repeat this same method of applying animation effects to Slides 3 and 4.

Besides specifying the type of animation, sound effects, and color after animation (dimming), you can also specify the order of events. In the case of Slide 4, you want the three bulleted items to appear first, and then the chart, and finally the media clip (sound effects). You'll now specify the order of these events.

To set the order of the events in custom animation:

1. If necessary, go to Slide 4, and then display the Custom Animation dialog box. Make sure the **Order & Timing** tab is visible. The Animation order list in this tab displays three items, Text 2 (the bulleted list), Chart 3 (the graphic chart), and Media 4 (the sound effect).

2. Click **Text 2**, and then click the **Move Up** button ⬆ once or twice until Text 2 is at the top of the list.

TROUBLE? If the item won't go all the way to the top, click the top item and then click the Move Down button to move the item down below Text 2.

3. Click and move the other items until the order is Text 2 at the top, Chart 3 in the middle, and Media 4 on the bottom. See Figure 3-22.

Figure 3-22   SETTING CUSTOM ANIMATION ORDER FOR SLIDE 4

order of animation

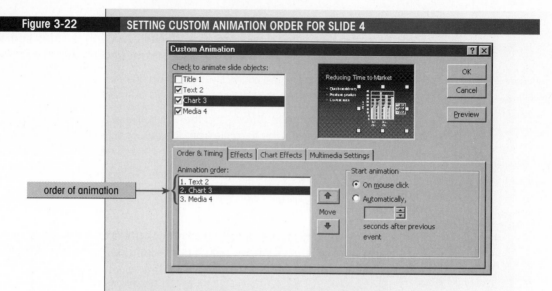

Next you'll make sure the sound effect starts immediately after the chart appears, without your having to click the mouse.

4. Click **Media 4**, and then if necessary set **Start animation** to **Automatically**. Now you won't have to press the Spacebar or click the mouse a separate time to play the sound file.

5. Click the **OK** button on the Custom Animation dialog box, and then save the presentation using the default filename.

Now when Patricia gives her presentation, her audience will see the slide transitions and animation effects and hear the sound effects.

Patricia realizes that all of the slides may not be appropriate for both audiences (the Inca Imports' board of directors and the company stockholders). For example, she doesn't want to take the time in her presentation to the board of directors to go over Slide 2, "Meeting Your Needs." The best solution is for her to temporarily hide that one slide, so it won't even show up during the one presentation.

Hiding Slides

To demonstrate to Patricia how to hide and unhide slides, you'll now hide Slide 2, go through the presentation, unhide Slide 2, and go through the presentation again.

To hide a slide:

1. Go to Slide 2, click **Slide Show** on the menu bar, and then click **Hide Slide**. While you're still in Normal View, nothing changes. You can still see and edit the "hidden" slide. It will be hidden only in Slide Show View. You'll now see your slides in Slide Show View.

2. Go to Slide 1, and then click the **Slide Show View** button 🖳 to view the presentation. As you can see, the first slide "dissolves" onto the screen. This is the transition effect that you applied earlier.

3. Press the **Spacebar** to go to the next slide. As you can see, instead of displaying Slide 2, "Meeting Your Needs," PowerPoint went directly to Slide 3, "Providing Quality Produce." You also observe the effect of animation: no bulleted items appear yet. You'll have to press the Spacebar or click the left mouse button to animate the text's appearance onto the screen.

4. Press the **Spacebar** to display the first bulleted item. As the text flies from right to left, you also hear the "whoosh." These are the animation effects you applied to this and the other slides with bulleted lists.

5. Display all of the bulleted items, one at a time, until you get to the last one, "Free of pesticides." See Figure 3-23.

| Figure 3-23 | SLIDE SHOW VIEW OF SLIDE 3 |

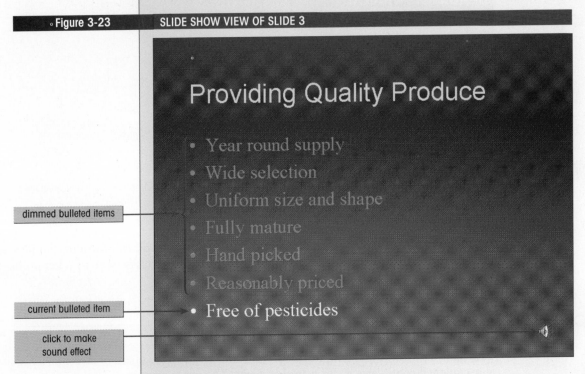

dimmed bulleted items

current bulleted item

click to make sound effect

6. Click 🖑 on the sound clip icon. PowerPoint plays the clapping sound.

7. Go to the next slide (Slide 4) and display all the animated objects and listen to the sound effect, which plays automatically after the other objects appear.

8. Finally, view Slide 5, which contains the organization chart, and then return to Normal View.

Now that you've seen how to hide a slide, you should go back and "unhide" it, so it will be available for Patricia's presentation to the stockholders.

To unhide a slide:

1. Go to Slide 2, click **Slide Show** on the menu bar, and then click **Hide Slide**. This toggles Hide Slide to off for Slide 2.

2. Go to Slide 1, again switch to Slide Show View, and then press the **Spacebar**. This time you see Slide 2.

3. After viewing Slide 2, return to Normal View.

4. Save the presentation using the default filename.

You've now completed Patricia's slide show. Before preparing materials for her audiences, Patricia wants to rehearse the presentation.

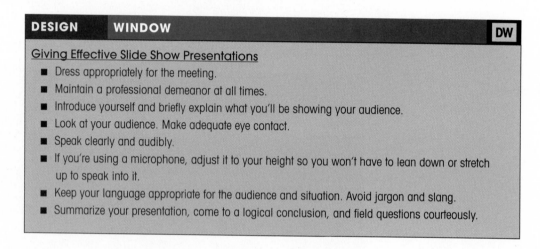

Patricia is now confident that her presentation will go smoothly, providing the needed information to her audiences in an engaging manner. Your final tasks are to help her produce the materials she'll need for her presentation.

Preparing **Presentation Materials**

Patricia will present the electronic (on-screen) slide show to the board of directors in a suitably equipped conference room at Inca Imports. The conference room at the stockholders' meeting, however, doesn't have the equipment necessary to run an electronic slide show, so Patricia plans to use 35mm slides.

Preparing 35mm Slides

Inca Imports, like most small businesses, lacks the facilities to make 35mm slides, but most U.S. cities have service bureaus that can convert computer files into 35mm slides. PowerPoint also supports the services of Genigraphics Corporation, a service bureau that handles 35mm slides, color overheads, and posters. PowerPoint contains the software necessary to prepare and deliver a file to Genigraphics. If you send the file to a Genigraphics facility, the company will create 35mm slides of the presentation and mail them back to you. Whether using Genigraphics or another service, you need to first change the output format to 35mm Slides in the Page Setup dialog box. You also need to change the output format if you decided to print overheads, for which you may want to change the orientation of printing from portrait (which is taller than it is wide) to landscape (which is wider than it is tall).

Patricia uses PowerPoint to prepare and deliver a file to Genigraphics, and within a few days, receives her 35mm slides from them.

In addition to preparing a presentation as 35mm slides or overheads, you can also save one or more of your slides as graphic images for use in other software, for example, to insert into a Word document. PowerPoint allows you to save slides in a variety of graphic formats including JPEG File Interchange Format (*.jpg), Device Independent Bitmap (*.bmp), and Tag Image File Format (*.tif). To save one of the slides as a graphic, you would display the Save As dialog box, change the file type to the desired graphic format, and click the Save button. PowerPoint would then ask you if you wanted to save all the files or just the current one. You would click Yes to save them all as individual image files, or click No to save just the current slide.

Patricia has one last, important step in getting ready: making sure her presentation will run even if PowerPoint isn't installed on the computer in the boardroom where she will give her presentation. She knows that she doesn't need PowerPoint to be installed because she can use the PowerPoint Viewer. She also wants to make sure that whatever computer she uses, the fonts (Arial and Book Antiqua) are available, so she will save the presentation with embedded fonts.

Preparing the Presentation to Run on Another Computer

PowerPoint **Viewer** is a separate program that you can use to give your slide show on any Windows 95/98/2000 or Windows NT computer. The Microsoft PowerPoint license allows you to create a Viewer disk and to install the Viewer program on other computers without additional charge.

Patricia asks you to use the Pack and Go Wizard to create a Viewer disk (or set of disks) that contains the PowerPoint Viewer files and a copy of her presentation. Patricia can then use the Pack and Go disk to install the Viewer and run the presentation file on any computer. Although Patricia can't change any of the slides using the PowerPoint Viewer, she is able to review the entire slide show, including special effects.

To save a file with embedded fonts and use Pack and Go:

1. Click **File** on the menu bar, click **Save As** to display the Save As dialog box, click **Tools** on the dialog box toolbar, and then click **Embed TrueType Fonts**.

2. Click the **Save** button in the dialog box, and then click the **Yes** button when you're asked if you want to replace the existing file. The file Annual Report is now saved with the fonts embedded, so it will have the same appearance on other computers that might not have those fonts.

3. Click **File** on the menu bar, and then click **Pack and Go**. The Pack and Go Wizard appears on the screen.

   TROUBLE? If the Pack and Go feature isn't installed, PowerPoint will ask you if you want to install it now. Click Yes if you have the Office 2000 or PowerPoint 2000 CD; otherwise click No and skip this section.

4. Place a formatted, blank 3½-inch floppy disk in the disk drive. You'll need two other formatted, blank 3½-inch floppy disks, a total of three, to hold all the necessary files.

5. Go through the Wizard answering the questions as best you can. If you're uncertain about a question, accept the default setting. When you get to the window on Links, click the check box to indicate that you do indeed want to embed TrueType fonts. When you get to the question about the View, you should choose to include the Viewer, since another computer might not have it. After going through the Wizard, click the **Finish** button.

You give the Pack and Go disks to Patricia so she can show her presentation on any computer. You have completed Patricia's presentation. She believes that the graphics, sound, and special effects for the on-screen slide show will help her audience stay focused on her presentation. She thanks you for your help.

Session 3.2 QUICK CHECK

1. How would you insert a chart (graph) into a slide?

2. What is an organization chart?

3. How would you insert an organization chart into a slide?

4. Define the following terms
   a. transition effect
   b. animation effect
   c. sound effect

5. Describe in general terms (not in specific steps) how you would do the following:
   a. add a transition effect to a slide
   b. add sound to an animation effect on a slide

6. What is Genigraphics?

7. What is the PowerPoint Viewer?

REVIEW ASSIGNMENTS

After Angelena Cristenas, Vice President of Operations at Inca Imports, reviews Patricia's presentation (using the Viewer disk), she asks you to create a similar presentation that will describe Inca Imports' benefits to new employees. Complete the following for Angelena:

1. If necessary, start PowerPoint and make sure your Data Disk is in the appropriate disk drive.

2. Create a new blank presentation with a title slide. Title the slide "Employee Benefits" and subtitle it "Inca Imports International."

3. Using the Slide Master, change the color scheme as follows: background color, light blue; text and lines color, dark green; shadow color, medium gray; and title text color, red. Keep the default color for the other items.

Explore   4. Change the level-one bullet style to small red squares. (*Hint*: On the Slide Master, click the placeholder where you want to change the bullet, click Format on the menu bar, click Bullets and Numbering, and then in the dialog box, make the desired changes in the character and color of the bullet. If you need additional help, use the Office Assistant.)

Explore   5. Change the background style to the textured background called "Blue Tissue Paper." (*Hint*: Click the Background fill list arrow in the Background dialog box, click Fill Effects, and then select the desired texture.)

6. Change the Slide Master title font to Arial, and the text alignment to left alignment.

7. Insert the **MachPicc** scanned image (from the Tutorial.03 Tutorial folder on your Data Disk) into the Slide Master. Resize it to a height of 1.5 inches, with the aspect ratio preserved. Position the logo in the lower-right corner of the text box of the Slide Master slide text style box, near the text "Object Area for AutoLayouts." Adjust the Title Master so that it doesn't contain the graphic and the title is centered, not left aligned.

8. Add a new slide with the Bulleted List layout. Make the title of the new slide "Basic Benefits." Type the following first-level bulleted list items: "Medical and Dental Insurance," "Group Term Life Insurance," "Disability Insurance," "Occupational Accidental Death & Dismemberment Insurance," and "Master Retirement Plan."

9. Insert all the slides from the existing presentation file Benefits from the Tutorial.03 Review folder on your Data Disk into the current presentation, following Slide 2.

10. Delete the background image from Slide 5 only.

11. To Slides 2 through 5, add the preset animation effect called "Appear." In each of these slides, set the after animation effect to dim the previous items to a gray color. Set the sound effect in the animation to Laser.

12. To Slide 5, titled "Retirement Benefits Calculation," add the animated GIF picture of a pencil and clipboard found in the Business category of the Motion Clips Gallery.

13. To the final slide, titled "For More Help," add the sound wave file **Ringing** (found in the Review folder), specifying that you want it to ring automatically when the slide is displayed, and then place the sound icon to the right of the first bulleted item on the slide.

Explore　14. In Slide 6, remove the bullets that appear to the left of the address of the benefits office. (*Hint*: Delete them as you would any other text character.)

Explore　15. Use the Handout Master to set the layout of the printed handouts so that they will automatically reflect the date they were printed in the upper-right corner. (*Hint*: Press the Shift key and the Outline View button, click View on the menu bar, click Header and Footer, and then make sure the Notes and Handouts tab is selected.)

16. Save the presentation as **Supplemental Benefits** in the Tutorial.03 Review folder on your Data Disk, print the presentation in black and white as handouts (six slides per page), and then close the file.

CASE PROBLEMS

Case 1. Sweet Bouquet, Inc. Jennifer McBride decided to combine her love of flowers and candy as a home business. Her business has since grown, and her company, Sweet Bouquet, Inc., now includes 53 franchises in 40 cities nationwide. She has decided to create a PowerPoint presentation that she will use (and modify) for a variety of audiences, such as the company's board of directors, employees, and potential franchise owners. Jennifer has asked you to create a custom design template for her company and to finalize the presentation that she has started. Do the following:

1. Open a blank presentation (with the Default Design), and then create a custom color scheme. Although you should follow the suggested general colors as guidelines, you'll have to decide on specific shades: Set the background to brown, the text and lines to white, the shadows to green, and the title text to yellow. Set the other four items to four different shades of blue. Apply these colors to all the slides in the presentation.

2. On the Slide Master, change the title font to 40-point bold Arial. Set the title text alignment to left.

Explore

3. Also on the Slide Master, change the level-one bullet from a round, white character to a picture of a yellow sunburst. (*Hint*: Click Picture on the Bullets and Numbering dialog box.)

4. On the Title Master, set the title font to 48-point bold Arial. Set the title text alignment to center.

5. Also on the Title Master, include the bitmapped image **SBouquet** (the company logo) located in the Cases folder of the Tutorial.03 folder on your Data Disk.

6. Move the logo so it's centered between the top of the slide and the top of the title.

Explore

7. Change the background on the logo from white to transparent, so that no white appears around the logo. (*Hint*: Click the Set Transparent Color button on the Picture toolbar.)

8. Save the presentation as a design template to the Tutorial.03 Cases folder on your Data Disk, using the filename **Sweet Bouquet**.

9. Close the current presentation, and then open the presentation **SBouquet** from the Tutorial.03 Cases folder on your Data Disk.

10. Change the design template of the presentation from its current Default Design to the **Sweet Bouquet** design template.

11. Save the file presentation to the same folder using the filename **Sweet Bouquet**. (This won't overwrite your design template, because the files have different filename extensions: .pot and .ppt.)

12. On Slide 2, insert the animated GIF picture of a bee on a pair of flowers or on a sunflower, found in the Movie Gallery under the category Plants.

13. Also on Slide 2, insert the sound wave file **SBouquet** (found in the Tutorial.03 Cases folder). Set it up so the sound effect automatically plays during a slide show. Move the sound icon to the lower-right corner of the slide. You might want to display this slide in Slide Show view, so you can see the animation and hear the sound.

14. Go to Slide 4. Insert an organization chart with Jennifer McBride, President, at the top; below her: Candice Slowinski, V.P. of Marketing, and Carlos Young, V.P. of Operations; below Candice Slowinski: Stella Carlson, Sales Director, Dean Bradford, Advertising Director, and Sharon Wong, Franchise Liaison; below Carlos Young: Sarah Peacock, Director of Accounting, and Stanley Levoisier, Director of Human Resources; and below Sarah Peacock: Charles Bonfanti, Chief Accountant, and Cindy Boutelle, Auditor. Use the default box and text colors if the text is legible; if not, change the text color.

15. Increase the size of the organization chart so that it fills most of the space on the slide below the title. Make sure the text is still legible in Slide Show View after you expand the chart.

16. Go to Slide 5. Change the Slide Layout to Chart, which contains only a title and a chart. For the labels in columns A through D of the datasheet, type the years 1996 (column A), through 1999 (column D). Then do the following:

    a. For the row labels (in rows 1 and 2), type "Gross Income" and "Net Profit." Delete row 3.
    b. For the data in row 1 (from cell A1 to cell D1), type the values 1.1, 1.9, 2.7, and 4.2. For data in row 2 (from cell A2 to D2), type the values 0.1, 0.4, 0.8, and 1.2.
    c. To the chart, add the Z-axis title "Amount in $Millions." Rotate this title so that it appears vertically parallel to the vertical Z-axis, with the text going from bottom to top.

17. Go to Slide 6. Using the right-center resize handle of the bulleted list text box, decrease the width of the box to about one-half its current size. It should be positioned on the left side of the slide.

18. Insert into this slide a scanned picture of the founder, Jennifer McBride, by inserting the picture file **Jennifer** from the Tutorial.03 Cases folder. Position the picture in the blank area on the right side of the slide.

19. To each of the slides with bulleted lists, add animation ("Wipe Down") with no sound effect. Apply light-blue dimming.

20. To all the slides, apply the slide transition effect "Box Out."

21. Save the presentation using the default filename.

Explore 22. Go to Slide 4 and save only that slide as a graphic file in the Tag Image File Format (*.tif) using the filename **Sweet Organization**.

23. Review the presentation in Slide Show View. Fix any problems you might see.

24. Print your presentation as handouts with six slides per page.

Case 2. SafetyFirst America Carl Cardova is President of SafetyFirst America, a company that designs and builds automotive safety components and systems, including airbags, seat belts, and child restraints. Sales approach $300 million annually. The company's clients include all the major automotive companies in North America, Europe, and Japan. Carl wants you to create a PowerPoint presentation that describes the company, including current and future products. Officers within the company will use the presentation in meetings with clients, subcontractors, and others. Because Carl will not give on-screen slide shows, he wants you to make black-and-white (grayscale) overhead transparencies from the presentation. Do the following:

1. Start a new, blank presentation in PowerPoint.

Explore 2. Change the Page Setup so that slides are sized for an Overhead presentation and use Portrait orientation. (*Hint*: Both of these features are found in the Page Setup dialog box.)

3. Select the Standard color scheme that has a white background, black text, and various shades of gray for the other objects.

4. Using the Slide Master and Title Master, change the title text (on both masters) to bold Arial. Leave the other font attributes and alignments set to the default.

Explore 5. On the Slide Master, change the level-one bullets to small, solid black squares. (*Hint*: On the Slide Master, click the placeholder where you want to change the bullet, click Format on the menu bar, click Bullets and Numbering, and then in the dialog box, make the desired changes in the character and color of the bullet. If you need additional help, use the Office Assistant.)

6. On the Title Master, insert the company logo, **Safety** (a TIFF image), from the Tutorial.03 Cases folder.

7. Resize the image to 60% of its original size, move it to the blank area above the title on the Title Master, so that the image is centered between the top of the slide and the top of the title text.

8. In Normal View, go to Slide 1, and then type the title "A Company Profile," and the subtitle "Saving Lives Through Technology."

9. Increase the width of the subtitle text box so that all the text fits on one line.

10. Use the Draw Align or Distribute feature to align the center of the company logo with the center of the title text box and subtitle text box.

11. Insert all the slides from a previously prepared presentation, **Safety**, located in the Tutorial.03 Cases folder on your Data Disk.

12. Go to Slide 2, insert the picture file **Cordova** (a picture of the company presidents) from the Tutorial.03 Cases folder, increase its size to 150% of normal, and position it to the right of the quote from the president.

13. Go to Slide 3 and insert a clip-art image of freeway overpasses (located in the Transportation category of the Clip Gallery).

14. Reduce the image size and center it in the blank area below the text on the slide.

15. Go to Slide 5. Create a chart showing the number of airbags sold between 1996 and 2001. The values are, respectively, 102, 188, 208, 196, 184, 177.

Explore 16. Delete any label or data in all the rows of the datasheet except row one, by clicking the gray row number button to select the entire row, and then pressing the delete button.

Explore 17. On the chart, click the legend box (where it shows the bar color and the name of the row label (the default name is "East"), and then delete it.

18. Label the Z-axis of the chart with the text "Seatbelts Sold (in Millions)." Rotate the text by 90 degrees so that it's parallel to the axis.

19. Go to Slide 6. Create an organization chart with Carl Cordova, President, at the top, and below him: Betty Samuelson, Research Director; Ann Scalora, Development Director; and Chun-Kit Fun, Marketing Director.

20. Save the presentation, using the filename **SafetyFirst Overheads**.

21. Print the presentation on plain paper as handouts, four overheads per page.

Case 3. Hone Travel Agency: Middle East Tours Matthew Hone owns and operates a small travel agency that specializes in tours to the Middle East, primarily Israel and Egypt. He wants you to help him prepare a presentation using pictures taken with a digital camera. He will use this presentation in "kiosk" mode—that is, it will run continuously on a computer in the lobby of his travel agency. Do the following:

1. Start a new, blank presentation, and create a color scheme that matches the mood of the Middle East, with earth tones such as browns, tans, yellows, golds, and possibly a reddish color for titles.

2. On the master slides, change the title fonts to something exotic; suggested fonts include Davida, Calligr421, Benguiat, Lucida, and Harrington. Keep the main text font set to Times New Roman. Because you'll need room for pictures on the slides, change the title text to 32 points, the level-one bulleted text to 28 points, and the level-two bulleted text to 24 points.

3. Decrease the height of the title text box and move it closer to the top of the slide to allow more room for the bulleted list text box, and then increase the size of the bulleted list text box. You might have to make additional adjustments to the size of the text boxes after you've made a few slides with text and pictures.

Explore 4. On the Slide Master, change the level-one bullet to a yellow or red starburst, whichever shows up better with your color scheme, but contrasts with the main text. (*Hint*: Click Picture on the Bullets and Numbering dialog box.)

5. Use a title slide for the first slide in the presentation, with the title text "TOURS TO THE MIDDLE EAST," and the subtitle text, "Making Memories for a Lifetime."

6. Also on the first (title) slide, insert the company logo file, **TravLogo**, found in the Tutorial.03 Cases folder on your Data Disk, and then center it attractively above the title. Resize it until you believe it's the appropriate size.

7. Add subsequent slides, each with text and a picture. You'll have to adjust the dimensions of the bulleted list text box on each slide so that the text doesn't overlap the picture. Resize the picture as desired. Depending on its shape, position the picture either on the right side of the slide or on the bottom. The following is a list of the picture files in the Tutorial.03 Cases folder (given in the suggested order of the slides), along with some descriptive text that you can use for the bulleted text of your presentation. (Don't feel that you have to use all the text, but the picture on each slide should have two to six bulleted items.)

   a. **Hone**, picture of Matthew Hone, tour guide for trips to the Middle East. He has been the owner for eight years, traveled to the Middle East and guided tours there more than 30 times, and graduated from college with a degree in Travel and Tourism with a minor in Middle East Studies, and he speaks fluent Arabic and Hebrew.

   b. **TelAviv**, picture of Jaffa (foreground) and TelAviv (background) on the shores of the Mediterranean Sea. Jaffa was the principle port area of Palestine from biblical times to the early 1900s, and was home for many Zionist settlers before Tel Aviv was built. Tel Aviv was started from a 32-acre purchase in 1909, is now the capital of Israel, is located on a gorgeous strip of beach along the Mediterranean, has pizza parlors, nightclubs, samba sessions at the beach on summer evenings, and theatres, and is the country's commercial center.

   c. **OldJeru**, picture of the Old City of Jerusalem, with the Dome of the Rock in the center of the picture and the Mount of Olives in the Background. Jerusalem is the spiritual center for three great world religions: Judaism, Islam, and Christianity. It has been a holy city for over 3,000 years and is one of the oldest, continuously inhabited cities in the world.

   d. **Galilee**, picture of the Sea of Galilee, located in northern Israel in the center of fertile hills and valleys, also called Lake Tiberius and Sea of Kinneret. It is 13 miles long and 7½ miles wide.

   e. **Masada**, picture of Masada, located in southern Israel near the shores of the Dead Sea. Masada is a natural fortress 1,300 feet high. Its summit is a plateau 1,900 feet long and 650 wide. Masada was the site of one of the most heroic and tragic events in Jewish history.

   f. **Giza**, picture of the Sphinx and Great Pyramids in Giza, Egypt. Giza is a suburb of Cairo. The pyramids were tombs for the Egyptian pharaohs and their queens. The Sphinx of Giza is both a guardian and a symbol of royalty.

Explore 8. Apply animation effects to all the slides with bulleted lists, such that the picture comes on first followed by each of the bulleted items. (*Hint*: Use the up and down arrows in the Animation order section of the Custom Animation dialog box to set the order of animation.) Set Start animation to "Automatically," with one second for the picture and three seconds for the bulleted text. Set the animation effect for the bulleted items to "Fly from Left," the animation effect for the picture on each slide to "Fly from Right," the sound to "No Sound," and the dimming to "Don't Dim."

Explore 9. To all the slides apply the transition effect called "Checkerboard Down," with the speed of transition set to "Slow." Set the slide transition to advance automatically. To determine how much time you should allow for each slide before it advances, count the number of bulleted items and multiply that by 5. This usually works well for bulleted items that automatically appear after 3 seconds, although you might want to make adjustments in timing after you see the slide show a time or two. For the title slide (with no bulleted list), have it advance automatically after 4 seconds. (*Hint*: You can set all of these features by clicking Slide Show and then clicking Slide Transition.)

Explore 10. Set the slide show to loop continuously, that is, to start over with Slide 1 after completing the last slide. (*Hint*: Click Slide Show, click Set Up Show, and then click the Browsed at a kiosk option button.)

11. Save the presentation with embedded fonts to the Tutorial.03 Cases folder on your Data Disk using the filename **Middle East Tours**.

12. Run the slide show and let it automatically cycle through the slides a couple of times to make sure it works in kiosk mode. Fix any problems you see in design or timing.

13. Certain Middle East tours don't go into Egypt, so Matthew wants to hide the slide that contains the picture and information about Giza. Hide the picture and run the slide show again in kiosk mode. After viewing it, save the presentation again, using the default filename.

14. Print the presentation as handouts, with four handouts per page, in color or in grayscale.

Case 4. *Presentation on a Sporting Goods Store* You have just opened a sporting goods store and would like to create a presentation for potential employees or investors. Do the following:

1. Create an attractive and readable color scheme for your presentation.

2. Modify the fonts and text alignment on the Slide Master and Title Master.

3. Add a graphic to the Title Master. You can select one from the Clip Gallery, from some other clip-art library, or from images you create using graphics software or a scanner.

Explore

4. Create a custom background to the Slide Master (by using either a gradient fill or textured background) that corresponds to your presentation.

5. Create a title slide and at least three other slides with bulleted lists.

6. Include at least one animated GIF picture in your presentation.

7. On a bulleted list slide or on a new slide, prepare a chart showing realistic information about sales, profits, and/or numbers of certain items sold during each quarter for the previous year. (You might be able to get real information from the annual report of your local sporting goods store.)

8. On a new slide, prepare an organization chart showing the management, sales, and clerical personnel. Use real or imaginary names and positions.

9. Add transition effects to all the slides in the presentation.

10. Add animation and sound effects to each slide that contains a bulleted list.

11. Save the presentation to the Tutorial.03 Cases folder, using the filename **Sporting Goods**.

12. Print the presentation as handouts, with four slides per page.

13. Create Pack and Go disks so that you can give your presentation on a computer that doesn't have PowerPoint installed.

LAB ASSIGNMENTS

The New Perspectives Labs are designed to help you master some of the key computer concepts and skills presented in each chapter of the text. If you are using your school's lab computers, your instructor or technical support person should have installed the Labs software for you. If you want to use the Labs on your home computer, ask your instructor for the appropriate software. See the Read This Before You Begin page for more information on installing and starting the Lab.

Each Lab has two parts: Steps and Explore. Use Steps first to learn and review concepts. Read the information on each page and do the numbered steps. As you work through the Lab, you will be asked to answer Quick Check questions about what you have learned. At the end of the Lab, you will see a Summary Report of your answers to the Quick Checks. If your instructor wants you to turn in this Summary Report, click the Print button on the Summary Report screen.

When you have completed Steps, you can click the Explore button to complete the Lab Assignments. You can also use Explore to practice the skills you learned and to explore concepts on your own.

Multimedia brings together text, graphics, sound, animation, video, and photo images. In this Lab you will learn how to apply multimedia and then have the chance to see what it might be like to design some aspects of multimedia projects.

1. Click the Steps button to learn about multimedia development. As you proceed through the Steps, answer the Quick Check questions. After you complete the Steps, you will see a Quick Check Report. Follow the instructions on the screen to print this report.

2. In Explore, browse through the STS-79 Multimedia Mission Log. How many videos are included in the Multimedia Mission Log? The image on the Mission Profile page is a vector drawing. What happens when you enlarge it?

3. Listen to the sound track on Day 3. Is this a WAV file or a MIDI file? Why do you think so? Is this a synthesized sound or a digitized sound? Listen to the sound track on page 8. Can you tell if this is a WAV file or a MIDI file?

4. Suppose you were hired as a multimedia designer for a multimedia series on targeting fourth- and fifth-grade students. Describe the changes you would make to the Multimedia Mission Log so it would be suitable for these students. Also, include a sketch showing a screen from your revised design.

5. When you view the Mission Log on your computer, do you see palette flash? Why or why not? If you see palette flash, list the images that flash.

6. Multimedia can be effectively applied to projects such as encyclopedias, atlases, and animated storybooks; to computer-based training for foreign languages, first aid, or software applications; for games and sports simulations; for business presentations; for personal albums, scrapbooks, and baby books; for product catalogs and Web pages.

   Suppose you were hired to create one of these projects. Write a one-paragraph description of the project you would be creating. Describe some of the multimedia elements you would include. For each of the elements, indicate its source and whether you would need to obtain permission for its use. Finally, sketch a screen or two showing your completed project.

INTERNET ASSIGNMENTS

The purpose of the Internet Assignments is to challenge you to find information on the Internet that you can use to create effective documents. The actual assignments are updated and maintained on the Course Technology Web site. Log on to the Internet and use your Web browser to go to the Student Online Companion to accompany this text at **www.course.com/NewPerspectives/office2000**. Click the PowerPoint link, and then click the link for Tutorial 3.

SESSION 4.1

In this session, you'll apply a design template from another presentation; learn about importing, linking, and embedding; and then use OLE techniques as you create a presentation. Specifically, you'll embed a Word table into your slide presentation, modify the table in PowerPoint, link an Excel chart into your presentation, and modify the chart. Finally, you'll add tab stops to one of the slides and then generate a summary slide.

Planning the Presentation

Before you begin to help create Angelena's slide show, she discusses with you her plans for the presentation:

- **Purpose of the presentation**: To propose a major expansion, present advantages and disadvantages of the expansion, and elicit further discussion from Inca Imports' executive officers
- **Type of presentation**: Proposal of a new idea
- **Audience**: Executive officers of Inca Imports: Mark Featherstone, Vice President of Finance; Carl Vetterli, Vice President of Sales and Marketing; Enrique Hoffmann, Director of Marketing; Montgomery Lender, Director of Sales; Carlos Becerra, Quality Assurance Manager; and Norma Lopez, Customer Service Manager
- **Audience needs**: To understand the advantages and disadvantages of the expansion so that the executive officers can make an informed decision
- **Location of presentation**: Company boardroom, with computer projection system
- **Format**: Electronic slide show, with imported, embedded, and linked graphics, sound, and spreadsheets

With the presentation carefully planned, Angelena created several slides for her presentation. She created the presentation using the design template Sunny Days, but she now decides that she would like to use the design that she created in another presentation, "Establishing a New Office." You'll begin to complete her presentation by opening it and then applying a design template from another presentation.

Applying a Design Template from Another Presentation

You have already learned how to apply a design template from a template file. You can use the same method to apply a design from any other presentation file. You'll do that now.

To apply a design template from another presentation:

1. Start PowerPoint, and then open the file **Proposal** from the Tutorial.04 Tutorial folder on your Data Disk. Make sure that the PowerPoint window is maximized and that the Office Assistant is hidden or turned off. See Figure 4-1. The title page appears on the screen with the name of the two presenters, Patricia Cuevas (President of Inca Imports) and Angelena Cristenas (Vice President of Operations).

| Figure 4-1 | TITLE PAGE OF PRESENTATION |

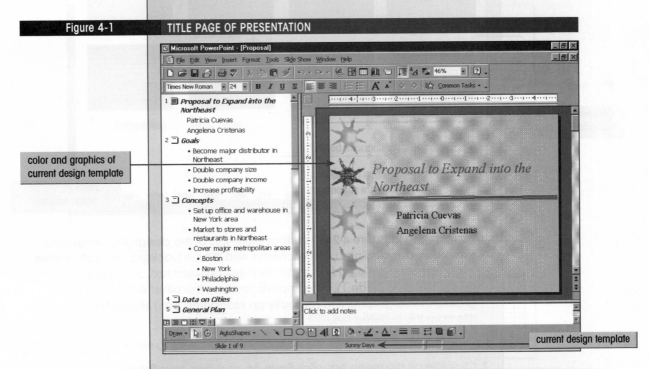

color and graphics of current design template

current design template

2. Click the **Common Tasks** button on the Formatting toolbar, and then click **Apply Design Template**. The Apply Design Template dialog box opens with a list of templates in the Presentation Designs folder. You won't use one of these template files but rather a normal presentation file.

3. Change the **Look in** folder to **Tutorial** (within the Tutorial.04 folder on your Data Disk), and then change the Files of type list box to **All PowerPoint Presentations**. The dialog box displays all the presentation files within the folder.

4. Click **NewOff**, and then click the **Apply** button. The "Proposal to Expand into the Northeast" now has a new design.

5. Click the **Slide Sorter View** button ⊞. See Figure 4-2.

Figure 4-7	SLIDE WITH LINKED CHART

Another method for linking the Excel chart with the PowerPoint presentation is to use the Paste Special command. Select the Excel chart that you want to link from within the Excel program, click the Copy button on the Standard toolbar, switch from Excel to PowerPoint, and then use the Paste Special command on the Edit menu in PowerPoint to link the chart. The Paste Special method is especially handy when you don't want to link an entire file to a PowerPoint presentation.

Reviewing the linked chart, you notice that the text of both the legend and the axes is too small to read. Moreover, the black text on a dark background is illegible. You'll take advantage of the link between PowerPoint and Excel to modify the chart by changing the axes text to a 16-point white font (with transparent background) and the legend text font size to 18 points.

To modify the linked chart:

1. Double-click anywhere on the chart. PowerPoint starts Excel with the Expenses workbook opened.

2. If necessary, click the **Maximize** button ▣ on the Excel window so that Excel fills the entire screen, and move the Chart toolbar so that it doesn't obscure the object. See Figure 4-8.

Figure 4-8   **EXCEL WINDOW**

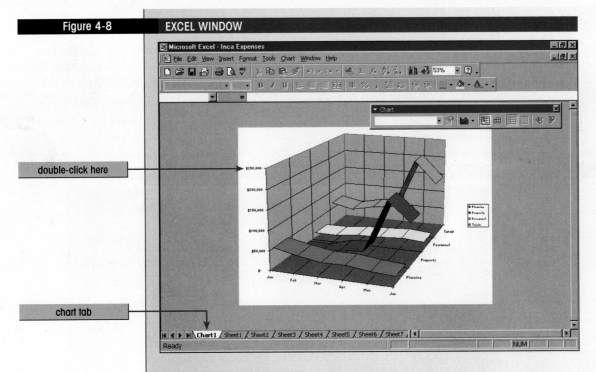

double-click here

chart tab

3. Double-click **$250,000** or any of the other numbers along the **Value Axis** (vertical axis). The Format Axis dialog box opens.

   TROUBLE? If you're not sure which axis to double-click in this and subsequent steps, move the pointer to the axis and read the ScreenTip.

4. Click the **Font** tab, change the **Size** to **16**, change the font **Color** from Automatic to white, change the **Background** from Automatic to **Transparent**, and then click the **OK** button. Notice that you can no longer read the numbers because they are a white font on a white background. They will, however, be legible in PowerPoint with the dark blue background.

5. Double-click one of the months on the **Category Axis** (horizontal axis) to open the Format Axis dialog box, change the font size to **16**, change the font color to white, change the background to **Transparent**, and then click the **OK** button.

6. Double-click one of the **Series Axis** (3-D line) labels along the right edge of the chart, change the font size to **16**, change the font color to white and the background to **Transparent**, and then click the **OK** button.

7. Double-click the **Legend** box, change the font size to **18**, and then click the **OK** button. You can leave the color and background with their default values.

8. Save the changes in the Excel spreadsheet using the default filename **Inca Expenses**, and then exit Excel.

Now that you have enlarged the font size to make the slide more readable, you'll enlarge the chart as much as possible.

To resize the chart:

1. Make sure the chart in Slide 7 is still selected, drag the bottom-right resize handle to the right and down, all the way to the bottom of the slide area, drag the upper-left resize handle left and up, until the pointer is on the left edge of the Inca logo, and then deselect the chart.

2. Click the **Slide Show View** button to see how the chart looks in full-screen view. See Figure 4-9.

Figure 4-9	COMPLETED SLIDE IN SLIDE SHOW VIEW

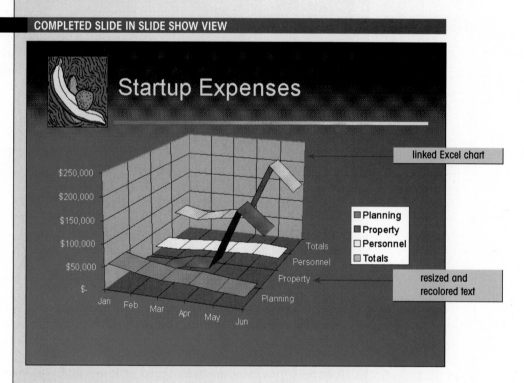

3. Press the **Esc** key to exit Slide Show View and return to Normal View.

4. Save your work using the current filename.

You have now linked and edited an Excel chart from PowerPoint. If you decide later to make further changes to the data in the workbook, you can do so either by directly starting Excel and opening Expenses or by double-clicking the chart from within PowerPoint. Either way, any changes made to the workbook will be automatically reflected in both files.

Your next change to Angelena's presentation is to add information to Slide 6. You'll then need to format the text by adding tab stops.

Adding Tab Stops

A **tab** adds space between the left margin and the beginning of the text on a particular line, or between the text in one column and the text in another column. (If you were creating several long columns of data, however, you'd probably want to use a table instead of tabs.)

When you press the Tab key, PowerPoint inserts a tab from the current location of the insertion point to the next tab stop. The default tab stops in PowerPoint occur every

0.5 inch along the slide and are left-aligned. However, you can easily add, remove, or change the location of these tab stops. You can also change the tab stop alignment style from left-aligned to centered, right, or decimal.

In Slide 6, you'll tab between each item in the timeline and its proposed date of accomplishment.

To insert tabs and change the tab stop:

1. Go to Slide 6, click ⌶ at the end of the phrase "Relocate Angelena," press the **Tab** key, and then type **August 2001**. You have finished typing one of the four items of the plan; you're now ready to type the others.

2. Click ⌶ after "Establish office," press the **Tab** key only once, type **December 2001**, click ⌶ after "Relocate current employees," press the **Tab** key, type **January 2002**, click ⌶ after "Hire new employees," press the **Tab** key, and then type **March 2002**. Deselect the text box. Your Slide 6 should look like Figure 4-10.

| Figure 4-10 | SLIDE AFTER INSERTING TABS AND TEXT |

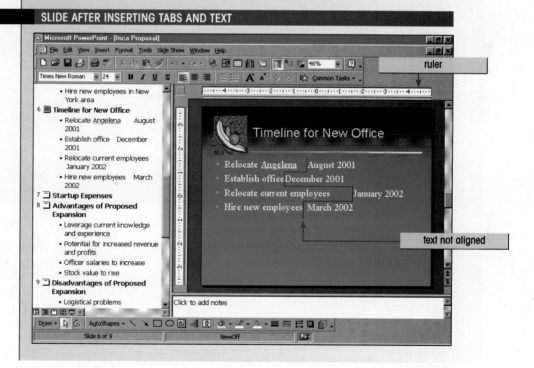

You can see that, after pressing the Tab key only once between each task and each date, the dates column isn't aligned, and one of the dates is too close to the first column. You can easily solve this problem by adding a tab stop. (Avoid pressing the Tab key two or three times to create more space between the task and the date; changing tab stops will give you more flexibility if you later want to edit the text.)

To add a tab stop:

1. If the Ruler doesn't already appear on your slide, click **View** on the menu bar, and then click **Ruler**. The Ruler appears below the Formatting toolbar.

2. Click anywhere in the bulleted list text box to select it. Notice that the default tab stops are indicated by small tick marks at the bottom of the Ruler. Make sure the current tab stop alignment selector is ⊾, shaped like a capital "L." If a different tab stop alignment style appears on the Ruler, click the tab alignment selector one or more times until ⊾ does appear.

3. Click ⌖ at about 5.5 inches on the tab bar at the bottom of the ruler. The 5.5 inches refers to the distance from the left edge of the text box. PowerPoint inserts a left-aligned tab stop at that location and removes the default tab stops (tick marks) to the left of the new tab stop. The dates in the second column of text move so that they are aligned at 5.5 inches. See Figure 4-11.

Figure 4-11	SLIDE AFTER INSERTING TAB STOP

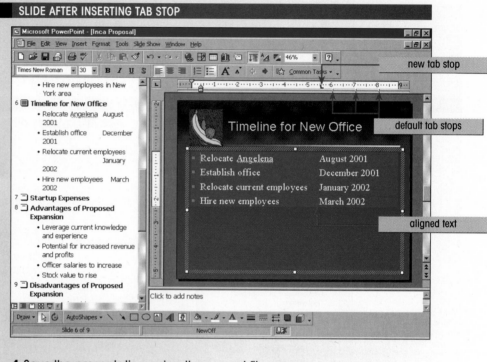

4. Save the presentation, using the current filename.

If, after you add a new tab stop to the ruler, you decide you want it in a different location, you can drag it to where you want it. If you decide you want to remove a tab stop, you can drag it off the ruler to delete it.

You have now embedded and linked objects and inserted a tab stop in Angelena's presentation. Reviewing the presentation to this point, Angelena realizes that she needs a slide listing all the topics in her presentation, that is, a summary slide.

Creating a Summary Slide

At the end of most presentations, you should summarize your key points. Often, you'll want to create a summary slide containing the titles of all or most of the slides in the presentation. Or, you might want a table of contents slide, with those same titles. Whether you use the summary slide at the end or as a table of contents at the beginning, PowerPoint will help you automatically generate the summary slide.

REFERENCE WINDOW   **RW**

<u>Creating a Summary Slide</u>
- Go to Slide Sorter View.
- Select the slides whose title you want as items in the summary slide.
- Click the Summary Slide button on the Slide Sorter toolbar. PowerPoint inserts a new slide in front of the first selected slide.

Angelena wants the summary slide to serve as a table of contents. You'll now use the Summary Slide feature in PowerPoint to create the summary slide automatically.

To create a summary slide:

1. Switch to Slide Sorter View. Here, you'll select Slides 2 through 9.

2. Click Slide 2, press and hold down the **Shift** key, click Slide 9, the last slide in the presentation, and then release the **Shift** key. Now all the slides of the presentation, except the first one, are selected.

3. Click the **Summary Slide** button 🖻 on the Slide Sorter toolbar. PowerPoint automatically inserts a new slide as Slide 2, which is now the selected slide.

4. Double-click the new Slide 2 to return to Normal View, with the new slide in the Slide Pane.

5. Change the title of Slide 2 from "Summary Slide" to "Contents of Presentation." See Figure 4-12.

6. Save your presentation using the default filename.

| Figure 4-12 | SUMMARY SLIDE |

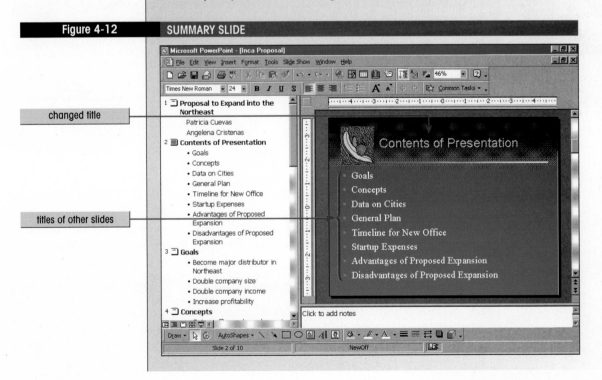

changed title

titles of other slides

The summary slide is now part of the presentation. You have made excellent progress on Angelena's presentation, which is now about finished.

Session 4.1 QUICK CHECK

1. How does applying a design template from another presentation differ from applying a design template from the Template folder?

2. Define or describe:
   a. import
   b. embed
   c. link
   d. OLE

3. If you modify a linked object, such as an Excel chart, in PowerPoint, what happens to the original disk file created by Excel?

4. If you insert a picture created using scanning software and hardware, is the picture file imported, embedded, or linked?

5. Why would you link an object rather than embed it?

6. Why would you add or modify a tab stop in a slide?

7. How do you automatically create a summary slide?

SESSION 4.2

In this session, you'll learn how to create and edit hyperlinks to slides within a presentation and hyperlinks to other presentations, and to add action buttons to slides. You'll also learn about rehearsing a presentation and about generating meeting notes and action items. Finally, you'll learn how to create a custom toolbar, publish the presentation on the World Wide Web, and collaborate with others on a presentation.

Creating and Editing Hyperlinks

Angelena decides that Slide 2, the summary slide, can also serve as a table of contents. She therefore asks you to create hyperlinks between each of the items in Slide 2 and the corresponding slide in the presentation, and then to create hyperlinks from each of the slides back to Slide 2. A **hyperlink** (short for "hypertext link," also called a "hot link" or just a "link") is a word, phrase, or graphic image that you click to "jump to" (or display) another location, called the **target**. Text hyperlinks are usually underlined and appear in a different color than the rest of the document. The target of a hyperlink can be a location within the document (presentation), a different document, or a page on the World Wide Web.

To create a hyperlink to another slide in the presentation:

1. If you took a break after the last session, make sure PowerPoint is running, that Inca Proposal is open, and that Slide 2 is in the Slide Pane in Normal View.

2. Drag I across the word "Goals" to select the entire word, which will become the hyperlink text.

3. Click the **Insert Hyperlink** button 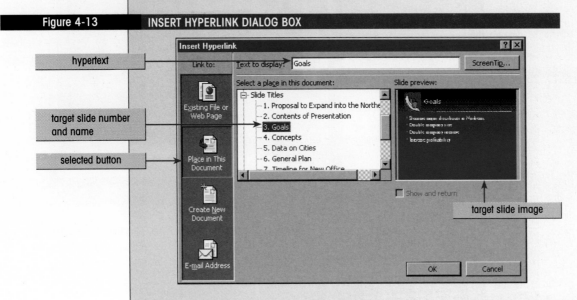 on the Standard toolbar, and then click the **Place in This Document** button in the Link to section on the left side of the Insert Hyperlink dialog box.

4. Click **3. Goals**. The Insert Hyperlink dialog box now indicates that Slide 3 is the target name. See Figure 4-13.

Figure 4-13   **INSERT HYPERLINK DIALOG BOX**

5. Click the **OK** button in the Insert Hyperlink dialog box. The word "Goals" remains selected.

6. Click in a blank area of the slide to deselect the bulleted list. The word "Goals" now appears as light blue and underlined, indicating that the word is a hyperlink. (Recall that you can specify the hyperlink color when you set the presentation color scheme.)

7. Repeat this same procedure to add hyperlinks for all the other bulleted items on Slide 2. Slide 2 should then look like Figure 4-14.

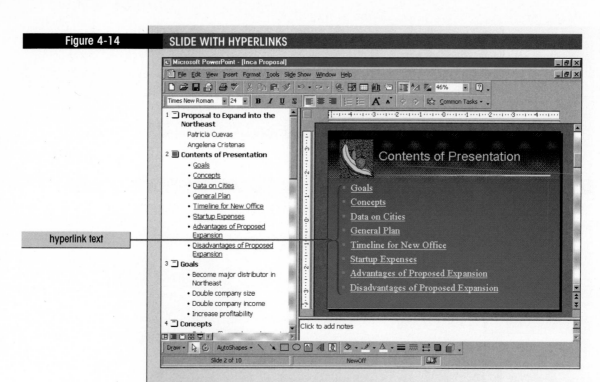

Figure 4-14   SLIDE WITH HYPERLINKS

TROUBLE? If you make a mistake, repeat the procedure. The Edit Hyperlink dialog box will then appear. You can then change the target of the hyperlink.

8. Save the presentation using the default filename.

Now that you have added hyperlinks from Slide 2 to all the other slides, you need a hyperlink from all the other slides back to Slide 2. In this way, Angelena will be able to easily jump to a topic, jump back to Slide 2, and then jump to another topic.

To create hyperlinks from the slides back to Slide 2:

1. Go to Slide 3, click the **Text Box** button on the Drawing toolbar, click ↓ near the lower-right corner of the slide, and then type **Return to Contents**.

2. Select the text **Return to Contents**, click the **Insert Hyperlink** button , set the hyperlink target to Slide 2, "Contents of Presentation," and then click the **OK** button to return to Slide 3.

3. Position the hyperlink text box as shown in Figure 4-15, and then deselect the text box.

Figure 4-15   SLIDE WITH NEW HYPERLINK

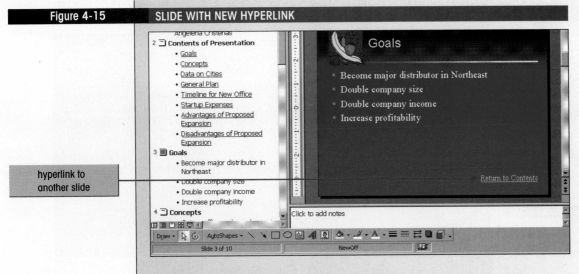

hyperlink to
another slide

TROUBLE? If the hyperlink text isn't located as shown in Figure 4-15, move it, by clicking anywhere in the text box, and then dragging the edge of the text box.

4. Test the link by going to Slide Show View, clicking the hyperlink on Slide 3, and then returning to Normal View. Fix the hyperlink if it doesn't work.

Now you'll copy the hyperlink on Slide 3 to the other slides.

5. Click anywhere in the hyperlink on Slide 3 to select it, click the edge of the text box, and then click the **Copy** button on the Standard toolbar.

6. Go to Slide 4, and then click the **Paste** button on the Standard toolbar.

7. Go to Slide 5, and then again paste the hyperlink onto the slide. Repeat this for Slides 6 through 10.

8. Save the presentation using the default filename.

With all the items on Slide 2 hyperlinked to the other slides, and then back again, you're ready to test the results.

To use a hyperlink to jump to a specific slide:

1. With Slide 2 still in the Slide Pane, click the **Slide Show View** button.

2. Click on the **General Plan** hyperlink. PowerPoint immediately displays Slide 6, "General Plan."

TROUBLE? If the hyperlink jump fails, return to Normal View, select the text "General Plan" on Slide 2, and then click the Insert Hyperlink button. PowerPoint then displays the Edit Hyperlink dialog box, allowing you to change the hyperlink target.

3. Click on the **Return to Contents** hyperlink. PowerPoint again displays Slide 2. See Figure 4-16. This time, however, the hyperlink text is gray, indicating (in your color scheme) that the hyperlink has been followed.

Figure 4-16   SLIDE WITH HYPERLINKS

Contents of Presentation

- Goals
- Concepts
- Data on Cities
followed hyperlink
- General Plan
- Timeline for New Office

4. Try all the other hyperlinks to make sure they work, and then return to Normal View.

TROUBLE? If one or more of the hyperlinks doesn't work, fix it as described above in the previous Trouble.

If your presentation includes custom shows (that is, two or more shows within one presentation file), you can also use PowerPoint to automatically create an agenda slide. You would create a summary slide as you did above, select the bulleted item, and then click Action Settings on the Slide Show menu. You would then click Hyperlink to, click Custom Shows, and then select the show you want to jump to. To return to the agenda slide after the last slide of the custom show, simply select the Show and return check box.

In addition to creating hyperlinks among the slides, you can also add action buttons that have essentially the same effect. For Angelena's presentation, you'll add an action button that will add a link to another presentation.

Adding **Action Buttons**

An **action button** is a ready-made icon for which you can easily define hyperlinks to other slides or to other documents. You can use one of the 11 predefined action buttons in PowerPoint, such as Action Button: Sound, or create your own custom one.

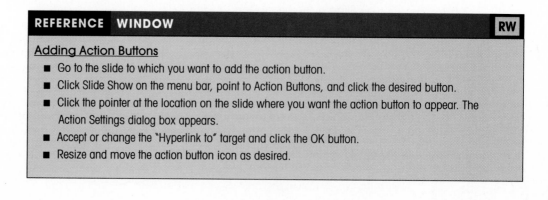

REFERENCE WINDOW   RW

Adding Action Buttons
- Go to the slide to which you want to add the action button.
- Click Slide Show on the menu bar, point to Action Buttons, and click the desired button.
- Click the pointer at the location on the slide where you want the action button to appear. The Action Settings dialog box appears.
- Accept or change the "Hyperlink to" target and click the OK button.
- Resize and move the action button icon as desired.

Angelena wants you to add a link to her presentation on establishing a new office. You'll do this by adding an action button.

To add an action button to link to another presentation:

1. Go to Slide 6, "General Plan."

2. Click **Slide Show** on the menu bar, point to **Action Buttons**, and then click the **Action Button: Document** button ▷.

3. Click ➕ roughly centered between the last bulleted item in Slide 6 and the bottom of the slide. The Action Setting dialog box opens. See Figure 4-17.

Figure 4-17	ACTION SETTINGS DIALOG BOX

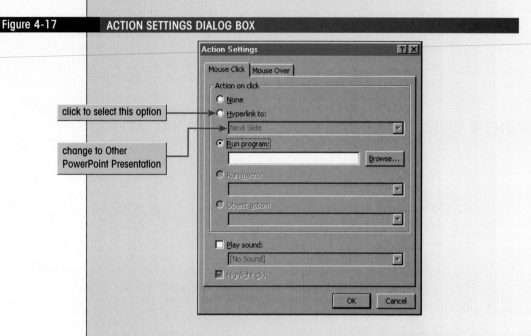

click to select this option

change to Other PowerPoint Presentation

4. Click the **Hyperlink to** option button, click the **Hyperlink to** list arrow, and then click **Other PowerPoint Presentation**.

5. In the Hyperlink to Other PowerPoint Presentation dialog box, click **NewOff** in the Tutorial.04 Tutorial folder on your Data Disk, click the **OK** button, click **1. Establishing a New Office** in the Slide title text box if necessary, and then click the **OK** button.

6. Click the **OK** button to close the Action Settings dialog box. If necessary, move the action button to the location shown in Figure 4-18.

Figure 4-18	SLIDE WITH ACTION BUTTON

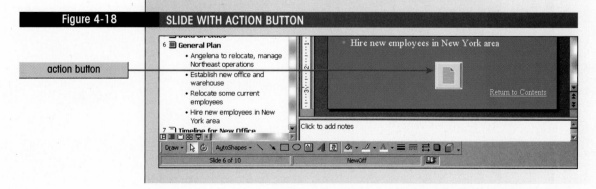

action button

7. Switch to Slide Show View with Slide 6, "General Plan," on the screen.

8. Click 🖰 on the action button. The slide "Establishing a New Office" from the NewOff presentation appears on the screen.

9. Go through the entire NewOff presentation, until you reach the blank slide at the end, and then press the **Spacebar** once more. PowerPoint automatically returns to Slide 6 of the Inca Proposal presentation.

10. Return to Normal View, and then save the presentation using the default filename.

Angelena looks at your work so far and is pleased with your progress. The presentation now includes an imported table from Word, an Excel chart, a summary slide that you're using as a table of contents, hypertext links to other slides in the presentation, and a hypertext link to another presentation. In the next session, you'll help Angelena ensure that her presentation will run smoothly and be available to all of her intended audience.

Viewing a Slide Show with Embedded or Linked Objects

When you present a slide show using a presentation with embedded or linked files, those files usually must be available on a disk so that PowerPoint can access them. For example, if you embed a video clip or sound effect, the video or sound file must be available on the hard drive, on a CD in the CD-ROM drive, or on a floppy in the system on which you're showing the presentation. This is because a copy of the embedded or linked file is often *not* included within the PowerPoint file itself, only the path and filename for accessing the linked file. Therefore, you should view the presentation on the system that will be used for running the slide show to make sure it has the necessary embedded or linked files. If embedded or linked objects don't work, you'll have to edit the object path so that PowerPoint can find the objects on your disk.

To view the slide show:

1. Display Slide 1 of the presentation in the presentation window, and then click 🖳. Slide 1 appears, filling the entire screen.

2. Click the left mouse button (or press the **Spacebar**) to advance to Slide 2, "Contents of Presentation."

3. Continue through the slide show sequentially or use the hyperlinks to move through it in any order. When you get to Slide 6, make sure you also view the linked slide show.

4. When you reach the end of the slide show, return to Normal View.

Angelena is pleased with how well the embedded and linked objects work in her slide show. She now asks you to print a hard copy of the slides.

To print the presentation:

1. Preview the slides in Grayscale Preview to make sure that all the slides are legible. If you see a problem (such as the axes on the Excel Chart on Slide 8), make the necessary changes to solve the problem. If you make changes for grayscale printing, be sure to return the presentation to its color form after printing it.

2. Print the slides as handouts, six slides per page.

3. Switch to Slide Sorter View so you can see all the slides on your screen at once. See Figure 4-19.

Figure 4-19	COMPLETED PRESENTATION

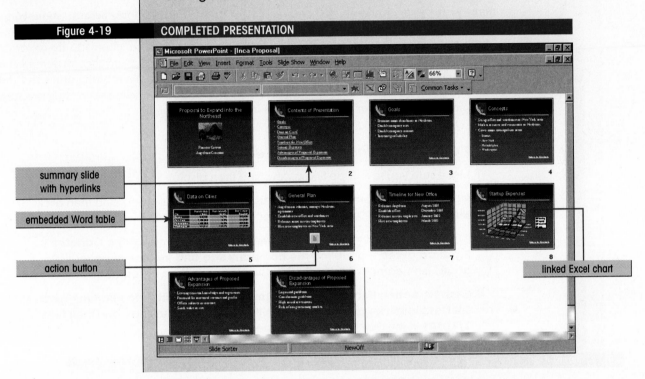

summary slide with hyperlinks

embedded Word table

action button

linked Excel chart

With the PowerPoint presentation completed, Angelena is ready to rehearse her presentation.

Rehearsing the Presentation

After double-checking your presentation for completeness and accuracy, you should always rehearse it. This will ensure that your presentation will go smoothly and be as professional as possible. As Angelena rehearses her presentation, she realizes that this might be a good opportunity to set automatic slide timings. **Slide timings** allow slides to advance after being on the screen for a specified amount of time. For example, the second slide would appear 30 seconds after the first one, the third slide 20 seconds after the second one, and so on. To set the slide timings, you would click Rehearse Timing on the Slide Show menu, after which PowerPoint would immediately go into Slide Show view and display the toolbar. You would then proceed through the slide show at the desired rate, and PowerPoint would record how long you spend on each slide. At the end of the slide show, PowerPoint would ask you if you wanted to accept the timings so that you could run the slide show automatically.

As Angelena rehearses the slide show, she realizes that the length of her comments and the time the participants use to make their comments and suggestions can't be accurately anticipated, so that automatic slide timings would not be useful in this case. In fact, automatic timing is best used for unattended (kiosk) slide shows, not for live presentations. (You'll have a chance to use automatic slide timings in Case Problem 4.)

Anticipating that the audience will make meaningful comments, you suggest to Angelena that she keep track of her audience's comments, using the PowerPoint Meeting Minder feature.

Generating Meeting Notes and Action Items

The PowerPoint **Meeting Minder** feature allows you to record meeting notes, save the notes with the presentation, and then print the notes. Furthermore, because some comments made during a presentation will be in the form of action items (decisions to be followed up on after the meeting), the Meeting Minder feature also automatically creates a new, final slide in the presentation, listing these action items. You can then review all the action items at the end of the presentation. You can also export the meeting notes and the action items to a Word document. Angelena asks you to help her rehearse creating meeting notes and action items for two of the slides in her presentation.

To create meeting notes and action items:

1. Make sure you're in Slide Show View, and then display Slide 3, "Goals."

2. Right-click anywhere in the slide to display the shortcut menu, and then click **Meeting Minder**. The Meeting Minder dialog box opens.

3. If necessary, click the **Meeting Minutes** tab, and then type **Anne Carleton Bradford asked if doubling the company size and income were realistic goals. Isn't competition in the Northeast worse than in southern California?**

4. Click the **Action Items** tab, type **Form ad hoc committee to examine goals** in the Description text box, type **Carl** in the Assigned To text box, and then type **7/15/01** in the Due Date text box. See Figure 4-20.

Figure 4-20	MEETING MINDER DIALOG BOX

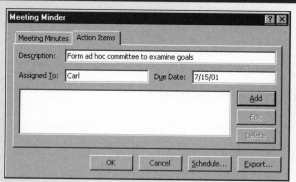

5. Click the **Add** button, and then click the **OK** button.

6. Go to Slide 7, "Timeline for New Office," open the Meeting Minder, and add an Action Item with the description **Hire a personal secretary for Angelena**, with the task assigned to **Angelena** and a due date of **10/30/01**, click the **Add** button, and then click the **OK** button. The list now has two action items.

While you were creating the action items, PowerPoint was automatically creating a new slide containing these action items. You'll now look at the action items.

7. Go to the last slide (Slide 11) of the presentation, the new "Action Items" slide. See Figure 4-21.

| Figure 4-21 | SLIDE WITH ACTION ITEMS |

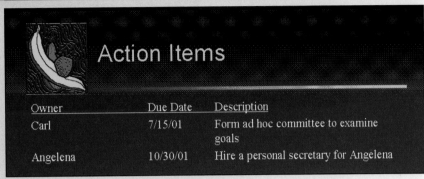

Owner	Due Date	Description
Carl	7/15/01	Form ad hoc committee to examine goals
Angelena	10/30/01	Hire a personal secretary for Angelena

8. Read the slide, go to Slide Sorter View, and then delete the Action Items slide. You don't want to keep this slide because Angelena used it only for rehearsal purposes.

When you save the presentation, the action items won't be saved because you deleted the slide, but the meeting notes will be saved. You can view the meeting notes at any time by opening the presentation, clicking Tools on the menu bar, clicking Meeting Minder, and then clicking the Meeting Minutes tab. The Meeting Minder dialog box also allows you to export the notes to Word by clicking the Export button and following any subsequent instructions.

Several days later, Angelena makes her presentation, which is well received, but unfortunately, several members of the executive council could not attend the meeting. Angelena therefore decides to make her presentation available on the Internet.

Before saving the presentation in a form that others can see on the Internet, however, Angelena wants you to set up PowerPoint for sharing her PowerPoint presentations with other people, particularly other Inca Imports' employees. Therefore, you'll first create a custom toolbar with icons that will help Angelena share presentations with others.

Creating and Customizing a Toolbar

All the toolbars in PowerPoint, including the Menu bar, Standard toolbar, Formatting toolbar, and Drawing toolbar, are customizable, that is, you can add or delete button (or text) commands to meet your own needs and your own working style. Furthermore, you can create a new toolbar using methods similar to customizing a toolbar.

Creating and Customizing a Toolbar

- Right-click any toolbar, click Customize, and then click the Commands tab on the Customize dialog box.
- If you want to create a new toolbar, click the Toolbars tab, click the New button, type the name of your toolbar, and then click the OK button.
- To add a command to a toolbar (new or old), select a desired category, select the desired command, and then drag the command button onto the toolbar.
- To delete a command from a toolbar, drag the command button from the toolbar into any non-toolbar region of the PowerPoint window.
- After adding and deleting the desired commands, click the Close button on the Customize dialog box.

You'll now create a toolbar named "Sharing," and add several commands to help Inca Imports employees share their presentations with others.

To create and customize a toolbar:

1. In Normal View, right-click anywhere on any toolbar in the PowerPoint window. A shortcut menu appears.

2. Click **Customize** on the shortcut menu. The Customize dialog box opens.

3. If necessary, click the **Toolbars** tab, click the **New** button to open the New Toolbar dialog box, type **Sharing** (the name of your new toolbar), and then click the **OK** button. The new Sharing toolbar appears on the screen, but without any commands. You're now ready to customize the new toolbar by dragging command buttons onto it.

4. Click the **Commands** tab on the Customize dialog box, and then make sure **File** is selected in the **Categories** list.

5. Scroll down the **Commands** list, and then drag the **Mail Recipient** button onto the Sharing toolbar. See Figure 4-22.

Figure 4-22	CREATING A NEW TOOLBAR

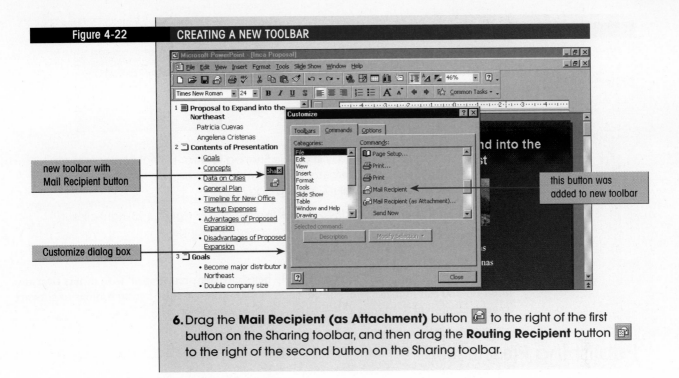

6. Drag the **Mail Recipient (as Attachment)** button to the right of the first button on the Sharing toolbar, and then drag the **Routing Recipient** button to the right of the second button on the Sharing toolbar.

The new toolbar now has three buttons, all relating to sending presentations via e-mail. Next, you'll add a group of commands related to publishing a presentation as a Web page.

To add new group of commands to the toolbar:

1. Scroll up the **Commands** list, and then drag the **Save as Web Page** button to the end of the Sharing toolbar.

TROUBLE? If necessary, drag the Sharing toolbar to another location so that it doesn't cover important parts of the Customize toolbar.

2. Right-click the **Save as Web Page** button on the Sharing toolbar, and then click **Begin a Group** on the shortcut menu. This inserts a break line before that button on the toolbar.

3. Using the same method, add the **Publish as Web Page** button and **Web Page Preview** button to the Sharing toolbar.

You're now ready to add two last buttons as a new group.

4. Change the **Categories** from File to **Slide Show**, and then drag **Online Broadcast** to the toolbar. This command appears as text only because it doesn't have an associated command button.

5. Set the Online Broadcast to begin a new group, so that a break line appears between it and the Web Page Preview button.

6. Add to the Sharing toolbar the command **Meet Now** in the **Tools** category.

7. Click the **Close** button, and then drag the new Sharing toolbar down below the lower-right corner of the Slide Pane, but above the Drawing toolbar, so that it remains a floating toolbar. See Figure 4-23.

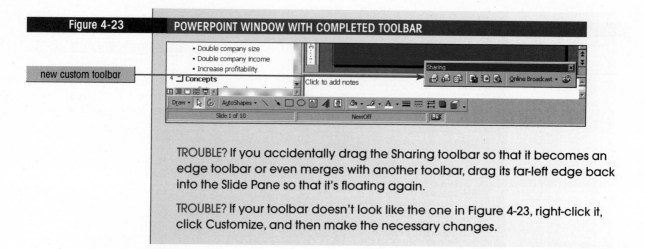

Figure 4-23

POWERPOINT WINDOW WITH COMPLETED TOOLBAR

new custom toolbar

TROUBLE? If you accidentally drag the Sharing toolbar so that it becomes an edge toolbar or even merges with another toolbar, drag its far-left edge back into the Slide Pane so that it's floating again.

TROUBLE? If your toolbar doesn't look like the one in Figure 4-23, right-click it, click Customize, and then make the necessary changes.

Angelena now has a toolbar that will help her share her presentation with others over the Internet. You can now use some of the command buttons on the Sharing toolbar to convert Angelena's presentation into a Web page.

Publishing Presentations on the World Wide Web

The **World Wide Web** (also called the "Web" or "WWW") is a global information-sharing system that allows you to find and view electronic documents, called **Web pages**. Organizations and individuals make their Web pages available by placing them on high-capacity hard disks called **Web servers**, which users can access electronically by specifying the address in a Web browser, software that retrieves and displays Web pages on a computer screen. The electronic location of a Web page is called a **Web site**. Most companies and many private computer users operate their own Web sites.

Most Web sites contain a **home page**, a Web page that contains general information about the site. Home pages are like "home base"—they are a starting point for online viewers. They usually contain hyperlinks, targeting other documents or Web pages, that online viewers can click to locate the information they need.

To prepare Angelena's PowerPoint presentation (or any presentation) for viewing on the World Wide Web, you first have to convert it to a special format called HTML (Hypertext Markup Language).

Saving Presentations as HTML Documents

HTML (Hypertext Markup Language) is a special language for describing the format of a Web page so that it can be viewed by a Web browser. The **HTML markings** in a file tell the browser how to format the text. Fortunately, you don't have to learn the Hypertext Markup Language to create HTML documents; PowerPoint does the work for you. You can easily save any PowerPoint presentation as an HTML document using the PowerPoint Save as Web Page command. This command automatically creates a set of HTML documents (or pages), one page for each slide, plus an index page. The index page includes hyperlinks to all the slides in the presentation. Furthermore, if your presentation includes any type of graphics, PowerPoint usually converts them to separate files, in GIF or JPEG format. Finally, PowerPoint creates still other files that help users view and navigate through the Web pages. All these files are stored in a separate folder, which is given a name based on the original PowerPoint presentation file.

If you want to edit the resulting HTML documents, you'll have to use either a word processor that supports HTML editing (for example, Microsoft Word 2000) or, better still, a dedicated HTML editor (for example, Microsoft FrontPage 2000). PowerPoint doesn't support direct editing of HTML documents.

You'll now save the PowerPoint presentation NewOff and your current presentation ("Inca Proposal") as a set of HTML documents. You'll save the HTML documents to the target browser Microsoft Internet Explorer 5.0, but you could also save it to other target browsers such as Microsoft Internet Explorer or Netscape Navigator 3.0, or even all of the above.

To save a presentation as a set of HTML documents:

1. Open the presentation file **NewOff** located in the Tutorial.04 Tutorial folder on your Data Disk.

2. Click the **Save as Web Page** button on the Sharing toolbar you created earlier. The Save As dialog box opens, with the save as type listed as Web Page. See Figure 4-24.

Figure 4-24	SAVE AS DIALOG BOX

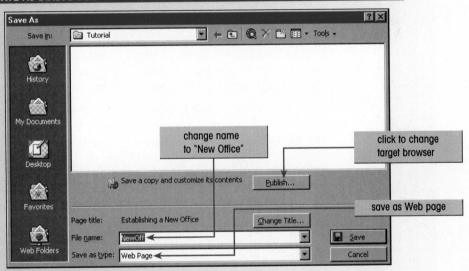

TROUBLE? If the Sharing toolbar doesn't appear on the screen, right-click any toolbar, and then click Sharing. If the Sharing toolbar doesn't appear on the list of toolbars, click File on the menu bar, and then click Save as Web Page.

If you wanted to change the target browser to Microsoft Internet Explorer 4.0, you would click the Publish button on this dialog box, and then change the browser support option. You'll leave IE 5.0 as the browser.

3. Set the **Save in** folder to **Tutorial** (in the Tutorial.04 folder on your Data Disk), change the File name to **New Office**, and then click the **Save** button. PowerPoint creates an HTML page named **New Office**, with the filename extension *.htm. PowerPoint also creates a new directory named New Office_files, which contains 26 files, including an HTML file for each slide, a .gif or .jpg file for each graphic, and other types of files to help your Web browser properly display the slide show.

4. Close the New Office presentation.

Having saved New Office as an HTML file, you now need fix the hyperlink in Inca Proposal so that its target is the HTML file New Office rather than the presentation file NewOff. Then you'll save Inca Proposal as a Web page.

To change the hyperlink target and save the presentation as a Web page:

1. With Inca Proposal in the PowerPoint window, go to Slide 6.

2. Right-click the action button to open the shortcut menu, point to **Hyperlink**, and then click **Edit Hyperlink**. The Edit Hyperlink dialog box (which looks the same as the Insert Hyperlink dialog box, except that the information about the current hyperlink appears in the dialog box) appears on the screen. You now want to change the target file from NewOff.ppt to the Web page New Office.htm.

3. Click the **Hyperlink to** list arrow, click **Other File**, if necessary change the Look in list arrow to the Tutorial.04 Tutorial folder, if necessary change the Files of type to **All files**, click **New Office**, and then click the **OK** button.

4. Click the **OK** button. Now you're ready to save Inca Proposal as a Web page.

5. Save the presentation as a Web page, using the procedure previously described. Keep in mind that the document in the PowerPoint window is now an HTML file, not a presentation file, and therefore any changes you make and save will be saved to the HTML file, not to the presentation file.

Now that you have saved the presentation as Web pages, you're ready to see how they look in a Web browser.

Viewing a Presentation in a Web Browser

Eventually, Angelena will give a copy of the two Web pages and their accompanying folders to the Inca Imports' computer support technician, who will post the files on the company Web server. For now, however, you can still view the presentation in a browser.

To view the presentation in a Web browser:

1. Click the **Web Page Preview** button 🔲 on the Sharing toolbar (or click **File**, and then click **Web Page Preview**). PowerPoint opens your Web browser (for example, Microsoft Internet Explorer) with the Web page in the browser window.

2. If necessary, maximize the browser window so it fills the screen. See Figure 4-25.

Figure 4-25   PRESENTATION WEB PAGE IN BROWSER

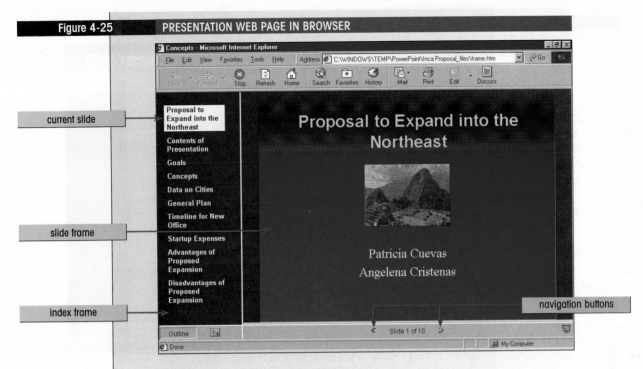

TROUBLE? If PowerPoint opened another program, such as Microsoft Word, or if you received an error message, a Web browser might not be installed on your computer. Consult your instructor or technical support person for assistance.

As you can see, the first slide of your presentation appears in the browser, an outline of the slides appears along the left edge, and a toolbar appears at the bottom of the window. This toolbar will help you navigate through the presentation.

TROUBLE? If you don't see the outline, click the Outline button at the bottom of the screen. You should also be aware that your Web page might look different if your default browser isn't Microsoft Internet Explorer 5.0.

3. Click the **Next Slide** button ▷ at the bottom of the screen. The browser now displays Slide 2 of your presentation.

4. Click the hyperlink **General Plan**. As you can see, the browser now displays the General Plan slide. This shows that when you saved your original presentation as a Web page, PowerPoint automatically translated the slide hyperlinks to Web page hyperlinks. PowerPoint cannot, however, change hyperlinks to other files because those other files may or may not be HTML files. That's why you had to edit the hyperlink on Slide 6. You'll see if that link to New Office now works.

5. Click the action button on Slide 6. As you can see, your browser now displays the Web page for the presentation "Establishing a New Office." See Figure 4-26.

In this session, you completed creating Angelena's presentation by linking an Excel chart and then modifying it. You then leaned how to add tab stops, generate meeting notes and action items as you run a slide show, create and customize toolbars, save presentations as Web pages, and use online meetings and broadcasts. Angelena thanks you for your help and offers you a position in the New York City office.

Session 4.2 QUICK CHECK

1. What is a hyperlink? What are two examples of hyperlink targets?

2. What is an action button?

3. How do you generate a new slide with an action item?

4. Why would you want to create a customized toolbar?

5. How do you save a presentation as an HTML document (Web page)?

6. In general terms, describe what a presentation looks like in the browser Internet Explorer 5.0.

7. In general terms, how do you broadcast a presentation on the Internet?

REVIEW ASSIGNMENTS

After seeing how effective Angelena's presentation was, Enrique Hoffmann, Director of Marketing, decides to use it as a model for his upcoming presentation on Inca Imports' competition. He asks you to help him create his presentation by doing the following:

1. If necessary, start PowerPoint and make sure your Data Disk is in the disk drive.

2. Open a new, blank presentation and create a title slide.

3. On the title slide, type the title "Competition in the Northeast" and the subtitle "Inca Imports International."

4. Import (insert) the Microsoft Word outline file **NEComp** from the Tutorial.04 Review folder on your Data Disk.

5. Format the presentation by applying the design template from the existing PowerPoint presentation file **NewOff** in the Tutorial.04 Tutorial folder.

6. Save the presentation using the filename **Competition in the Northeast**.

Explore 7. Go to Slide 2 and embed the graphic image **Graph** located in the Tutorial.04 Review folder. (*Hint*: Don't just insert the graphic but embed it as an object file.)

Explore 8. Edit the embedded object: Change the white background color to blue (to match the background of the slide), and change the light-blue border to yellow. (*Hint*: Use the Fill tool in Microsoft Paint, or some other appropriate tool if your bitmapped graphic editor is something other than Paint.)

9. Size and position the graphic attractively below the bulleted text.

10. Go to Slide 3 and add the phrase "and Year Established" to the slide title.

11. At the end of each of the bulleted items, insert a tab (one and only one tab) and type the year that each of the four companies was established. The years are 1964, 1982, 1978, and 1993, respectively.

12. Display the Ruler, and insert a left-aligned tab stop at 5.5 inches from the left edge of the bulleted list text box so that all the years are vertically aligned.

13. Make a copy of the Excel file **Sales** found in the Tutorial.04 Review folder, and then change its filename to **Inca Sales**.

14. Go to Slide 4, change the slide layout to Object, and then link the Excel chart from the **Inca Sales** file. If necessary, enlarge it to maximum size without covering the title of the slide.

Explore   15. Edit the Excel chart and, within Excel, change the chart area color to blue. (*Hint*: Double-click the background area to display the Format Chart Area dialog box, and then make the color change.)

16. Change the font color of all the text on the Excel chart to white, save your changes, and then exit Excel to return to PowerPoint.

17. Use the PowerPoint Summary Slide feature to create a summary slide from Slides 2 through 5. Change the title of the new Slide 2 from "Summary Slide" to "Presentation Objectives."

18. Create a hyperlink from each of the bulleted items on Slide 2 to the corresponding slide in the presentation.

19. Create a hyperlink using the text "Return to Objectives" (in 14-point Arial) from each of the slides back to Slide 2. Position the hyperlink text near the lower-right corner of the slide.

20. Save the presentation, and then print a copy of the presentation as black-and-white handouts (six slides per page).

21. Save the presentation as a set of Web pages to the Tutorial.04 Review folder on your Data Disk. View the document in a Web browser.

Explore   22. From within your browser, print the HTML page that contains the first slide of the presentation and then close the file. (*Hint*: You can print an HTML page in the same way you print a document from any Windows program.)

CASE PROBLEMS

Case 1. *Country Living Cabinetry and Furniture, Inc.*   Arnold Porter is Director of Marketing for Country Living Cabinetry and Furniture, Inc. (CLCF), which manages over 300 independent retail cabinet and furniture franchises. The company provides information to retailers on the best buys, coordinates hiring and training, and provides volume discount purchases. CLCF also provides consumer information services through a toll-free hotline. Arnold wants to prepare a presentation to introduce new sales representatives to the company's marketing system. Do the following:

1. Open a blank presentation and create a title slide. Use the title "Introduction to CLCF Marketing" and the subtitle "Training for Sales Representatives."

2. Import (insert) the Microsoft Word outline file **CLCFDoc** located in the Tutorial.04 Cases folder on your Data Disk to create the text for the remainder of the slides.

3. Apply the design template from the presentation file **CLCFPres** (from the Tutorial.04 Cases folder) to the presentation.

4. Save the presentation using the filename **Introduction to CLCF Marketing**.

Explore   5. On Slide 2,"Overview of Marketing Procedure," insert a tab after each bulleted item and then add the proposed dates for the marketing plan. The first mailing is 1/01, the second mailing is 3/01, telemarketing phone calls is 4/01, and the visit by field representatives is 5/01. Select the *right*-align tab stop, and position it at 8.5 inches. Then, drag the tab stop so that it's positioned as closely as possible to the right edge of the text box, at about 9.0 inches. (*Hint*: The right-align tab stop is shaped like a backward capital "L"; you can access it by clicking the tab alignment indicator on the left edge of the ruler.)

6. In the Cases folder of Tutorial.04, make a copy of the Excel file **CLCFData**, and change the name of the copy to **CLCF Success Data**.

7. On Slide 7, "Effectiveness of System," change the slide layout to Object, and then link in the Excel chart in the file **CLCF Success Data**.

8. To demonstrate the power of a linked object, change the data in cell B5 of Sheet1 of the Excel workbook from 8.1 to 12.4.

9. Change the background (Chart Area) fill color of the chart from White to No Fill, so that the chart background takes on the color of the slide background when you return to PowerPoint.

10. Make sure that the Chart1 tab is active so that the chart will appear as an object when you return to PowerPoint, save the Excel file, and exit Excel.

Explore 11. When you return to PowerPoint, resize the chart so that it is 4.5 inches in height, maintaining the current aspect ratio. Position the chart halfway between the bottom of the slide title box and the bottom of the slide itself. (*Hint*: To accurately adjust the chart size, right-click the chart and open the Format Object dialog box, and then click the Size tab.)

12. To the bottom of Slide 1, add a set of four action buttons, as shown in Figure 4-27. Accept the suggested (default) hyperlink target of each button as follows (left to right, as they appear in Figure 4-27): First Slide, Previous Slide, Next Slide, and Last Slide. Set the size of each button to 0.5 by 0.5 inch. Make sure that the buttons are aligned and distributed as shown in Figure 4-27.

Figure 4-27

13. After sizing and positioning the four action buttons, select all four of them, and then copy them to all the other slides in the presentation. If necessary, move the chart up on Slide 7 so that it doesn't crowd the action buttons.

14. View the presentation in Slide Show View, and test all the action buttons.

15. Save the presentation as a set of Web pages to the Tutorial.04 Cases folder on your Data Disk, and then view the document in a Web browser.

16. Open the file **CLCFPres** and save it as a set of Web pages, using the filename **CLCF Presentation**. Then close the file.

17. On Slide 9 ("Summary") of "Introduction to CLCF Marketing," insert the hyperlink text "More about CLCF," and set the target of the link to the Web pages of "CLCF Presentation."

18. Save the Web file, and then view the Web page in your Web browser. Test the hyperlink and action buttons.

Explore

19. From within your browser, print the Web page that contains Slide 7, "Effectiveness of System," and then close the browser. (*Hint*: You can print a Web page in essentially the same way you print a document from any Windows program. If you're using Internet Explorer 5.0, be sure you select the As laid out on screen option button so both frames will be printed.)

Case 2. XPressions, Inc.   Annie Camberlango is Vice President of XPressions, Inc., a company that designs logos for other companies, clubs, and organizations. Through a manufacturer in Hong Kong, XPressions makes T-shirts, mugs, pens, pencils, and other items that contain the logo. Margaret is preparing a presentation for prospective clients to inform them of the products and services of XPressions, Inc. Do the following:

1. Open the presentation file **XPres** and save it as **XPressions Products and Services**.

Explore

2. Export the outline to a Word document (as an outline only), and save it (as a Word document) to the Tutorial.04 Cases folder on your Data Disk, using the filename **XPressions Outline**. (*Hint*: Use the Send To command on the File menu to send the presentation to Microsoft Word.)

3. From within Word, print the outline.

4. Into Slide 1, import (insert) the sound wave **XIntro** (from the Tutorial.04 Cases folder), which is an introduction by Stephen Zabriskie, President of XPressions, Inc. Move the sound wave icon to the lower right corner of the screen. Select the Multimedia Settings tab in the Custom Animation dialog box so that sound plays during the transition to the slide.

5. In Slide 2, "Our Mission," import a clip-art image (from the Clip Gallery) of people interacting, such as shaking hands.

6. Reduce (as necessary) the size of the clip-art image so that you can position it just below the main text.

7. In Slide 4, "Our Expressions," import the image file **XPencil** from the Tutorial.04 Cases folder. Position the item to the right of the main text and resize it as necessary to make it attractive.

8. Add a new Slide 5 to your presentation, using the Object layout. Use the slide title, "Our Success."

9. Make a copy of the file **XSales** located in the Cases folder of Tutorial.04. Give the copy the filename **XPressions Sales**. Remember, you can make a copy by displaying the filename in Windows Explorer or on an Open dialog box (with All Files selected) from within PowerPoint.

10. In the new Slide 5, link the Excel worksheet **XPressions Sales** from the Tutorial.04 Cases folder on your Data Disk. The worksheet containing XPressions sales will appear.

11. Modify the chart so it's legible and its color scheme matches that of the XPressions presentation.

12. To the three slides with bulleted lists, add the Appear build effect, with light purple (one of the preset colors) as the dimming color.

13. To all the slides, add the Box Out transition effect.

14. Add a summary slide based on Slides 2 through 5, and then move the summary slide to make it Slide 6.

15. Save the presentation and print it as a handout with six slides per page.

16. On the new Slide 6, add the hyperlink to the target Web page http://www.xpressions.com. The text of the hyperlink should be "Visit us at www.xpressions.com". Because this is a fictitious link, don't try to go there.

17. Save the presentation as a Web page in the Cases folder of Tutorial.04 of your Data Disk.

18. Preview the Web page version of the presentation.

Explore   19. From within your browser, print the Web page that contains Slide 5, "Our Success" and then close the browser. (*Hint*: You can print a Web page in essentially the same way you print a document from any Windows program. If you're using Internet Explorer 5.0, be sure you select the As laid out on screen option button so both frames will be printed.)

Case 3. Debby's Gym and Spa   Debby Flickinger is owner and operator of Debby's Gym and Spa. She wants to create a presentation about her gym for employees to give to potential customers and for posting on the World Wide Web. Do the following:

1. Open the presentation file **Debby's** from the Cases folder in Tutorial.04 on your Data Disk.

2. Import into the Slide Master and into Title Master the company logo file named **DebLogo** located in the Cases folder.

3. On the Slide Master and Title Master, modify the position and font of the text placeholders, and resize and position the graphic (logo) to make the slides attractive and readable.

4. Create a slide color scheme that matches the logo and apply it to the Slide Master and Title Master.

5. Create a gradient fill background for the slide masters.

6. Return to Normal View and save the presentation as **Debby's Gym and Spa**.

7. Import at least three graphics from the Microsoft Clip Gallery or from some other source to appropriately illustrate points made on the slides.

8. Link the Excel chart in the file **DebChart** on Slide 7, "Usage During Typical Day."

9. Modify the chart as necessary to make the colors and fonts compatible with your color scheme.

10. Add appropriate action buttons to each of the slides.

11. Add appropriate transitions, animation, and sound to the slides.

12. Save the presentation and print it as handouts in grayscale with six slides per page. Don't forget to check the presentation in grayscale beforehand to ensure that all the text and graphics are visible.

13. Save the presentation as a Web page, and then view the presentation in your Web browser.

Explore   14. From within your browser, print the Web page that contains Slide 7, "Usage During Typical Day," and then close the browser. (*Hint*: You can print a Web page in essentially the same way you print a document from any Windows program. If you're using Internet Explorer 5.0, be sure you select the As laid out on screen option button so both frames will be printed.)

Case 4. A Favorite Foreign Country   Create a slide show on a foreign country and then prepare to present it to the class. Your slide show should include specific information about the selected country as detailed below. Do the following:

Explore

1. Create a title slide with an interesting title, using your name for the subtitle.

2. Get information about your selected country from the World Wide Web. Try searching the Web using words like "(country) economy" and "(country) information."

3. Create at least eight slides on such topics as geography, people, government, economy, communications, transportation, military, and travel.

4. Include at least six pictures, including a map, of your country. You can get a map by saving a picture from the Internet, from a clip-art collection, or by scanning a picture from an encyclopedia.

5. Create a slide color scheme appropriate for the topic. Make sure the text and graphics are legible and attractive.

6. Apply slide transitions and animation to all the slides with bulleted lists.

7. Use Excel to create a chart (or Word to create a table) on some aspect of the country, for example, on the gross national product over a five-year period, and then link the chart (or table) to one of the slides. Adjust the colors and fonts to make the chart (or table) legible.

8. Create a Summary Slide. Change its title to "Presentation Summary," and move the slide to the end of your presentation.

9. Check the spelling of all the text on your slides.

10. Rehearse your presentation, setting automatic slide timings. Make any other needed changes.

11. Save the presentation using the name **Report on (Country)**.

12. Check to make sure all the slides are legible in grayscale, and then print your presentation as grayscale handouts, six slides per page.

13. Create a slide titled "References" and include at least one hyperlink to material that you got from the Web.

14. Save the presentation as a set of HTML documents to the Tutorial.04 Cases folder on your Data Disk and then view the document in a Web browser.

LAB ASSIGNMENTS

The Internet: World Wide Web

One of the most popular services on the Internet is the World Wide Web. This Lab is a Web simulator that teaches you how to use Web browser software to find information. You can use this Lab whether or not your school provides you with Internet access.

1. Click the Steps button to learn how to use Web browser software. As you proceed through the Steps, answer all of the Quick Check questions that appear. After you complete the Steps, you will see a Quick Check Summary Report. Follow the instructions on the screen to print this report.

2. Click the Explore button on the Welcome screen. Use the Web browser to locate a weather map of the Caribbean Virgin Islands. What is its URL?

3. A Scuba diver named Wadson Lachouffe has been searching for the fabled treasure of Greybeard the pirate. A link from the Adventure Travel Web site **www.atour.com** leads to Wadson's Web page, called "Hidden Treasure." In Explore, locate the Hidden Treasure page and answer the following questions:

   a. What was the name of Greybeard's ship?

   b. What was Greybeard's favorite food?

   c. What does Wadson think happened to Greybeard's ship?

4. In the Steps, you found a graphic of Jupiter from the photo archives of the Jet Propulsion Laboratory. In the Explore section of the Lab, you can also find a graphic of Saturn. Suppose one of your friends wanted a picture of Saturn for an astronomy report. Make a list of the blue, underlined links your friend must click in the correct order to find the Saturn graphic. Assume that your friend will begin at the Web Trainer home page.

5. Enter the URL **http://www.atour.com** to jump to the Adventure Travel Web site. Write a one-page description of this site. In your paper include a description of the information at the site, the number of pages the site contains, and a diagram of the links it contains.

6. Chris Thomson is a student at UVI and has his own Web pages. In Explore, look at the information Chris has included on his pages. Suppose you could create your own Web page. What would you include? Use word-processing software to design your own Web pages. Make sure you indicate the graphics and links you would use.

INTERNET ASSIGNMENTS

The purpose of the Internet Assignments is to challenge you to find information on the Internet that you can use to create effective documents. The actual assignments are updated and maintained on the Course Technology Web site. Log on to the Internet and use your Web browser to go to the Student Online Companion to accompany this text at **www.course.com/NewPerspectives/office2000**. Click the PowerPoint link, and then click the link for Tutorial 4.

QUICK | CHECK ANSWERS

Session 4.1

1. They are the same, except that the presentation file will usually not be found in the Template folder, whereas the design template file will be.

2. **a.** Import means to insert a file that was created using one program into another program's file.

   b. Embed means to insert a file so that a one-way connection with the source program will be maintained.

   c. Link means to insert a file so that a two-way connection between the source program and the destination program will be maintained.

   d. OLE (object linking and embedding) supported programs let you embed or link objects from one program to another.

3. The file is modified.

4. imported

5. You might want any changes made to the linked file to take effect in both the source program and the destination program.

6. to align text vertically that was inserted after a tab

7. In Slide Sorter View, select the slides that you want in the summary, and click the Slide Summary button on the Slide Sorter toolbar.

Session 4.2

1. A hyperlink is a word, phrase, or graphic that you click to display an object at another location. Other slides within the presentation and other presentations.

2. An action button is a ready-made icon for which you can easily define hyperlinks to other slides or to other documents.

3. During a slide show, right-click on the screen and open the Meeting Minder. Click the Action Items tab, type an item, and then click Add. PowerPoint automatically generates the slide.

4. to increase the efficiency of your work by putting menu commands on a toolbar where they are more accessible

5. Click File and then click Save as Web Page.

6. A frame on the left contains a table of contents of the slides, the slide itself appears in a frame on the right, and navigation buttons appear at the bottom of the slide.

7. Announce to the participant the time and place of the broadcast, open the presentation that you're going to broadcast, click Slide Show, point to Online Broadcast, and click Begin Broadcast.

New Perspectives on

MICROSOFT®
POWERPOINT®
2000

TUTORIAL 5   PPT 5.03

Applying Advanced Special Effects in Presentations
Preparing a Presentation for a Trade Show

TUTORIAL 6   PPT 6.01

Creating Special Types of Presentations
Technical Presentations at the American Association of Food Buyers

Read This Before You Begin

To the Student

Data Disk

To complete the Level III tutorials, Review Assignments, Case Problems, and Additional Cases in this book, you need two Data Disks. Your instructor will either provide you with Data Disks or ask you to make your own.

If you are making your own Data Disks, you will need two blank, formatted high-density disks. You will need to copy a set of folders from a file server or standalone computer or the Web onto your disks. Your instructor will tell you which computer, drive letter, and folders contain the files you need. You could also download the files by going to www.course.com, clicking Data Disk Files, and following the instructions on the screen.

The following list shows you which folders go on each of your disks, so that you will have enough disk space to complete all the tutorials, Review Assignments, Case Problems and Additional Cases:

Data Disk 5

Write this on the disk label:
Data Disk 5: Level I Tutorial 5

Put these folders on the disk:
Tutorial.05

Data Disk 6

Write this on the disk label:
Data Disk 6: Level I Tutorial 6

Put these folders on the disk:
Tutorial.06

When you begin each tutorial, be sure you are using the correct Data Disk. See the inside front or inside back cover of this book for more information on Data Disk files, or ask your instructor or technical support person for assistance.

Using Your Own Computer

If you are going to work through this book using your own computer, you need:

- **Computer System** Microsoft PowerPoint 2000 and Windows 95 or higher must be installed on your computer. This book assumes a complete installation of PowerPoint 2000.

- **Data Disks** You will not be able to complete the tutorials or exercises in this book using your own computer until you have two Data Disks. You also need access to a hard drive or other high-capacity disk onto which you can save your work.

- **Course Lab[s]** See your instructor or technical support person to obtain the Course Lab software for use on your own computer.

Visit Our World Wide Web Site

Additional materials designed especially for you are available on the World Wide Web. Go to http://www.course.com.

To the Instructor

The Data files are available on the Instructor's Resource Kit for this title. Follow the instructions in the Help file on the CD-ROM to install the programs to your network or standalone computer.

For information on creating Data Disks see the "To the Student" section above.

You are granted a license to copy the Data Files to any computer or computer network used by students who have purchased this book.

OBJECTIVES

In this tutorial you will:

- Save a PowerPoint slide as a picture object, and copy a slide to another application

- Apply complex animation and sound effects to a presentation, including built-in sounds, recorded narration, and CD music tracks

- Download Microsoft clip art from the Internet

- Manipulate background objects in a slide

- Set up a self-running presentation

- Use drawings and diagrams from other applications in a PowerPoint presentation

- Create and modify digital photographs

APPLYING ADVANCED SPECIAL EFFECTS IN PRESENTATIONS

Preparing a Presentation for a Trade Show

CASE

Inca Imports at a Trade Show

With offices in Los Angeles and New York City, Inca Imports International is well established in both the western and eastern United States. The company is now one of the major fruit and vegetable importers in the country. So, Inca Imports' executives decided to participate as a major exhibitor at a trade show of the American Association of Food Buyers (AAFB) to be held in San Francisco later this year. A **trade show** is a convention, usually held biannually, annually or semiannually, in which people within one profession or industry gather to learn more about their profession, meet colleagues, and share ideas. The AAFB trade show is important to Inca Imports because over 5,000 food buyers from all over the country will attend. Enrique Hoffmann, director of marketing for Inca Imports, will help you create the main presentation for the Inca Imports booth at the trade show.

SESSION 5.1

In this session, you'll copy one of the slides of a presentation into a Microsoft Word document, and copy some of the slides in the presentation as miniature picture objects into another slide. You'll then enhance the presentation with complex animations and sound effects by applying motion and sound clips from the online Microsoft Clip Gallery, by inserting a CD audio track on a slide, and by recording a narration. Finally, you'll manipulate the background object so that it appears on some slides, but not on others.

Planning **the Presentation**

Before creating the presentation, Enrique and you sit down to plan the presentation:

- ■ **Purpose of the presentation**: To provide information about the products and services of Inca Imports
- ■ **Type of presentation**: Product/Services Overview
- ■ **Audience**: Attendees of the AAFB trade show—buyers from grocery store chains, independent grocery stores, restaurant chains, independent restaurants, military food services departments, and educational institutions.
- ■ **Audience needs**: To understand the advantages of purchasing produce from Inca Imports
- ■ **Location of presentation**: The exhibition hall of San Francisco's Moscone Convention Center, site of the AAFB trade show.
- ■ **Format**: Electronic slide show, for oral and self-running presentations.

With the above general plan for the presentation, Enrique started to create a presentation using the AutoContent Wizard, selecting the Product/Services Overview as the type of presentation under Sales/Marketing. He modified the text created by the Wizard, and then applied a custom-designed template to the presentation. He wants you to copy one of the slides into a Word document that briefly describes the Inca Imports exhibit at the convention.

Using **PowerPoint Slides in Other Applications**

Enrique informs you that the company has to send in a summary, consisting of one paragraph and one graphic, to the trade show organizers for placement in the trade show guide book. You'll begin by opening the presentation that Enrique started, selecting one of the slides, and copying it as a picture object into the Microsoft Word document.

To copy a slide into a Word document:

1. Start PowerPoint, and then open the file **TradeSho** from the Tutorial.05 Tutorial folder on your Data Disk. Make sure that the PowerPoint window is maximized and in Normal View, and that the Office Assistant is hidden or turned off. The title page of the trade show presentation appears in the Slide Pane. See Figure 5-1. The presentation includes a custom design (slide color scheme, background, color, fonts, background graphics, etc.) developed by a graphic designer under Enrique's direction.

THE TRADE SHOW PRESENTATION IN THE POWERPOINT WINDOW

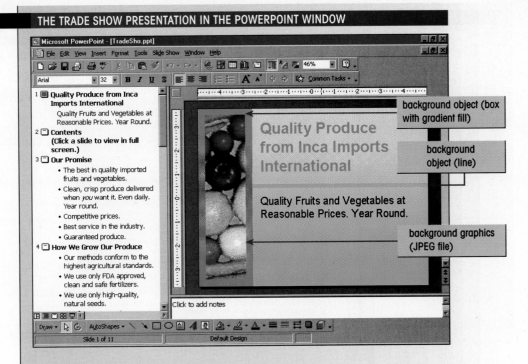

2. Save the presentation file as **Inca at Trade Show** to a high-capacity disk (your hard disk, a Zip disk, or the like.) You're now ready to copy a slide. Enrique wants you to put a copy of the title slide into the company summary document.

   TROUBLE? If you are using drive A for your Data Disk, you won't have enough space to save the files in this tutorial. If you don't have access to a hard drive or some other high-capacity disk, you should read through the steps anyway to learn the material in this tutorial.

3. Switch to the **Slide Sorter View**, and make sure Slide 1 (the title slide) is selected.

4. Click the **Copy** button on the Standard toolbar to place Slide 1 as a picture object on the Windows Clipboard.

5. Start Microsoft Word, and then open the file **CoSummry** from the Tutorial.05 Tutorial folder on your Data Disk, and save it to a high-capacity disk using the filename **Inca Company Summary**.

6. With the insertion point at the beginning of the Word document, click the **Paste** button . The image of Slide 1 appears at the beginning of the Word document. See Figure 5–2.

| Figure 5-2 | WORD DOCUMENT WITH COPIED GRAPHIC |

With the picture object in the Word document, you'll now want to resize and position it so that it appears to the left of the text paragraph, rather than above it.

To modify the picture object in Word:

1. Right-click the image to select it and to display a menu.

2. Click **Format Object** on the menu, click the **Size** tab, make sure the **Lock aspect ratio** check box is checked, and change the **Height** to **2** inches. This will decrease the size of the image in the document.

3. Click the **Layout** tab on the Format Object dialog box, click the **Square** wrapping style icon so that the text wraps to the right of the image, click the **Left horizontal** alignment option button so the picture will appear on the left side of the page, and then click the **OK** button. After a moment, the image is resized and the text wraps around the right side of the image.

4. Click anywhere in the document text to deselect the picture. See Figure 5–3.

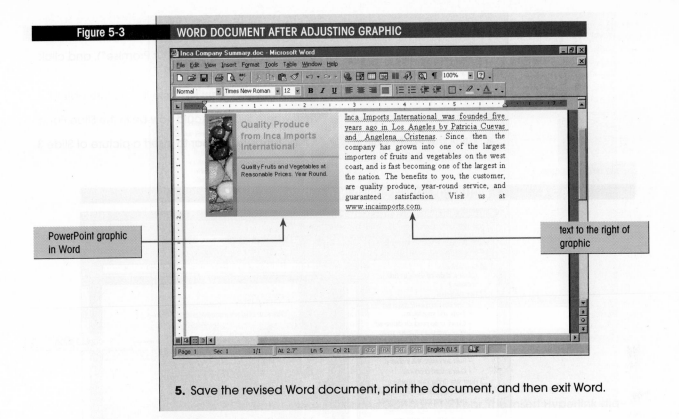

Figure 5-3   **WORD DOCUMENT AFTER ADJUSTING GRAPHIC**

PowerPoint graphic in Word

text to the right of graphic

5. Save the revised Word document, print the document, and then exit Word.

Having added the picture to the company summary, you can now give a copy of the document to Enrique so he can mail it to the trade show organizers to include in their guide book.

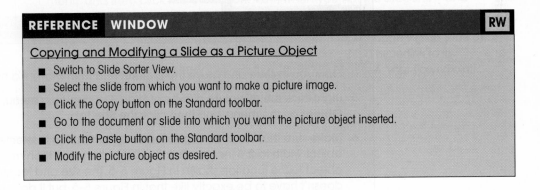

REFERENCE   WINDOW   **RW**

Copying and Modifying a Slide as a Picture Object
- Switch to Slide Sorter View.
- Select the slide from which you want to make a picture image.
- Click the Copy button on the Standard toolbar.
- Go to the document or slide into which you want the picture object inserted.
- Click the Paste button on the Standard toolbar.
- Modify the picture object as desired.

Next you'll copy some of the slides in your presentation to create miniatures in the Contents slide, and then you'll make each of the miniatures hyperlinks to their respective full-sized slides.

Figure 5-6 **SLIDE 2 WITH COPIES OF SIX SLIDE MINIATURES**

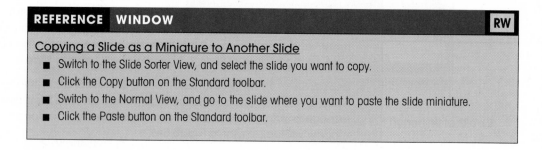

10. Save your presentation using the current filename.

REFERENCE WINDOW **RW**

Copying a Slide as a Miniature to Another Slide
- Switch to the Slide Sorter View, and select the slide you want to copy.
- Click the Copy button on the Standard toolbar.
- Switch to the Normal View, and go to the slide where you want to paste the slide miniature.
- Click the Paste button on the Standard toolbar.

In this example, you've used the picture objects of the slides as hyperlinks to the actual slides in the presentation, but you can design any PowerPoint slide and use it as a picture of any type on any other slide, or in any other Windows program. You can also save any or all of the slides in a presentation as picture files (in GIF, JPG, PNG, or BMP file format) by displaying the desired slide in the Slide Pane in Normal View, clicking File on the menu bar, clicking Save As, and then selecting one of the picture formats as the file type.

Applying **Complex Animation and Sound Effects**

Enrique wants you to make the presentation for the trade show as attractive and eye-catching as possible. You decide that one way to achieve that goal is to add animation and sound effects to the presentation. You'll begin by creating an animated process diagram for the harvesting and shipping processes of the Inca Imports fruits and vegetables.

Fortunately, the graphic artist, under Enrique's direction, has already created most of the graphics for the slide of the harvesting and shipping process, so you'll just do the animation.

You should understand, however, that anyone familiar with PowerPoint drawing can create this slide; you just have to know how to add text boxes, change the border and fill of the text box, and insert AutoShapes.

The goal of animating the process diagram is to make each object appear on the screen one at a time, in the sequence of the process.

To animate the process diagram:

1. Go to Slide 6, "How We Harvest and Ship Our Produce (continued)".

2. Click **Slide Show** on the menu bar, click **Custom Animation** to display the Custom Animation dialog box, and then click the **Effects** tab. Now you'll select all the objects (except the first one) for animation.

3. Click **Text 2** in the object list, scroll down to the bottom of the object list, press and hold down the **Shift** key, and then click **Down arrow 18**. All the objects (except the first) become selected.

4. In the **Entry animation and sound** section of the dialog box, click the list arrow for the animation list box, and then scroll down and select **Wipe**. All of the object check boxes (except the first) become selected and are assigned the Wipe animation.

5. In the section to the right of Wipe, click the list arrow, and select **Right**, so that all the objects wipe to the right when they appear on the screen. Later, you'll change some of these to wipe in other directions, or to do other types of animation. See Figure 5-7.

Figure 5-7	CUSTOM ANIMATION DIALOG BOX WITH OBJECTS SELECTED

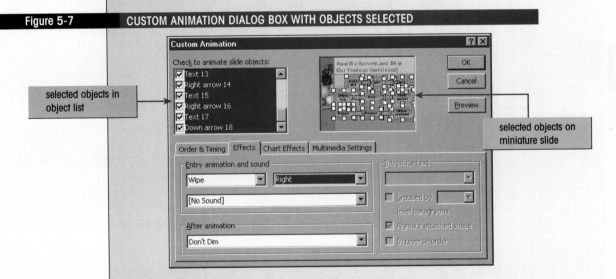

With the objects selected, you can now change the timing of each object— the time lapse between the appearance of a particular object and the previous object.

6. With the objects to be animated still selected, click the **Order & Timing** tab on the Custom Animation dialog box, click the **Automatically** button in the Start animation section of the dialog box, and then set the time (located below Automatically) to **00:01** second. Now there will be a one-second delay between appearances of objects. As you scroll through the list of objects, you

can see that the last object is Down arrow 18, but it is the third item in the animation order. Somehow Enrique added that object out of order, so you'll want to move that object so that it will animate at the right time.

7. Click **Down arrow 18** so it's the only object highlighted. Make sure you see that the Down arrow is selected in the slide miniature on the dialog box.

TROUBLE? If you click the check box next to the text, rather than the text itself, click the box again to keep it selected.

8. Click the **Move Down** button ⬇ to the right of the Animation order section until Down arrow 18 is just below Text 12 and above Text 13, in other words, until Down arrow 18 becomes object number 12 in the animation order. See Figure 5-8. Now the object is in the right place for the correct animation sequence.

TROUBLE? If the order of objects in your data file isn't the same as shown in Figure 5-8, fix your file so that it is.

Figure 5-8	CUSTOM ANIMATION DIALOG BOX AFTER MOVING AN OBJECT

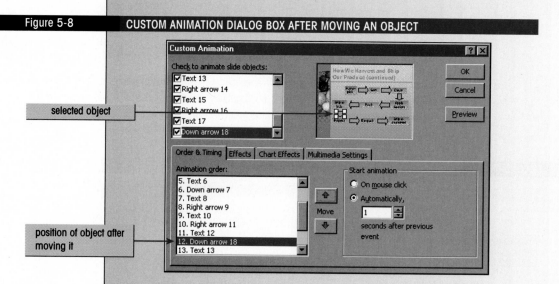

9. To see how the animation looks so far, click the **Preview** button on the dialog box. The miniature slide shows the animation.

Now you're ready to change the animation of some of the objects to make the animation more interesting.

To edit the animation effects:

1. With the Custom Animation dialog box still on the screen, click the **Effects** tab. Now you're going to change the animation wipe direction to match the direction of the arrows. You'll therefore have to change the down arrows and the objects that follow them to wipe down, and the left arrows and the objects that follow them to wipe left.

2. Select **Down arrow 7** and **Text 8**. Remember, if you want to select more than one object, hold down the **Ctrl** key while you click the objects following the first one.

3. Change the wipe direction from Right to **Down**.

4. Select from **Right arrow 9** to **Text 12**. Notice that Right arrows 9 and 11 are actually left arrows on the screen. To create them, Enrique copied one of the right arrows, and then flipped the objects horizontally so that they would actually point to the left.

5. Change the wipe direction from Right to **Left**.

6. In a similar fashion, change the wipe direction of **Down arrow 18** and **Text 13** to **Down**.

7. Change the Entry animation of Text 17 from Wipe to **Swivel**, click the **Sound** list arrow and change the sound from (No Sound) to **Applause**, and change the sound effect for Right arrow 16 to **Drum Roll**. This will add a dramatic effect to the last two objects in the diagram.

8. Click the **Preview** button on the dialog box to preview the animation and sound effects. If everything looks and sounds right, click the **OK** button, and then save the presentation using the current filename.

REFERENCE WINDOW   RW

Animating an Object
- Click Slide Show on the menu bar, click Custom Animation, and click the Effects tab.
- Select the object or objects that you want to animate using the same animation effect.
- Select an effect from the Entry animation and sound section of the dialog box.
- With the object(s) still selected, click the Order & Timing tab on the Custom Animation dialog box, click the Automatically button, and set the time that you want the animation delayed after the previous animation. Alternatively, you can specify that the animation takes place upon a mouse click.
- Click the OK button.

You've completed the animation effects for Slide 6, but Enrique also wants to add some background music and an animated GIF file to the slide. Unfortunately, the standard Office Clip Gallery doesn't include the desired music and GIF files that you need. So you decide to download some clip files from the Internet.

Downloading Clips from the Online Microsoft Clip Gallery

Microsoft provides a Web site with many picture and sound clips for you to use in your PowerPoint presentations. You'll now download an animated GIF file (motion clip) and a music file (sound clip) for use in the current presentation.

To download clips over the Internet:

1. Make sure your computer is set up for Internet access. This might require that you connect your computer modem to an outside phone line, or that your computer be equipped with direct-line Internet access.

2. Make sure you're still viewing Slide 6 in PowerPoint, and then click **Insert** on the menu bar, point to **Picture**, and then click **Clip Art**. The Insert ClipArt dialog box opens.

3. Click the **Clips Online** button at the top of the dialog box. You might now see a dialog box with the title "Connect to Web for More Clip Art, Photos, Sounds".

TROUBLE? If you don't see the "Connect to Web for More Clip Art, Photos, Sounds" dialog box, don't worry. Some PowerPoint software is set up to skip this step.

4. Click the **OK** button. Your Internet browser automatically runs and opens the Microsoft Clip Gallery Web page, probably with the URL *cgl.microsoft.com/clipgallerylive/default.asp*. See Figure 5-9.

TROUBLE? If you see a page with an Addendum to the Microsoft End User License Agreement, read the agreement and click the Accept button.

| Figure 5-9 | ONLINE MICROSOFT CLIP GALLERY |

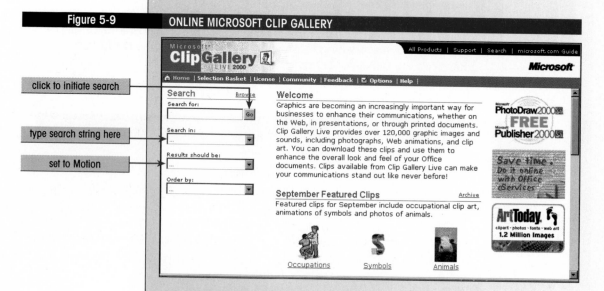

TROUBLE? If you get an error message that the Internet connection failed, you might want to run your Internet browser, and then repeat Steps 3 and 4 above.

You'll now search the online Clip Gallery for desired animated GIF and sound files.

5. Click in the **Search for** box on the Web page, and type **fruit**, because you want a clip-art image that relates to the fruits or vegetables of Inca Imports.

6. Click the list arrow of the **Results should be** selection box, and click **Motion**. This ensures that you will find animation clip art.

7. Click the **Go** button to the right of the Search for selection box. This initiates the search. After a moment or two (depending upon your connection speed), the Clip Gallery displays and animates a group of pictures. You'll download the picture showing two people picking fruit from a tree. See Figure 5-10.

Figure 5-10   **ONLINE MICROSOFT CLIP GALLERY WITH SELECTED MOTION CLIPS**

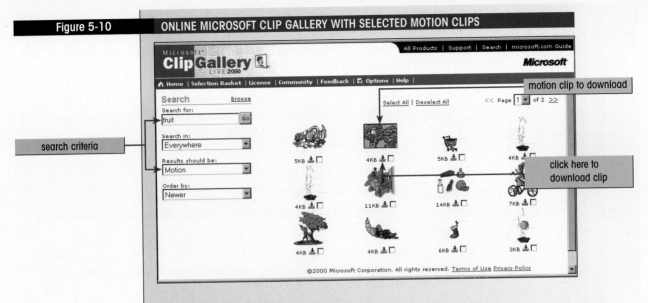

8. Click the **download button** (red arrow) just below the picture, as indicated in Figure 5-10. Within a second or two, the picture is downloaded and appears in the Insert ClipArt dialog box. This indicates that the picture was successfully downloaded.

   TROUBLE? If you can't find the animated picture of people picking fruit, try the search word "farms", or select a different animated picture file to download.

9. Click anywhere in the Web browser to bring its window to the forefront and hide the Insert ClipArt dialog box.

You've successfully downloaded the desired animated GIF picture. Now you'll download a music clip.

To download a music clip over the Internet:

1. Click in the **Search for** text box on the left side of the Microsoft Clip Gallery Web page, and replace **fruit** with **music**, because you want to search for music.

2. Change the **Results should be** from "Motion" to **Sounds**, and then click the **Go** button to initiate the search. The Microsoft Clip Gallery has many pages of sound clips that fit the broad search criteria of music.

3. Go through the pages of sound clips by clicking **>>** in upper-right corner of the Web page until you see the sound clip titled **Latin Joyful** and then download it in the same way you downloaded the motion clip.

4. Exit your Web browser and close the Insert ClipArt dialog box.

Having downloaded a motion clip and a sound clip, you're now ready to apply them to your PowerPoint presentation.

Applying the Downloaded Motion and Sound Clips

Enrique has asked you to add a motion clip and a sound clip to Slide 6 so that both clips "play" while potential clients view the animation that you added to the harvesting and shipping diagram. You'll begin by applying the motion clip.

To apply the motion clip to the slide:

1. Make sure Slide 6 is in the Slide Pane, click **Insert** on the menu bar, point to **Movies and Sounds**, and click **Movie from Gallery**. The **Insert Movie** dialog box opens.

2. In the Categories window of the dialog box, find and then click **Downloaded Clips**. The miniature image of the people picking fruit appears in the Downloaded Clips window. See Figure 5-11.

| Figure 5-11 | INSERT MOVIE DIALOG BOX WITH DOWNLOADED MOTION CLIP(S) |

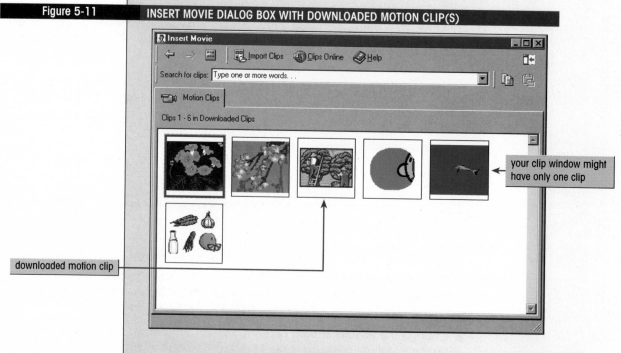

downloaded motion clip

your clip window might have only one clip

3. Click the miniature image that you want to insert into the slide, click the **Insert Clip** button , and then close the Insert Movie dialog box. As you can see, the motion image is inserted into your slide.

4. Move the **motion clip image** to the position shown in Figure 5-12—to the left of the "Hand-pick" text box—and then deselect the image.

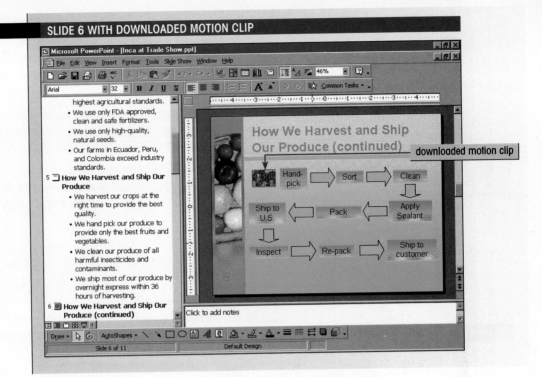

Figure 5-12 | SLIDE 6 WITH DOWNLOADED MOTION CLIP

When you run the slide show, the motion clip will animate automatically, and stay animated as long as the slide appears on the screen.

Now you'll download the sound clip and set it up to play in the background while the slide is on the screen in "Slide Show" mode.

To apply a sound clip for background playing:

1. Click **Insert** on the menu bar, point to **Movies and Sounds**, and click **Sound from Gallery**. The Insert Sound dialog box opens.

2. In the Categories window of the dialog box, find and then click **Downloaded Clips** (as before), click the sound clip icon for **Latin Joyful**, and then click the **Insert clip** button ⊡. PowerPoint will then give you a warning sound and ask when you want the sound clip to play. You'll have to close the **Insert Sound** dialog box before you can respond to the question.

3. Close the **Insert Sound** dialog box, and then click the **Yes** button to indicate that you want the sound clip to play as soon as the slide appears on the screen. Since you've animated the other objects on the screen, the sound clip won't play until all the objects appear because the sound clip is the last object. You can solve that problem by moving the object to the top of the Custom Animation list. Once you do that, however, the music will stop playing as soon as the next object appears. You can solve that problem by modifying the Multimedia Settings.

4. Click **Slide Show**, click **Custom Animation** to display the Custom Animation dialog box, click the **Order & Timing** tab on the dialog box, and then move **Media 20** to number 1 in the Animation order (by selecting it and clicking the **Move Up** button ⬆ until the item is at the top of the list).

5. With Media 20 still selected, make sure the Start animation settings are **Automatically** and **00:00** seconds (no delay in starting the sound).

6. Click the **Multimedia Settings** tab on the Custom Animation dialog box, make sure the **Play using animation order** check box is selected, click the **Continue slide show** option button so that the slide show continues while music plays in the background, and then click the **After current slide** option button so that music stops playing after the current slide.

7. Click the **OK** button on the Custom Animation dialog box to close it. You'll now hide the Sound icon because it has no function on the screen and might distract those who view the slide show.

8. Move the **Sound** icon 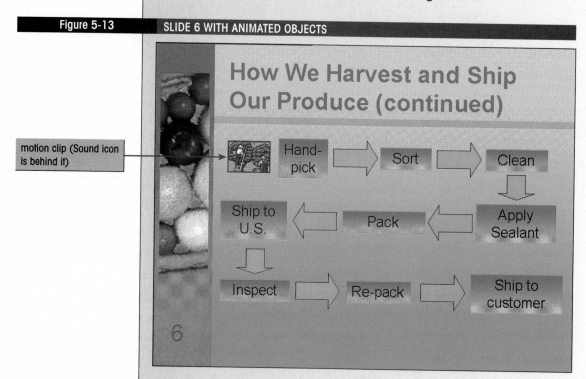 on top of the motion clip image of the fruit pickers, click **Draw** on the Drawing toolbar, point to **Order**, and click **Send to Back**. The Sound icon stays on the screen so the music plays, but the icon itself is hidden from view.

   TROUBLE? If you can't hide the CD icon, just leave it showing. Some releases of PowerPoint 2000 do not permit changing the layer of this object.

9. Click the **Slide Show** button on the View toolbar to see the animations and hear the background music of Slide 6. See Figure 5–13.

Figure 5-13	SLIDE 6 WITH ANIMATED OBJECTS

motion clip (Sound icon is behind it)

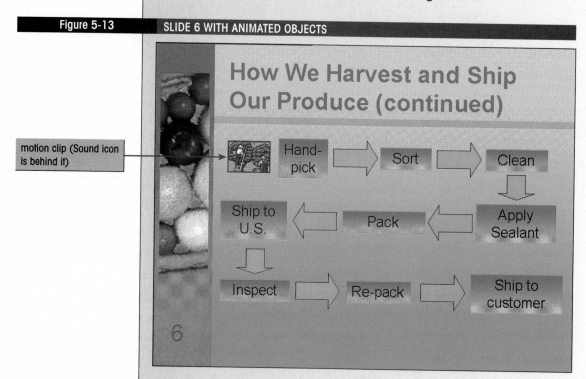

How We Harvest and Ship Our Produce (continued)

Hand-pick → Sort → Clean

Clean ↓ Apply Sealant

Ship to U.S. ← Pack ← Apply Sealant

Ship to U.S. ↓

Inspect → Re-pack → Ship to customer

6

10. If all of your changes appear correctly on Slide 6, save your presentation using the current file name.

    TROUBLE? If something doesn't work, such as the order or direction of animation, or the background music, carefully review the above procedures and adjust the animation order, the wipe direction, or the Multimedia Setting.

This completes the animation and sound effects of Slide 6.

REFERENCE WINDOW   **RW**

Downloading Clips from the Microsoft Clip Gallery

- Display the slide into which you want to insert a picture, motion, or sound clip.
- Click Insert on the menu bar, point to Picture or to Movies and Sounds, and click Clip Art, Movie from Gallery, or Sound from Gallery.
- Click Clips Online.
- Use the search feature of the Microsoft Clip Gallery to find one or more clips that you want, and click the download button.

Inserting a CD Audio Track into a Slide

Just as you can insert a music clip into a slide, you can also insert a CD audio track into a slide, provided your computer has a CD-ROM or DVD disk drive. Enrique wants you to insert some CD music into the final two slides of your presentation. You'll do that now.

To Insert a CD audio track into a slide:

1. Go to Slide 10 ("Whom You Should Contact"). This and the next slide are where Enrique wants CD music to play in the background.

2. Select a music CD that has a track you want to play in the background of Slides 10 and 11. For example, Enrique suggests that you select track 1 ("Strawberry Fields Forever") on CD1 of *The Beatles/1967-70* (the "Blue Album"), because Inca Imports International imports strawberries picked from its own fields in South America.

3. Place the music CD into the CD-ROM or DVD disk drive, and after you've verified that the music does indeed play properly, and you know the desired track, close the **music window** to stop the music.

4. Click **Insert** on the menu bar, point to **Movies and Sounds**, and then click **Play CD Audio Track**. The Movie and Sound Options dialog box opens.

5. Click the **Loop until stopped** check box in the Play options section of the dialog box, and then select the starting and ending track in the **Play CD audio track** section of the dialog box. In the case of playing the Beatles' "Strawberry Fields Forever", you would select track 1 as the starting and ending because you only want to play that one track. However, you can play two or more consecutive tracks.

6. Click the **OK** button, and when PowerPoint asks if you want sound to play automatically, click the **Yes** button. PowerPoint inserts a CD icon in the middle of the slide.

7. Drag the small **CD icon** from the middle of the slide to the lower-right corner. You now need to tell PowerPoint that you want to play the CD track of music in the background for two slides.

8. Click **Slide Show**, click **Custom Animation**, click the **Multimedia Settings** tab, click the **Play using animation order** check box, click the **Continue slide show** option button, and set the sound to **Stop playing After 2 slides**. See Figure 5-14.

Figure 5-14	CUSTOM ANIMATION DIALOG BOX WITH CD MUSIC CLIP OBJECT

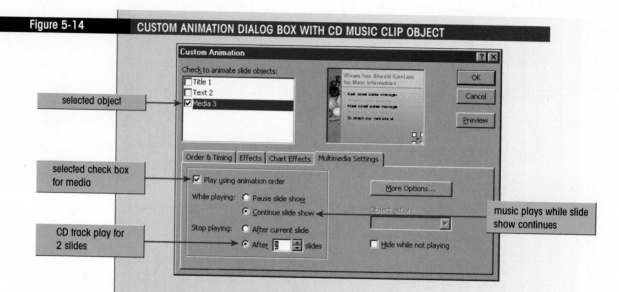

TROUBLE? If the Multimedia Settings are dimmed, deselect and re-select the Media 3 check box to make sure PowerPoint knows that a media object is selected.

9. Click the **OK** button, close the **Custom Animation** dialog box, and then save your presentation.

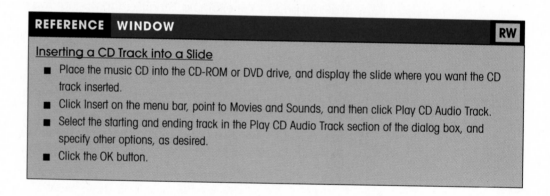

REFERENCE WINDOW   RW

Inserting a CD Track into a Slide

- Place the music CD into the CD-ROM or DVD drive, and display the slide where you want the CD track inserted.
- Click Insert on the menu bar, point to Movies and Sounds, and then click Play CD Audio Track.
- Select the starting and ending track in the Play CD Audio Track section of the dialog box, and specify other options, as desired.
- Click the OK button.

Your slide is ready to play a CD music track. Now you just have to make sure your music CD is inserted into the CD-ROM or DVD drive whenever you start the slide show. If the CD is not inserted when you run the slide show, the music will simply be omitted.

Adding Action Buttons to the Slides

You're probably already familiar with **action buttons**, which are ready-made icons for which you can easily define hyperlinks. You'll add action buttons to some of the slides in the presentation for Inca Imports. These action buttons will help those who view the presentation to navigate the slide show, without necessarily having to proceed in a specific order.

To add action buttons to the slides:

1. Go to Slide 3 ("Our Promise"). You'll add three actions to this slide, and then copy them to the other slides in the presentation. In some of the slides, you'll delete one or two of the action buttons.

2. Click **Slide Show** on the menu bar, point to **Action Buttons**, and click the **Action Button: Back or Previous button** ◀. The pointer becomes a cross hair +.

3. Drag the pointer + while holding down the **Shift** key, so that you draw a square near the center of the bottom of the screen, as shown in Figure 5–15, and then release the mouse. PowerPoint displays the Action Settings dialog box, with the default setting of the **Hyperlink to Previous Slide**, which is the setting you want.

4. Click the **OK** button on the dialog box to accept the hyperlink setting.

   TROUBLE? If the action button isn't in position, or isn't sized as shown in Figure 5–15, adjust the size or position now.

5. Repeat Steps 2 through 4, except this time, insert **Action Button: Home**, position the button immediately to the right of the previous one, make it the same size as the previous one, and link it to Slide 2 by clicking the **Hyperlink to** list arrow, clicking **Slide**, and selecting **Slide 2. Contents**. Click the **OK** button twice to close the two dialog boxes.

6. Repeat Steps 2 through 4, except this time, insert **Action Button: Forward or Next**, and set the hyperlink to the **Next Slide**.

| Figure 5-15 | SLIDE 3 WITH ADDED ACTION BUTTONS |

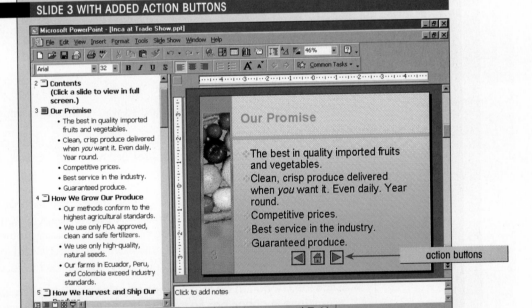

TROUBLE? If the action buttons don't have essentially the same positions and sizes shown in Figure 5–15, adjust the sizes and positions now.

7. Select the three action buttons on Slide 3 (by drawing a selection box around all three), and copy them to all the other slides (including Slides 1 and 2), using the copy-and-paste method.

8. Go to Slide 1 and delete the **Previous and Home action buttons** (leaving only the Forward action button), go to Slide 2 and delete the **Home** action button (leaving the Previous and Forward action buttons). Move the two buttons closer together.

9. Go to Slide 11 (the last slide) and remove the **Next action button** (leaving only the Previous and Home action buttons). Center the remaining two buttons.

10. Review all the slides to make sure the action buttons don't cover any text and, if necessary, move them out of the way; then run the slide show starting at Slide 1 to ensure that all the action buttons work properly. If all is correct, save your presentation.

Having set up action (navigation) buttons, you're now ready to add narration to the slides to help potential clients understand how to run the slide show.

Recording a Narration

Enrique told you that the PowerPoint presentation for the trade show will be **self-running**—on a computer at the Inca Imports exhibitor booth where trade show attendees can come by and run through the presentation on their own. (A self-running presentation runs without human interruption, but it *can* accept human intervention to advance to another slide or return to a previous one.) Enrique suggests that you add narration to the slides so that the attendees will know how to navigate through the presentation. You should always write a brief script for each of the slides so you won't hesitate while recording the narration. We'll assume that you've already done that, and you're ready to record the narration.

To record a narration:

1. Make sure your computer is equipped with a recording microphone.

   TROUBLE? If your system doesn't have a microphone, find a computer that does, attach a mic to your computer, or check with your instructor or technical support person.

2. Go to Slide 1, click **Slide Show**, click **Record Narration** to open the Record Narration dialog box, click the **Set Microphone Level** button, read the contents of the **Microphone Check** dialog box, hold the microphone where you want it while you record the slide show narration, and read aloud the text shown on the dialog box. PowerPoint automatically adjusts the microphone level for you.

3. Click the **OK** button on the Microphone Check dialog box, and click the **Link narrations in** check box so that the recorded sound files will be saved in the directory where your presentation file is saved.

   TROUBLE? If the directory path to the right of "Link narrations in" isn't the Tutorial.05 Tutorial folder on your Data Disk, click the Browse button and set the path to that directory.

4. Click the **OK** button on the dialog box. PowerPoint automatically starts the slide show. As you go from one slide to the next, you'll record a brief message at each one.

5. Talk into the microphone using a clear and steady voice: "Welcome to Inca Imports International. After you read the contents of this title slide, click the orange Forward button at the bottom of the screen to advance to the next slide."

6. Press the **spacebar** to go to Slide 2, and say into the microphone, "This is the Contents slide, or home slide. To jump directly to another location in the slide show, click one of the miniature slides below. To go to the next slide, click the Forward button. To go back to the previous slide, click the Back button."

7. Press the **spacebar** to go to Slide 3, and say into the microphone, "After looking over this slide, or any subsequent slide, click the Home button to return to the Contents slide, or click the Back or Forward button to go to the previous or next slide." Press the **spacebar** to go to the next slide, and the **Esc** button to halt the recording. PowerPoint displays a message asking if you want to save the timing, as well as the recordings, with each slide.

8. Click the **No** button. You've now recorded a narration with your slide show.

9. Go back to **Slide 1** and run the slide show to test your narration.

   TROUBLE? If the narration has mistakes, return to Normal View, click the Sound icon in the lower-right corner of the slide, and rerun the narration for that slide (Steps 2 through 7 above). Note that to save a narration of a particular slide, you must advance to the next slide, or the narration won't be saved.

10. Save the presentation.

REFERENCE WINDOW **RW**

Recording a Narration
- In Normal View, go to the slide where you want to start recording a narration, click Slide Show, click Record Narration, click the Set Microphone Level button, read the contents of the dialog box, hold the microphone where you want it while you record the slide show narration, and read the text shown in the dialog box.
- Click the OK button, click the Link narration in check box, and click the OK button.
- Talk into the microphone to record the narration for the current slide.
- Press the spacebar to go to the next slide (if desired), and record the narration for that slide, and then continue, as desired, to other slides.
- After completing the narrations, press the Esc key, and click the Yes or No button.

You've now recorded the narration for the presentation. The recording for each slide is saved in a separate sound wave (.WAV) file. Whenever you copy a presentation that has narration, be sure you copy all the sound files with it.

Manipulating **Background Objects**

The next task that Enrique wants you to perform to improve the trade show presentation is removal of the background on Slide 11, the final slide. As the slide now appears, the background picture of produce on the left side of the slide interferes with the similar but larger picture of produce that appears on the main part of the slide. You'll first remove the entire background, and adjust the size and location of the large graphic. Later you'll see how to add part of the background back into the slide.

To remove the background of a slide:

1. Go to Slide 11, click **Format** on the menu bar, and click **Background**. The Background dialog box opens.

2. Click the **Omit background graphics from master** check box to select it, and then click the **Apply** button. All three background objects disappear: the image of the produce, the green-to-red gradient box, and the horizontal orange bar below the title.

   TROUBLE? If you accidentally click the Apply to All button, click the Undo button on the Standard toolbar, and repeat the above step.

3. To improve the looks of the slide, click in the text **Try A Sample at Our Booth!**, adjust the height of that text box so that the line of text just barely fits within the text box, move the text box near to the upper left corner of the slide, and then increase the size of the graphic so it fills the entire width of the slide and comes nearer to the text at the top. See Figure 5–16.

Figure 5-16	SLIDE 11 AFTER REMOVING BACKGROUND AND RESIZING GRAPHIC AND TEXT BOX

The appearance of the slide still needs improvement, so you decide to add back in the horizontal orange bar below the slide title. Because PowerPoint doesn't allow you to add part of a background, you have to do a trick—you'll copy the background object from the master slide onto the current slide.

4. Click **View** on the menu bar, point to **Master**, and click **Slide Master**. PowerPoint goes into Master Slide View.

5. Click the horizontal orange bar to select it, click the **Copy** button, return to **Normal View**, and click the **Paste** button. A copy of the background orange bar appears on the slide.

6. Move the horizontal orange bar so it rests just on top of the produce picture and below the title, as shown in Figure 5–17.

| Figure 5-17 | SLIDE 11 WITH BACKGROUND OBJECT COPIED TO SLIDE |

7. Save the presentation.

TROUBLE? If the position of the text and the orange bar need adjustment to look like Figure 5–17, make those adjustments now.

These steps have demonstrated how you can omit background objects, copy one or more of the background objects, and use them in a slide.

You've almost completed the presentation. Your last set of tasks is to set up the presentation as a self-running slide show, so that it will run unattended.

Session 5.1 QUICK CHECK

1. Give two methods for saving a PowerPoint slide into another program.

2. If the ClipArt Gallery on your computer doesn't have some picture, motion, or sound clips that you want, where would you get additional clips?

3. True or False: While a sound clip associated with a slide is playing, PowerPoint can proceed with the animations of that slide.

4. True or False: PowerPoint provides a facility for omitting some background objects while displaying other background objects.

5. True or False: If you add several objects to a slide and want to animate them one at a time, they will always animate in the same order in which you added them.

6. Explain in general terms how you would set up a slide to play a CD music track.

SESSION 5.2

In this session, you'll set up the presentation to be self-running. You'll also see how to draw diagrams and illustrations using PowerPoint and other software, and how to use PowerPoint to label graphics. You'll then learn how to use digital photographs—those you scanned from photographic prints, or those you took using a digital camera—in your PowerPoint presentations, and how to edit the digital images and modify their size and compression level.

Setting Up a Self-Running Presentation

According to Enrique's instructions, you will set up the presentation as a self-running presentation. This often includes one or more of the following:

- **Automatic timing of slides:** You'll set up automatic timing in this section.
- **Manual timing:** This allows users to view the slide show at their own pace. In your slide show, users can still use the action buttons to move to a previous or subsequent slide without waiting for the automatic timing.
- **Hyperlinks:** The action buttons and other hyperlinks that you've already applied will allow users to speed up or change the order of viewing, but you'll set up the slide show so that if users don't use the action buttons, the slide show will proceed automatically.
- **Narration:** You've already added narration to some of the slides.
- **Kiosk browsing:** You'll set up the slide show for browsing at a kiosk, and automatic looping.

So regarding the things typically involved in a self-running presentation, the only items you have left to add are the automatic timing and kiosk browsing. But before applying those things, you'll also want to add slide transitions and animations of bulleted items. You'll add the transitions and text animations now, and then later add the automatic timing and kiosk browsing.

To add transitions and text animations:

1. Click the **Slide Sorter View** button to get into Slide Sorter View.

2. Select all the slides except the first one by clicking the second slide, holding down the **Shift** key, and clicking the last slide.

3. Click the **Slide Transition Effects** list arrow on the Slide Sorter toolbar, and click **Dissolve**.

4. Deselect the selected slides, select Slides 3 to 5 and 7 to 10 (the ones with bulleted lists), click the **Present Animation** list arrow, and click **Fly From Right**. See Figure 5–18.

| Figure 5-18 | SLIDES WITH TRANSITION EFFECTS AND PRESET ANIMATIONS |

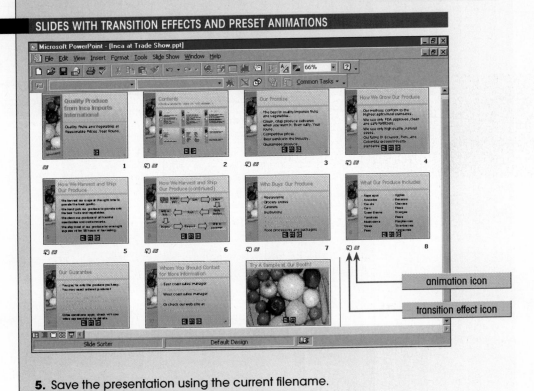

5. Save the presentation using the current filename.

Now when the trade show attendees run the slide show, they'll see transitions between slides, and each bulleted item will appear on the screen one at a time.

Rehearsing and Recording the Slide Timing

PowerPoint will keep track of the time you spend on each slide as you rehearse the presentation, and then allow you to set those times for automatic timing of a self-running slide show. You'll determine the timing now.

To determine timing of slides for a self-running slide show:

1. Make sure you're still in Slide Sorter View, select Slide 1, and then click **Rehearse Timings** button. PowerPoint automatically starts the slide show.

2. Read and look over each slide in the presentation, taking the amount of time

that you think an attendee will view each slide or bulleted item. Use the space-bar to advance from one bulleted item to the next, and from one slide to the next, according to your desired timing of each item. Don't use the action buttons. You should move along at a speed for moderately slow readers, but if you move too slowly, your viewers will become bored, or might wonder if the slide show is working properly.

3. When you're through all the slides, PowerPoint asks if you want to save the timing; click the **Yes** button. PowerPoint then saves the timing and displays the time on each miniature slide in Slide Sorter View. See Figure 5-19.

Figure 5-19

SLIDES WITH RECORDED DISPLAY TIMES

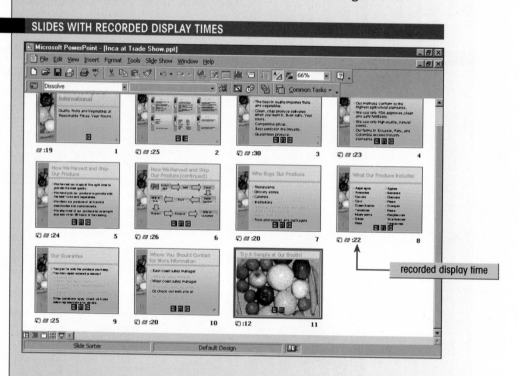

recorded display time

TROUBLE? If the times you selected are significantly different from those shown in Figure 5-19, you might want to adjust the times. To do so manually, select the desired slide in Slide Sorter View, click the Slide Transition button on the far left side of the Slide Sorter toolbar, and change the time setting under Automatically after.

4. Run the slide show to check the animation and timing. If you feel that a slide stays on the screen for too much or too little time, fix the delay time. As you go through the slide show, you notice that on Slide 8 the right column animates before the left column. You'll correct that problem now.

5. In Normal View, go to Slide 8, click **Slide Show** on the menu bar, click **Custom Animation**, click the **Order & Timing** tab, and then move **Text 2** so it's above Text 3.

6. Click the **Preview** button to ensure that the order of animation is correct, and then click the **OK** button.

7. Save the presentation using the current filename.

Applying Kiosk Browsing

The browse-at-a-kiosk feature in PowerPoint allows you to set up a presentation to be self-running—the slides and the animation proceed without human intervention through the entire presentation, and then continue by looping back to the beginning of the presentation. You'll now set up the trade show presentation for kiosk browsing.

> *To set up the presentation for browse at a kiosk:*
>
> **1.** Click **Slide Show** on the menu bar, and click **Set Up Show** to display the Set Up Show dialog box.
>
> **2.** In the Show type section of the dialog box, click the **Browsed at a kiosk (full screen)** option button, and then click the **OK** button.
>
> **3.** Save the presentation using the current filename.

Now when you run the slide show, it will continue to run until someone presses the Esc key. Each slide and bulleted list item will proceed one after another according to the automatic timing that you set up earlier. The use of the keyboard to navigate through the slide show is disabled, but those who view the slide show can still use the action buttons and other hyperlinks.

Drawing **and Modifying Diagrams and Illustrations**

You're already familiar with the PowerPoint drawing tools. For example, Enrique used the Block Arrows (types of AutoShapes) and text boxes (with borders and gradient fills) to create the diagram in Slide 6 of your presentation. If you want more sophisticated diagrams or illustrations, however, you might have to use a more sophisticated drawing software package. The most popular high-end drawing software includes Adobe Illustrator and Corel Draw. Because this type of software is complex and difficult to learn, it's meant primarily for skilled artists and draftspersons. Other people, with moderate artistic ability, however, might also find sophisticated illustration software useful in creating complex illustrations.

As an example of how illustration software is helpful, Enrique wants you to add a new slide with a map of the locations of Inca Imports' facilities in Latin America, including the types of fruits and vegetables produced at each site. Fortunately, one Inca Imports employee is an artist and was able to combine clip art, digital images, and software drawing tools to produce an attractive map, now saved in JPEG format. The results are shown in Figure 5–20.

Figure 5-20	DIAGRAM DRAWN WITH ILLUSTRATION SOFTWARE

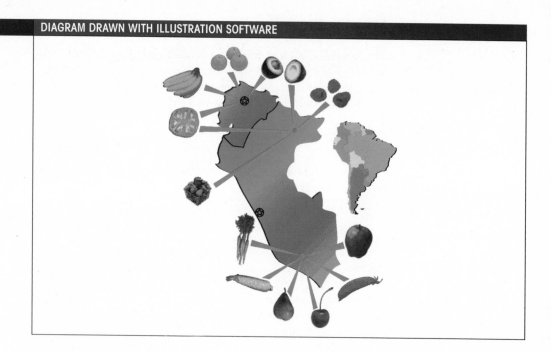

You'll import this drawing into PowerPoint, and then label the drawing using PowerPoint drawing tools.

To insert a graphic produced with illustration software:

1. Click Slide 8, select **Normal View**, click the **New Slide** button 🗔 on the Standard toolbar, click the **Title Only** AutoLayout, click the **OK** button, click the slide title placeholder, and type **Our Farm Locations in South America**. The new Slide 9 and its title are now part of the presentation.

2. Click **Insert** on the menu bar, point to **Picture**, click **From File**, change the directory location (if necessary) to the Tutorial.05 Tutorial folder on your Data Disk, click **ProdMap** (the produce map created using illustration software), and click the **Insert** button. The picture of the produce map appears in the slide. You'll now want to remove the white background on the graphic.

3. Make sure the graphic is still selected, and that the Picture toolbar appears on the screen. If it doesn't, click **View**, point to **Toolbars**, and click **Picture**.

4. Click the **Set Transparent Color** button 🖉 on the Picture toolbar, and then click anywhere in the white area of the produce map graphic. The white background disappears so that the picture blends better with the slide background.

   TROUBLE? If the color of the map becomes distorted when you apply the Set Transparent Color tool, don't worry. The picture will appear properly in Slide Show View.

5. Resize and position the map so that it appears as shown in Figure 5–21.

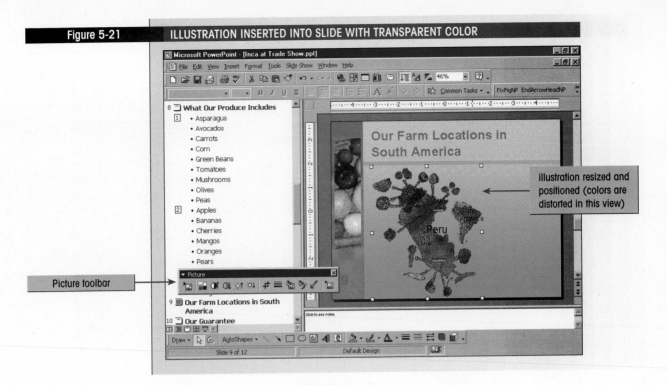

Figure 5-21 — ILLUSTRATION INSERTED INTO SLIDE WITH TRANSPARENT COLOR

You've now inserted the illustration into the new slide. Now you'll want to create some labels using the Text Box and Line features on PowerPoint's Drawing toolbar.

To add labels to the illustration:

1. Click the **Text Box** button 📄 on the Drawing toolbar, click the pointer ↓ near the middle of the map of Peru (the larger, green-to-orange map on the left), and type **Peru**.

2. Make sure the font size is **32** and the font style is **Arial**.

3. Add other text to the map and adjust its font, font size, and location, as shown in Figure 5–22. (You will need to re-select the text box tool for each.) All text should be in Arial font. The font size of "South America" is 20 points, "Ecuador" is 16 points, "Lima" is 14 points, and "Quito," "Iquitos," and "Arequipa" are 12 points.

Figure 5-22   ILLUSTRATION LABELED USING POWERPOINT DRAWING TOOLS

TROUBLE? If you're having trouble seeing and positioning the text, click the Zoom list arrow and set the Zoom value to 200%.

4. Click the **Line** button on the Drawing toolbar, and then draw a straight line from Peru on the small South American map to the word Peru on the large map, as shown in Figure 5–22.

5. With the line still selected, click the **Line Style** button on the Drawing toolbar, and click the **1½ pt** line. If necessary, click the **Line Color** button and set the line color to black. The slide is almost complete; you just have to add action buttons to it.

6. Go back to Slide 8, select the three action buttons at the bottom of the screen and copy them. Go to Slide 9, paste the action buttons onto the screen, and then drag the buttons to the right so that they aren't on top of the produce map graphic.

7. Switch to **Slide Sorter View**, add the **Dissolve** transition to the new Slide 9, click the **Slide Transition** button, set the Automatically after to **15** seconds, and click the **Apply** button.

8. Save your presentation using the current filename.

This completes the new Slide 9. The graphics on Slides 6 and 9 demonstrate the power of combining illustration software, clip art, digital photographs, PowerPoint drawing tools, and animation effects to make a complete illustration.

Creating and Modifying Digital Photographs

Digital photographs—pictures created by scanning photographic prints or taken using a digital camera—can be an important part of enhancing the quality of a PowerPoint presentation. For example, the background of your trade show presentation contains an image of fruits and vegetables. The following will help you understand how the picture was prepared for use in PowerPoint.

- The picture was taken using a digital camera and then uploaded to a computer. The photographer simply selected sample fruits and vegetables from his refrigerator, arranged them on a kitchen table, and took a flash picture of them.

- The resulting original digital photograph was 8×10 inches with a resolution of 1536×1024 pixels, for a total of 1.6 million pixels. (A **pixel** is a "picture element" or a little dot. A photograph is a rectangular array of these little dots. In a black-and-white photograph, the pixels are different shades of gray, from white to black. In color photographs, the pixels are different colors.)

- The original photograph was then edited using photo-editing software. The most popular high-end (most sophisticated) photo-editing software includes Adobe PhotoShop and Corel Photo-Paint. These are feature-laden programs designed for professional photographers and artists. Simpler (and cheaper!) photo-editing software includes Microsoft PhotoDraw, Adobe PhotoDeluxe, and many others.

- Editing the photograph included: (a) increasing the contrast and brightness, (b) applying an impressionist artistic effect (which the photo-editing software can do automatically), (c) changing the background color (the spaces between the fruits and vegetables) from white to green, (d) touching up some minor blemishes in the fruit, (e) copying (using a "clone tool") part of a carrot from one location to another in the picture, (f) rotating the picture 90 degrees, (g) cropping the picture so it's tall and skinny (see the uncropped version of the picture in the final slide of the trade show presentation), and (h) reducing the dimensions, and hence the total number of pixels, of the cropped picture.

- Finally the picture was saved and compressed (in JPEG format) so it would take up less disk space and load faster into PowerPoint.

You'll now add three other photographs to the presentation. Two of these were taken with a digital camera, but the other was taken with a regular 35mm single-lens reflex camera, developed at the local photo-processing store as a print, and then scanned into the computer. All three were extensively edited using photo-editing software. For example, one of the photographs is really a collage of 11 digital pictures, all merged into one photograph using photo-editing software. Here is a list of some other common photo-editing operations that help improve photographic quality of digital pictures:

- Removing "red eye," skin blemishes, shadows, distracting reflections, and unwanted background objects

- Enhancing the brightness, contrast, and saturation of a picture

- Enhancing specific parts of a photograph—whitening the teeth, changing the skin hue if it's too red or too yellow, adding a colorful background (or removing one), and moving an object from one place to another to improve composition

■ Changing the size of the picture. For example, the typical picture from a digital camera or scanner might be 8 × 10 or 4 × 6 inches, but you might want a long, narrow 2 × 8-inch picture.

■ Reducing the number of pixels, or increasing the compressions, so that the picture takes less disk space and loads faster. This is especially important for Web-page photographs, but can also be beneficial for PowerPoint presentation graphics.

■ Adding an artistic touch, such as those shown in Figure 5–23. A high-end photo-editing program supports dozens of such effects.

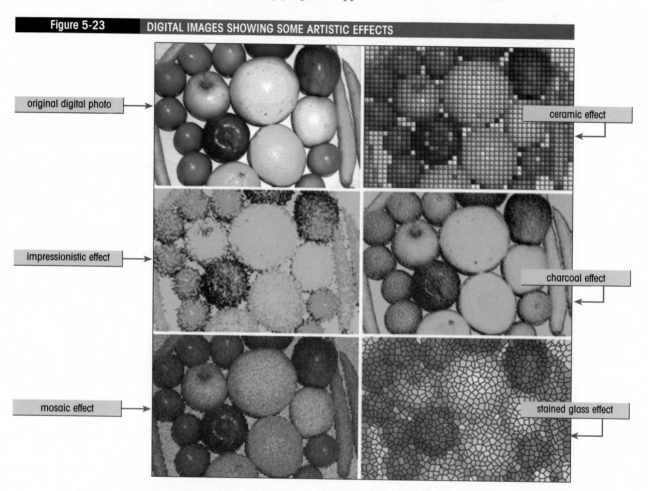

Figure 5-23 · DIGITAL IMAGES SHOWING SOME ARTISTIC EFFECTS

Let's add the three digital images to the presentation now.

To add digital images:

1. Go to Slide 7 in Normal View, and insert the image **Bldgs**, a collage of building photographs that represent businesses and institutions that might use produce supplied by Inca Imports International. Move the photo to the location shown in Figure 5-24.

Figure 5-24 SLIDE 7 WITH COLLAGE OF DIGITAL PHOTOGRAPHS

image made from digital photos

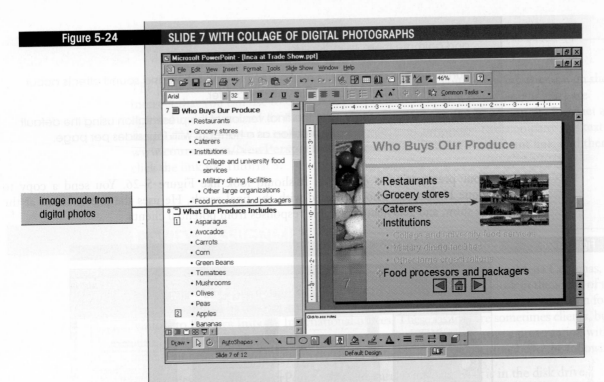

2. Go to Slide 11 and insert the photographs of the two sales managers. The filenames are **Tuesta** and **Arias**. Resize them so that they are both **1.5** inches in width, and then move them to the locations shown in Figure 5–25.

Figure 5-25 SLIDE 11 WITH DIGITAL PHOTOGRAPHS

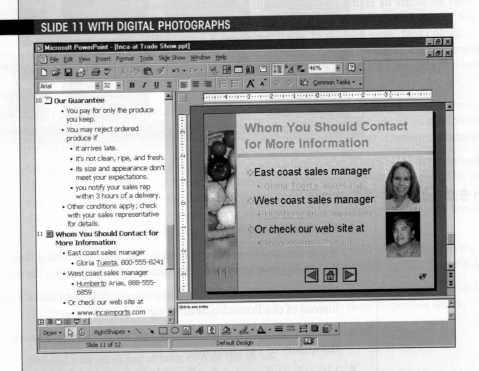

3. Open the **Custom Animation** dialog box (by selecting **Slide Show** on the menu bar and choosing Custom Animation), check **Picture frame 7** and **Picture frame 8** to animate them both, make sure the order of animation is such that Tuesta animates before Arias (but both animate after Text 2), set both photos to animate after **2** seconds, and select the **Spiral** animation effect.

Figure 6-4   SLIDE MASTER WITH LOGO AND RESIZED TITLE TEXT BOX

logo

resized title
text box

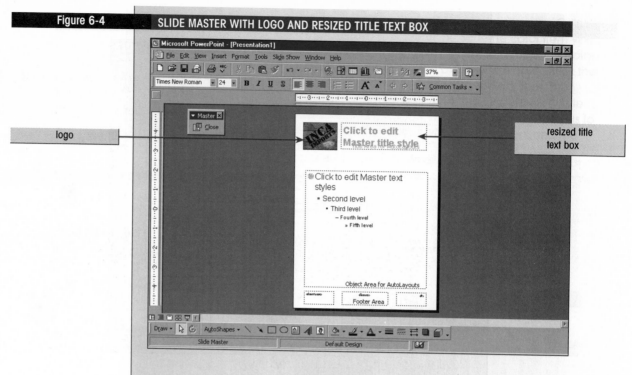

3. Using the **Drawing** toolbar, draw a rectangle that fits over the entire top part of the slide (logo and title) with some margin around the objects, fill the rectangle with yellow, and set the Line color to **No line**. See Figure 6–5 for the position and size of the rectangle, except that when you first draw it, the rectangle will cover the title text and the logo. Next you'll send the yellow rectangle behind the text and logo.

4. With the yellow rectangle still selected, click the **Draw** button on the Drawing toolbar, point to **Order**, and click **Send to Back**. Now you'll add a brown line.

5. Draw a line across the bottom of the rectangle, change the line color to brown, and change the thickness to **6 pt**.

6. Resize the **Master text** placeholder so that the top of it is closer to the brown line. The complete background objects should appear, as in Figure 6–5.

Figure 6-5 SLIDE MASTER AFTER ADDING BACKGROUND GRAPHICS AND RESIZING TEXT BOX

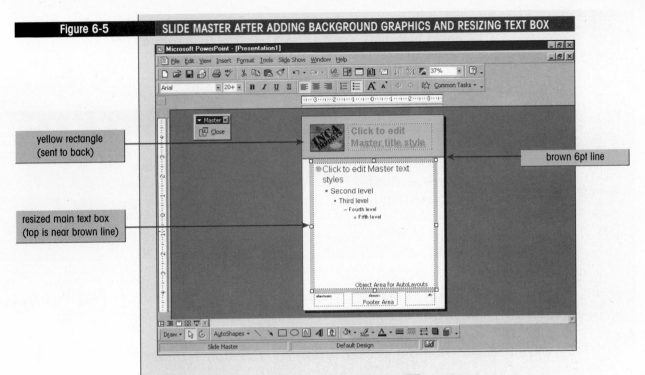

yellow rectangle (sent to back)

resized main text box (top is near brown line)

brown 6pt line

7. Click the **Insert New Title Master** button to create a Title Master.

8. On the Title Master slide, move the logo, change the size of the yellow rectangle, move the brown line to the bottom edge of the rectangle, change the size and position of the text placeholders, change the Master title style text to 48-point Arial bold, and change the title style alignment to **Center**, as shown in Figure 6–6. Your only task left on the Master slides is to make sure that the date, time, and footer are not displayed, and that the page number is displayed.

Figure 6-6 TITLE MASTER AFTER ADDING BACKGROUND ELEMENTS

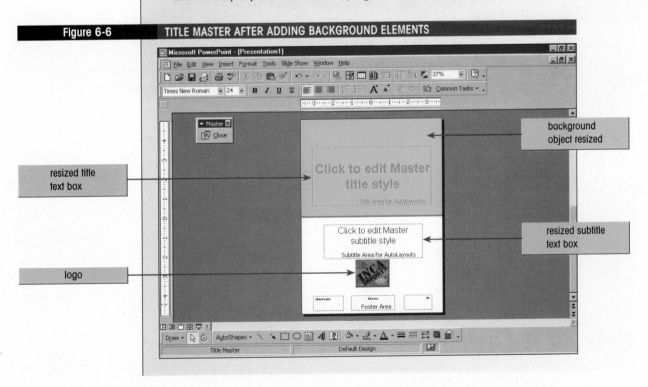

resized title text box

logo

background object resized

resized subtitle text box

9. Click **View** on the menu bar, click **Header and Footer**, click the **Slide number check box**, make sure the check boxes for Footer and for Date and time are unchecked, and then click the **Apply to All** button.

REFERENCE   WINDOW   **RW**

Changing the Order (Layer Level) of Objects
- Click the object that you want sent behind or in front of another object.
- Click the Draw button on the Drawing toolbar, and then point to Order.
- Click Bring to Front to place the object on the top (furthest front) level of objects, click Send to Back to place the object on the lowest (furthest back) level of objects, click Bring Forward to bring the object one level higher (forward), or click Send Backward to send the object one level lower (backward).

You have now completed the Master slides and are ready to save the PowerPoint file as a design template.

To save the presentation as a design template:

1. Return to Normal View, click **File** on the menu bar, click **Save As**, type **Inca Overheads Template** in the File name text box, and then change the Save as type list box to **Design Template (*.pot)**. You'll want to save this to your hard disk, a Zip disk, or some other high-capacity disk, because it might not fit on your Data Disk. Don't save it to the default Templates folder.

2. Locate the desired folder or your high-capacity disk in the Save in list box, and then click the **Save** button in the Save As dialog box. The template file is saved to your disk.

Now you should make sure that the colors and background objects will be readable and attractive if printed in grayscale.

3. Click the **Grayscale Preview** button 🖿 on the Standard toolbar. See Figure 6–7. The template design looks good in grayscale, so click 🖿 again to return to Normal (color) View.

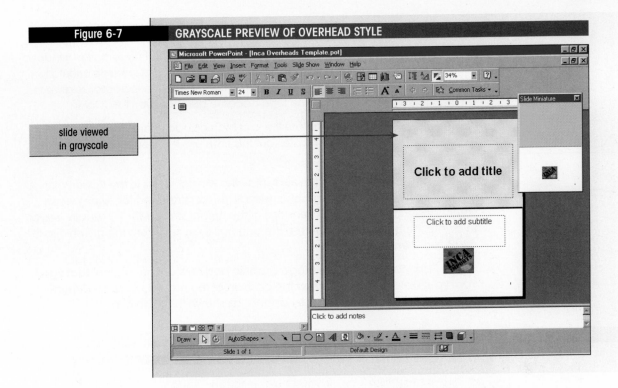

Figure 6-7 | **GRAYSCALE PREVIEW OF OVERHEAD STYLE**

slide viewed
in grayscale

You created a design template file for an overhead transparency presentation by changing the Page Setup to Overhead in Portrait orientation, and then specifying the color scheme and background objects. You also determined that the color scheme and background objects look good if you decide to print the overhead transparencies in grayscale. Next you'll follow essentially the same steps to create a design template for 35mm slides.

Creating a Design Template for 35mm Slides

The audience for Ana's presentation will be a small, professional group in a more formal setting than Richard's workshop, so Ana wants to use 35mm slides, the preferred medium of presentations at many formal professional meetings. She also knows that this won't be the last of her 35mm slide presentations, so she asks you to create a design template for Inca Imports professional slide presentations. To give Inca Imports a consistent image in all presentations given by its employees, you will use the same color scheme and logo as you did for the overhead transparency design, but the slide design will have some significant differences. For example, 35mm slides usually look better with white or light-colored text on a dark background. Moreover, you'll use a picture for the background instead of just color fills. And of course, you'll set the Page Setup for 35mm slides, in the normal Landscape orientation.

Setting up the Template for 35mm Slides

Just as you changed the Page Setup to Overheads for the overhead transparencies, you'll now change the Page Setup for 35mm slides.

To set up the design template for 35mm slides:

1. With the overhead transparency master still in the PowerPoint presentation window, click **File**, click **Page Setup**, set the page for **35mm Slides**, set the slide orientation to **Landscape**, and click the **OK** button. The width of the slide increases relative to its height. Don't worry now that the logo became distorted; you'll fix it later.

2. Save the file as a design template file to a high-capacity disk, just as you did the overhead transparency master, but this time use the filename **Inca 35mm Slides Template**.

3. Shift-click the **Slide View** button to display the Master slides in the PowerPoint window. As noted, the logo graphic was distorted (stretched too wide) when you changed the relative dimensions of the height and width. It's usually easier to delete the graphic and reinsert the original, than to restore the graphic to its original dimensions.

4. On the Title Master, delete the logo graphic and reinsert the original **IncLogo2** from your Data Disk. Then adjust the position of the graphic and the dimensions of the placeholders so they appear as shown in Figure 6–8.

| Figure 6-8 | TITLE MASTER SLIDE WITH MODIFIED BACKGROUND OBJECTS |

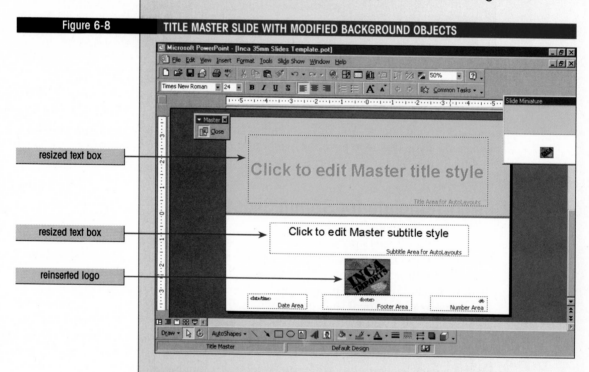

5. Display the Slide Master by scrolling up the vertical scroll bar, delete the logo graphic and reinsert the original from your Data Disk, just as you did on the Title Master. Then adjust the position of the graphics and the dimensions of the placeholders so they appear as shown in Figure 6–9. Notice that the title placeholder and the main text placeholder have to be widened, the text placeholder needs to be shortened slightly, the yellow rectangle has to be taller, and the brown line has to move down.

Figure 6-9 | SLIDE MASTER AFTER ADDING NEW BULLETS AND ADJUSTING MAIN TEXT BOX SIZE

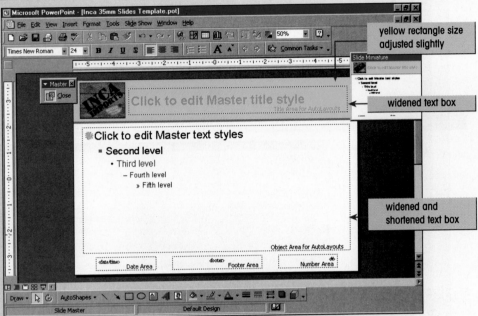

6. Delete the yellow rectangle background object at the top of both the Title Master and the Slide Master. Then, because you're going to add a dark background, you'll change the font colors.

7. Change the font color of the title text on both the title and master document to yellow, and change the subtitle text of the Title Master and the main (bulleted-list) text of the Slide Master from black to white. When you do this, you won't be able to read the placeholder text.

8. Save the presentation.

You're now ready to add the dark background picture.

Adding a Picture Background to the Master Slides

Up until now, you created presentations with plain white, plain colored, or gradient-fill backgrounds, but now you'll use a picture as the background. The picture file that you'll use is a digital photograph of produce (fruits and vegetables), similar to those you saw in the previous tutorial, except this photograph was darkened using photo-editing software.

To add a picture background:

1. With either the Title Master or Slide Master in the PowerPoint presentation window, click **Format** on the menu bar, and then click **Background**. The familiar Background dialog box appears on the screen.

2. Click the **Background Fill** list arrow, click **Fill Effects**, and then click the **Picture** tab. This tab on the dialog box allows you to select a picture, in this case an edited digital photograph, as the background to the slide.

3. Click the **Select Picture** button, and, if necessary, change the Look in location to **Tutorial** in the Tutorial.06 folder on your Data Disk, select the picture file **IncaBkGr**, and click the **Insert** button.

4. Click the **OK** button on the Fill Effects dialog box, and click the **Apply to All** button on the Background dialog box. This causes the picture to be the background for both the Title Master and the Slide Master. When you view the Slide Master, it will appear like Figure 6–10.

Figure 6-10   SLIDE MASTER AFTER ADDING BACKGROUND PICTURE

As you can see, the slide number is not visible because the text is black on a dark background. Instead of changing the font to white or a light color, you'll simply remove the page numbering, which isn't as important in a slide presentation as in an overhead transparency presentation. Slide numbers are not typically included because it's easier to write page numbers on a slide frame (the casing around the image—not seen by the audience) than on transparency film, and because it's easier to keep slides in order once you place them in a slide carousel. This also gives you the flexibility of reusing slides in different presentations because they can be expensive and time-consuming to produce.

5. Click **View** on the menu bar, click **Header and Footer**, and click the **Slide number** check box to deselect it.

6. Click the **Apply to All** button to remove the page number from both the Slide Master and the Title Master.

7. Click the **Normal View** button 🖳 and save the template file using the current filename (**Inca 35mm Slides Template**) and location. See Figure 6–11.

Figure 6-11   **TITLE MASTER OF 35MM SLIDE TEMPLATE**

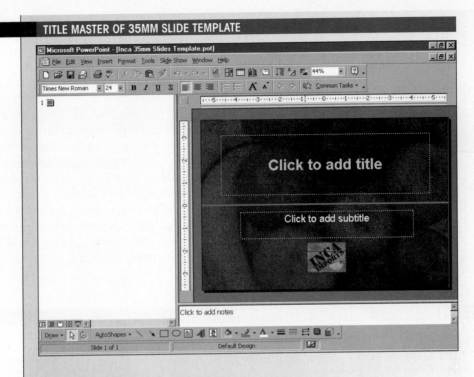

8. Close the presentation, but leave PowerPoint open.

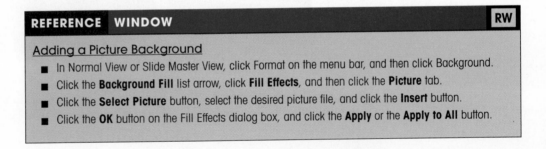

REFERENCE WINDOW   **RW**

Adding a Picture Background
- In Normal View or Slide Master View, click Format on the menu bar, and then click Background.
- Click the **Background Fill** list arrow, click **Fill Effects**, and then click the **Picture** tab.
- Click the **Select Picture** button, select the desired picture file, and click the **Insert** button.
- Click the **OK** button on the Fill Effects dialog box, and click the **Apply** or the **Apply to All** button.

In this design template, you used a picture background. Before using a picture background in your other presentations, keep in mind the following:

- Make sure the picture is very light overall (for use with dark-colored text) or very dark (for use with light-colored text). If you use a picture with normal colors (usually the case in correctly exposed digital photographs), the text won't be legible.
- Make sure the picture is low contrast. If you use a picture with normal contrast, it will distract from the text.
- Make sure that even though the picture is low contrast, the viewers can still tell what the picture represents, without actually having to get information from the picture. In the case of your slide template, the viewers will see that the background represents produce, but they don't have to be able to distinguish, for example, between the apples and tomatoes.
- If you're not absolutely sure that a particular picture fulfills the above three criteria, don't use it. Instead, pick a solid-color, gradient, texture, or pattern background.

You asked Ana and Richard to check over your two design templates. They are pleased with the results and instruct you to go ahead and use them to make the overhead and 35mm presentations.

Making Overhead Transparencies

Richard has started to write the text and create the graphics for his overhead presentation. He wants you to apply your overhead transparency design template to the current version of his presentation, and then print the overheads. Before doing so, you have to make sure you purchase and use the right type of transparency film (in 8½ × 11-inch sheets). Carefully read the specifications on the package of transparency sheets before you purchase or print them. Make sure the package says that the film is designed specifically for the type of printer you have—laser printer or inkjet printer—because the two aren't interchangeable. See Figure 6–12. Furthermore, ordinary transparency film sheets designed for color felt-tip pens and markers are not acceptable for printers; the film melts inside the printer and doesn't properly hold printer ink.

Figure 6-12	SAMPLES OF THE TWO TYPES OF TRANSPARENCY FILM

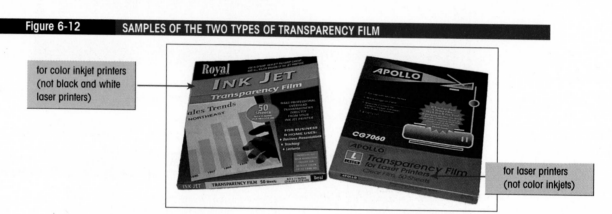

for color inkjet printers (not black and white laser printers)

for laser printers (not color inkjets)

Now you'll apply the overhead transparency design template to Richard's presentation, which he has already prepared using a blank (default) design template.

To apply the overhead transparency design template to a presentation:

1. Open the presentation file **IncaOver** located in the Tutorial.06 Tutorial folder on your Data Disk. You should now see the title slide, "Better Nutrition for a Healthier World."

2. Click the **Common Tasks** button on the Formatting toolbar, and click **Apply Design Template**.

3. Change the Look in location to the Tutorial.06 Tutorial folder where you saved the design templates, click the template filename **Inca Overheads Template**, and click the **Apply** button on the dialog box. The first overhead with the proper design appears in the Slide Pane. To see all the slides at once, go to **Slide Sorter View**. See Figure 6–13.

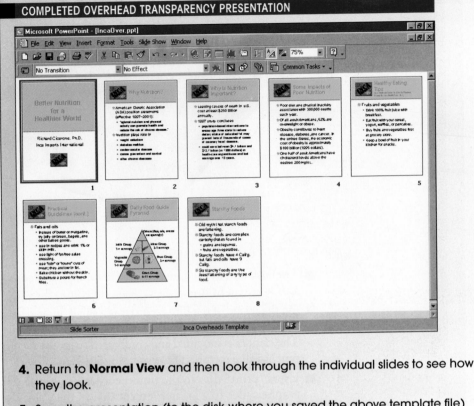

Figure 6-13   COMPLETED OVERHEAD TRANSPARENCY PRESENTATION

4. Return to **Normal View** and then look through the individual slides to see how they look.

5. Save the presentation (to the disk where you saved the above template file) using the new filename **Inca Overheads Workshop**.

6. Print the presentation on normal paper as handouts with four slides per page.

7. Close the presentation, but leave PowerPoint open.

Richard likes the look of his presentation overheads. He will complete all the slides in the presentation, and then print the presentation on color inkjet transparency film. On the other hand, he might decide to save some time and expense and print the presentation on black-and-white transparency film in grayscale using his laser printer. Either way, he has a professional and consistent look to his presentation overheads.

Using a Film Recorder to Prepare 35mm Slides

A **film recorder** is an instrument that takes pictures of computer graphics files, including PowerPoint presentations, using 35mm slide film. See Figure 6–14.

Figure 6-14   FILM RECORDER

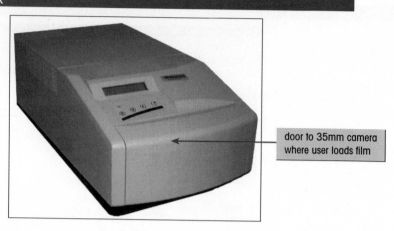

door to 35mm camera
where user loads film

The instrument works as follows:

- The instrument is connected to a computer and configured on the computer as if it were a printer.

- On the inside of the film recorder is a small, high-resolution monitor and a 35mm camera. The user loads regular 35mm color slide film into the camera. The camera is mounted and configured (with the proper focus and exposure time) to take pictures of the monitor inside the film recorder.

- Users "print" files to the film recorder, exactly as if they had printed the graphics files to a printer, except that in the Print dialog box, they set the film recorder as the name of the "printer." The film recorder then automatically takes pictures of the "printed" files.

- After the film recorder takes the pictures of the file, the user unloads the film and takes it to a photo processor for developing and mounting, just as you would pictures from any other camera.

For example, Ana will take the PowerPoint presentation that you helped her prepare, load it onto the computer to which the film recorder has been connected and installed, load the 35mm film into the film recorder camera, "print" the presentation to the film recorder, and take the film to a photo processor for developing and mounting.

You'll now apply your 35mm slide template to Ana's presentation file.

To apply the 35mm slide design template to a presentation:

1. Open the presentation file titled **Inca35mm** from the Tutorial.06 Tutorial folder on the Data Disk using the same method that you used to apply the overhead template.

2. Apply the design template **Inca 35mm Slides Template** located on your Data Disk.

3. Go through the presentation slide by slide, making sure that all the text and graphics are properly formatted and legible.

4. View the presentation in **Slide Sorter View** to see all the slides at once. See Figure 6-15.

COMPLETED 35MM SLIDE PRESENTATION

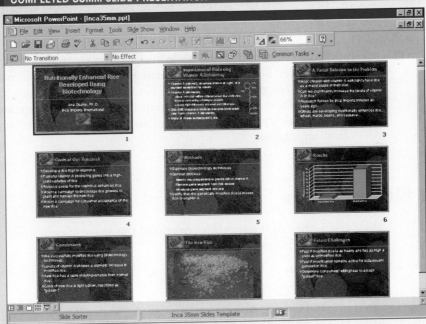

5. Return to **Normal View**, save the presentation as **Inca 35mm Slide Presentation** to the high-capacity disk where you saved the other files in this tutorial.

6. Print the presentation as handouts with four slides per page.

7. If desired, close PowerPoint.

When you apply a design template to an existing presentation, keep in mind that you often have to make one or more of the following modifications:

- Recolor or select different clip art, digital photographs, and other imported graphics, so that they match the design template color scheme. In the case of Ana's presentation, the chemical structure of vitamin A on Slide 2 was already yellow, which made it visible with the dark background of the new design template, but often such graphics are black, or other dark colors on a white background, so that when you change the background color, the graphic is hard to see.

- Reload or resize the imported graphics. This is essential if the relative dimensions of the new design are significantly different from the old design. You saw this when you converted the overhead transparency template to the 35mm slide template; you originally imported the new Inca Imports logo with the pages set up in Landscape orientation, and then the graphics became distorted when you applied the design template that had Portrait orientation. In that case, you simply reloaded the logo, rather than trying to resize it.

- Recolor organization charts, data charts, graphs, and other graphic objects created in PowerPoint, so that these objects are visible. For example, in Ana's 35mm slide presentation, she already modified the colors of the chart in Slide 6 so they would match the dark picture background and color scheme of your design template. If Ana had not done this, you would have had to do the changes yourself to make the chart legible.

■ Resize text boxes or change font sizes. When the presentation undergoes a font change (in size and style), sometimes the font doesn't fit properly, or the hard returns are in the wrong place. Fortunately, all the text fit properly when you applied the 35mm design template to Ana's original presentation.

You give the Inca 35mm Slide Presentation file to Ana, who uses a film recorder to make 35mm slides. She could also send the PowerPoint presentation to a service bureau (a company that can print 35mm slides, banners, posters, and other types of media), which can convert a PowerPoint file into 35mm slides. Service bureaus are located in almost all major cities in the United States, and online service bureaus, such as Genigraphics, are available from anywhere.

Session 6.1 QUICK CHECK

1. List four advantages overhead transparencies have over 35mm slides, and one disadvantage.

2. True or False: It's easy to print overheads in grayscale even when the presentation was designed in color.

3. Give two reasons why you usually want to print overhead transparency film with a white (blank) background.

4. In general terms, explain how you would use a digital photograph as a slide background.

5. What are two attributes of a good background picture for slides with text?

6. What is a film recorder and how does it work?

SESSION 6.2

In this session you'll create two poster presentations, one made up of a banner and individual pages, and another to be printed on one large 6 × 4-foot poster sheet of paper. You'll also create a presentation for the World Wide Web, with customized and animated action buttons.

Creating a Poster Presentation

A **poster presentation** is generally a presentation given at a professional meeting in which the information is formatted as a poster, or in the space of a poster. The poster size is generally about 6 × 4 feet in Landscape orientation. Often the presenters or authors stand by their mounted poster at a designated time and place—during the so-called "poster session" of the conference—to answer questions, pass out business cards, and sometimes distribute hand outs. See Figure 6–16.

| Figure 6-16 | EXAMPLE POSTER PRESENTATIONS |

single-page poster
presentation

mulitple-page poster
presentation

Poster sessions are a popular method of presentation at academic and professional conferences in science, engineering, social sciences, education, and humanities.

For example, after giving her presentation in oral form, Ana Tuesta was invited to give a poster presentation at the AAFB conference so that she had more time to present ideas and answer questions in a less formal setting. She now asks you to help her prepare a PowerPoint poster presentation.

PowerPoint poster presentations can be formatted in two ways: as a **multiple-page poster** (with the title slide and each of the information slides printed on separate sheets of paper) or as a **single-page poster** with multiple frames (or slides) on one large printout. Both types of presentations are shown in Figure 6–16. Ana asks you to prepare both formats so that she can choose which she wants to use for her presentation.

Creating a Multiple-Page Poster Presentation

You'll start by preparing a multiple-page poster. For example, Figure 6–17 shows a scientist at the AAFB conference standing by his multiple-page poster during the poster session of the conference. The poster includes the title printed as a banner, and each of the presentation slides printed on a separate sheet of paper. As in the case shown in Figure 6–17, you'll set up the pages in Landscape orientation, but you can also use Portrait orientation.

7. Click the **Slide View** button [img] on the View toolbar to switch to Slide View, and edit the subtitle so all the text is on one line. You'll have to insert a comma and space after "Ph.D." to separate the author's title from the company name.

8. Save the presentation using the default name.

You're now ready to insert a miniature copy of the all the slides onto this one slide.

To copy slides from the multiple-page poster presentation to the single-page poster presentation:

1. Keeping the Inca Single-Page Poster file in the PowerPoint presentation window, open **Inca Multiple-Page Poster**. Now you'll copy Slides 2 through 9 from this presentation to the other one.

2. Switch to **Slide Sorter View** of Inca Multiple-Page Poster, select Slide 2, copy it to the Windows clipboard by pressing the **Ctrl+C** keys. Switch to **Inca Single-Page Poster** in Normal View, and paste the slide onto the single slide by pressing the **Ctrl+V** keys.

3. Make sure the Picture toolbar is open (if it isn't, right-click the slide you just copied, and click **Show Picture Toolbar**), click the **Format Object** button [img] on the Picture toolbar, click the **Size** tab, make sure the **Lock aspect ratio** check box is checked, and change the **Width** to **1.25** inches.

   Now you'll draw a brown border around the slide miniature to make it stand out as a separate slide.

4. Click the **Colors and Lines** tab on the Format Object dialog box, change the line color to brown, click the **OK** button, and then move the slide to the position of the first slide in Figure 6–24.

| Figure 6-24 | COMPLETED SINGLE-PAGE POSTER PRESENTATION |

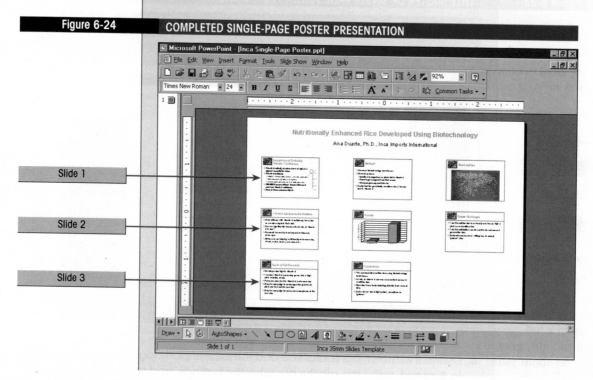

5. Repeat the above procedure to copy, paste, resize, and draw a border around the other seven slides in the slide show, until your presentation window in Slide View looks like Figure 6–24. You have completed the single-page poster presentation. You can now save it and print a copy.

6. Save the presentation using the default filename **Inca Single-Page Poster** to your hard disk, to a Zip disk, or to some other high-capacity storage medium. This is necessary because the presentation file is too big to store on a floppy disk.

7. Print a copy of the poster on an 8.5 × 11-inch sheet of paper, either in color or grayscale.

8. Close both files in the PowerPoint presentation window, but leave PowerPoint open.

You now give a copy of both poster presentation files to Ana. She decides she wants a single-page poster presentation, so she takes the file to a local service bureau, where she has it printed on a 6 × 4-foot sheet of glossy poster paper. The result is clear, easy-to-read, attractive, and professional. Ana successfully uses the poster during her presentation at the poster session of the AAFB conference.

Publishing a Web Presentation with Custom Action Buttons

You're probably already familiar with the concept of publishing a PowerPoint presentation on the Web. After you complete a PowerPoint presentation, you can save it as an HTML file—a Web-browser readable file.

After Ana makes her presentation on the biotechnologically modified rice, she decides she will post the presentation on the Inca Imports company Web site. She asks you to add navigation (action) buttons to the slides, but instead of using PowerPoint's built-in action buttons, she wants you to use customized ones to give the presentation a more unique look. Furthermore, she wants you to set the action buttons to animate and make a sound when the user passes the pointer over them.

You ask the company artist to create two small JPEG files, using a fruit (like a pear) as a pointer to go to the previous or next slide. The artist has created the two JPEG files using a photo-imaging program, so you're now ready to import them into the slide show, resize the custom action buttons, and hyperlink them to the previous or next slide. Then when you publish the presentation as a Web page, you'll specify that you want to use your own navigation buttons, not the ones normally created by PowerPoint.

To add custom action buttons to the slides:

1. Open the file **Inca 35mm Slide Presentation**, which you created earlier and saved to your Data Disk.

2. On Slide 1, insert the graphics (JPEG) file **NextBtn** (located in the Tutorial.05 Tutorial folder), resize it so that its width is exactly **1.5** inches (while maintaining the aspect ratio), and move it to the lower- right corner of the slide. See Figure 6–25.

Figure 6-25   SLIDE 1 WITH CUSTOM ACTION BUTTON

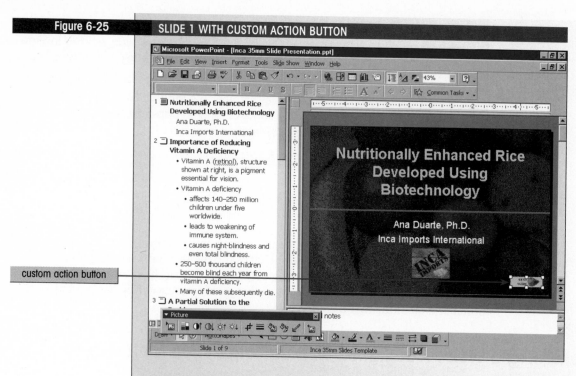

custom action button

3. With the graphic still selected, click the **Insert Hyperlink** button , click the **Place in This Document** icon in the **Link to** section of the dialog box, select **Next Slide** (you'll have to scroll up to see it) in the **Select a place in this document** section of the dialog box, and click the **OK** button. The graphic is now an action button, which, during a slide show or Web presentation, will cause the presentation to advance to the next slide. You'll add one more feature to the customized action button: make it become highlighted and make a sound when the user passes the pointer over it.

4. If necessary, select the custom action button, click **Slide Show** on the menu bar, click **Action Settings** to display the Action Settings dialog box, and click the **Mouse Over** tab. See Figure 6-26.

Figure 6-26   ACTION SETTINGS DIALOG BOX FOR CUSTOM ACTION BUTTONS

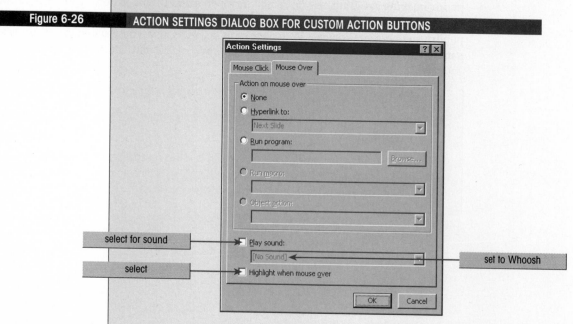

select for sound

select

set to Whoosh

5. Click the **Highlight when mouse over** check box, click the **Play sound** check box, click the **Play sound** list arrow, and click **Whoosh**. This becomes the sound effect when the user passes the pointer over the button.

6. Click the **OK** button, copy the custom action button to Slide 2, move the button closer to the center of the screen. Insert the JPEG file **PrevBtn**, resize it to a width of **1.5** inches (keeping the same aspect ratio), and move it to the left of the **Next Slide** custom action button. See Figure 6–27.

| Figure 6-27 | SLIDE 2 WITH BOTH CUSTOM ACTION BUTTONS |

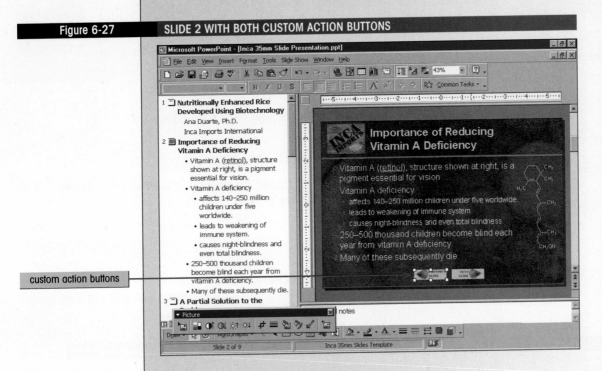

custom action buttons

7. Make this graphic an action button to go back to the previous slide, and add the **Mouse Over Action Settings** as you did for the other button.

8. Copy the two custom action buttons from Slide 2 to Slides 3 through 9, and then on Slide 9, change the **Next Slide** action button so it's hyperlinked to Slide 1. This causes the last slide to cycle back to the first slide of the presentation. Now all the slides have action buttons to move forward or backward in the presentation.

9. Go through the presentation in **Slide Show View** to make sure the action buttons work properly, and then save the presentation file to your Data Disk using the filename **Inca Web Presentation**.

REFERENCE WINDOW **RW**

Applying Mouse Over Action Settings to an Action Button

■ Select the Action button.

■ Click Slide Show on the menu bar, click Action Settings to display the Action Settings dialog box, and click the Mouse Over tab.

■ Click the Highlight when mouse over check box.

■ If desired, click the Play sound check box, click the Play sound list arrow, and select a sound—Whoosh.

■ If desired, click the Highlight when mouse over check box.

■ Click the OK button.

Now you're ready to publish this presentation as a Web page.

To publish the presentation as a Web page:

1. Click **File** on the menu bar, click **Save As**, change the Save as type from Presentation (*.ppt) to **Web Page (*.htm, *.html)**.

2. Rather than clicking Save at this point, click the **Publish** button on the Save As dialog box. This allows you to customize the Web page. The Publish as Web Page dialog box opens.

3. Deselect the **Display speaker notes** check box, and make sure all the other options are like those in Figure 6–28. (Note that your file location will vary from that shown here.)

| Figure 6-28 | PUBLISH AS WEB PAGE DIALOG BOX WITH DESIRED SETTINGS |

make sure this is deselected

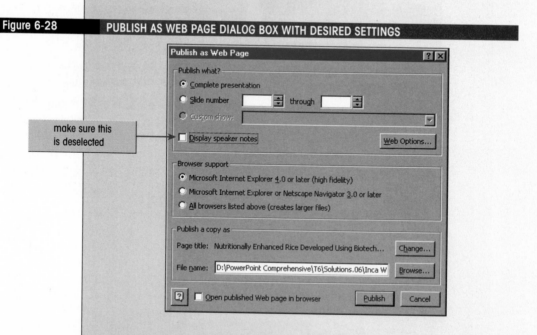

4. Click the **Web Options** button, and deselect the **Add slide navigation controls** so that PowerPoint doesn't create its own action buttons, and click the **Show slide animation while browsing** check box to select it. Those who view the Web page will see all the animation, just as they would when viewing the slide show in a presentation, and they will use your custom-animated navigation buttons.

5. Click the **OK** button on the Web Options dialog box, and then click the **Publish** button on the Publish as Web Page dialog box.

6. Close the presentation file, and then run your Web browser (if it didn't run automatically). The browser doesn't have to be connected to the Internet, because you'll open your Inca Web Presentation into the browser from the disk where you saved the files.

7. On your browser, click **File** on the menu bar, click **Open**, and then browse until you find the file **Inca Web Presentation** on your Data Disk, select it, and click the **Open** button. If necessary, click the **OK** button to complete the open operation. See Figure 6–29.

 Figure 6-29   **SLIDE 1 VIEWED IN A WEB BROWSER**

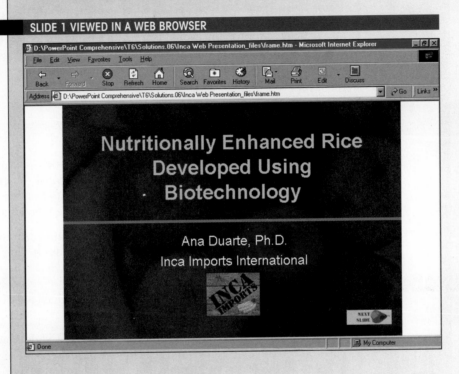

8. Click the **Next Slide** button to go to the next slide in the Web presentation, and then look through all the slides.

TROUBLE? If your animation of the action buttons doesn't work, don't worry. This type of animation often doesn't translate well to a Web page.

9. Close the Web browser, close the **Inca Web Presentation** file, and close PowerPoint.

Ana is pleased with your work in creating a Web version of her slide presentation. She gave the HTML file and accompanying folder to the Inca Imports network administrator for posting on the company Web page.

Richard and Ana thank you for all your help in making their presentations at the AAFB so successful.

Session 6.2 QUICK CHECK

1. What are the general steps required to print a banner prepared in PowerPoint?

2. List three instances when you might need to prepare a poster presentation.

3. What is the difference between a multiple-page poster presentation and a single-page poster presentation?

4. List one advantage and one disadvantage of a single-page poster over a multiple-page poster.

5. True or False: If you want action buttons to advance one slide forward or one slide back, you have to use the PowerPoint action buttons found on the Slide Show menu.

6. In general terms, how would you set up a hyperlink object (text or graphic) to become highlighted and make a sound when the user passes a pointer over it?

REVIEW ASSIGNMENTS

After Richard and Ana enjoyed success in their presentations at the meetings of the AAFB, they start to think about future presentations at professional conferences. They decide to make a joint presentation on genetically engineered pinto beans. After they create the text and graphics for the presentation, they ask you to do the following:

1. Start PowerPoint, open the file **ZincBean** from the Tutorial.05 Review folder on the Data Disk, and save the file as **Zinc-Rich Beans 35mm Slides** to your high-capacity disk.

2. Verify that the Page Setup for 35mm slides.

3. Go to Slide 7 and insert the picture file **PintoBns**, which is a digital photograph of the new pinto beans.

4. Add the logo file **IncLogo3** to the Title Master and Slide Master slides. Size and position it to look attractive and readable. Adjust the size and position of the text boxes so all the text is still legible. Set appropriate fonts, font colors, and font sizes.

5. Knowing the colors of the logo and the beans on Slide 6, set up an appropriate, coordinated color scheme for the presentation.

6. Add the background picture **BkgrDNA** to all the slides in the presentation.

7. Change the bullets of the first two levels of bullets to two different pictures that you get from the Clip Gallery. If you can't find picture bullets that you want, get some from the online Microsoft Clip Gallery Live.

8. Complete the presentation design by adding any other appropriate background objects, such as lines and squares. Be creative and tasteful.

9. Change the colors of the elements of the chart on Slide 6 to match the color scheme of the presentation.

10. Review all the slides in the presentation to make sure they are attractive and well-formatted.

11. Save the presentation using the current filename.

12. Print the presentation as handouts with four slides per page.

13. Delete all but the first slide in the presentation, delete the text on the first slide so it contains only the background objects, and save the presentation as a design template (*.pot) file to the Tutorial.06 Review folder on the Data Disk using the filename **Inca 35mm Bean Template**. Ana and Richard now have another choice for a design template for Inca Imports presentations.

14. Modify the template that you just saved so it works well for creating overhead transparencies. (For example, remove the background picture, set the background color to white, fix any distortions in the background objects, and change the Page Setup.)

15. Save this as a design template file using the new filename **Inca Overhead Bean Template**.

16. Open the presentation file **ZincBean** again.

17. Apply the Inca Overhead Bean Template to the presentation.

18. Go through the presentation one slide at a time to make sure all the text and graphics are readable, attractive, and well-formatted

19. Save the presentation as **Zinc-Rich Beans Overheads**.

20. Print the overhead transparency presentation as a handout with four slides per page.

CASE PROBLEMS

Case 1. Canyon Glen Park   Harvey McNaughton is superintendent of parks in Whistler, British Columbia, Canada, which is a town famous for its skiing, but which hosts numerous conferences and festivals during the summer. Locals and visitors alike take advantage of the city parks, including the largest one, Canyon Glen. This park has facilities for picnicking, volleyball, and softball, as well as a small amphitheatre. Harvey is also in charge of the Whistler jogging trail that passes through Canyon Glen. The jogging trail is 22 miles of paved path not only for jogging but also for walking, biking, and roller-skating (in-line skating). Harvey has been invited to give a presentation at the Annual Canadian Conference on Parks and Recreation and has asked you to help him prepare his presentation graphics. Harvey will give his presentation using 35mm slides, but he also wants you to create custom navigation (action) buttons for the presentation and publish it as a Web page on the Whistler Web site. Do the following:

1. Create a design template for 35mm slides, using the graphic file **BkgrTree** (located in the Tutorial.06 Cases folder of your Data Disk) as a picture background for all the slides.

2. Choose your color scheme based partly on the colors in the background picture and the colors in the other graphics you'll use, which are the JPEG files that begin with the word **Park** and which are located in the Tutorial.05 Cases folder. In other words, the color scheme should include greens, yellows, grays, and possibly other colors.

3. Use the JPEG file **ParkSign** as a logo that goes on all the slides.

4. On your slide masters, select appropriate, attractive, and readable fonts, font sizes, and font attributes, as well as appropriately sized and positioned text boxes.

Explore ▶ 5. Use the picture file **Bullet** (a picture of a stone at Canyon Glen) from the Tutorial.06 Cases folder to make bullets for all the level-one bulleted items in the presentation. *Hint:* As you carry out the normal method for inserting a picture as a bullet from the Clip Gallery, click the Insert Clip button, and then insert the desired picture. From then on, you can use that picture as a bullet in any presentation.

6. Select a normal round bullet, but color it gray, to serve as the level-two bullets.

7. If you want, apply any other background objects that you think would look attractive.

8. Save the presentation as a design (*.pot) template to your Data Disk using the filename **Canyon Glen Slide Template**, and close the file.

9. Open the file **ParkShow**, and save it as the presentation (*.ppt) file **Canyon Glen Slide Presentation**.

10. Apply the Canyon Glen Slide Template to the presentation.

11. Add the graphics files **ParkJog** (picture of the jogging trail), **ParkPic** (picture of one of the covered picnic areas), and **ParkRivr** (picture of the river that passes through the park) to the presentation—selecting the appropriate slide onto which each picture should be inserted.

12. Go through all the slides to make sure they are attractive and legible. Check to make sure the graphics don't overlap the text.

13. If necessary, adjust the colors of the organization chart so it is legible.

14. Save the 35mm slide presentation using the default filename (**Canyon Glen Slide Presentation**).

15. Print a copy of the presentation as a handout with four slides per page.

16. Prepare the presentation for publication as a Web page by adding custom navigation (action) buttons **NavNext** and **NavBack** to each of the slides.

17. Make the navigation buttons cyclical—the Back button on Slide 1 hyperlinks to the last slide, and the Next button on the last slide hyperlinks to Slide 1.

18. Set the custom navigation buttons to become highlighted and to make a sound when the pointer passes over them.

19. Save the file as a Web page using the filename **Canyon Glen Web Page**. Tell PowerPoint to omit putting in its own navigation objects.

20. Review the Web page in your Web browser. If you notice problems, fix them and then save the Web page again.

Case 2. Palm Computer for College Students The teacher in your Computer Applications class asks you to prepare a presentation on palm computers (for example, PalmPilot, Palm III, IV, or V, Visor, Visor Deluxe) for college students. The presentation should answer the questions: Who should buy a palm computer? Why should a student use a palm computer? What are some of the applications on a palm computer? What are the advantages? What are the disadvantages and inconveniences? Do the following:

1. Talk to students who have palm computers. Ask them the above questions. If you use one yourself, you can answer the questions. If you like, go into a palm computing chat room on the Internet, and ask the participants to provide information for your presentation.

2. Get on the Internet, do an Internet search for Web pages on palm computers, and gather information. Reviews of new palm products are good source of information on the pros and cons of palm computers.

3. Organize your presentation in PowerPoint overhead transparency format, 8.5 × 11 inches in size and Portrait orientation.

4. Include at least eight pages, one of which can be the title page.

5. If you like, use the five graphics files that start with "palm ...", located in the Tutorial.06 Cases folder of your Data Disk. You should include at least five pictures (photos, clip art, GIF animation files) in your presentation. You can get many pictures of models of palm computers from the Internet.

6. Use pictures for the level-one bullets on your bulleted list slides.

7. Design the presentation with a white background and with other colors that match the figures.

8. After you determine the color scheme, check to make sure the slides are still legible in grayscale.

9. Prepare, as desired, appropriate background objects, including a logo, if you have access to graphics software.

10. After completing the presentation, save it using the filename **Palm Multiple-Page Overhead**.

11. Change the format and layout of the presentation so that each slide is in Landscape orientation.

12. Go through each slide to make sure the graphics, background objects, text boxes, etc., are not distorted, but attractive and readable.

13. Copy all the individual slides to one large slide in preparation to make a single-page poster presentation.

14. On your single-page overhead presentation, don't include a separate title page, but rather make the title (and byline) as large-font headings at the top of the page.

15. Save the presentation using the filename **Palm Single-Page Overhead**.

16. Print the single-page overhead presentation on a single piece of 8.5 × 11-inch paper, unless your instructor tells you to print it on large, poster-sized paper.

Case 3. *Jayhawk Foreign-Language Institute* You recently accepted employment at the Jayhawk Foreign-Language Institute headquartered in Lawrence, Kansas. This company has on-site language-training institutes in six countries. Your task is to prepare a 35mm slide presentation and a single-page poster presentation on the language institute in Guadalajara, Mexico. Do the following:

1. Open the presentation file named **Jayhawk**, and save it to your disk using the filename **Jayhawk in Guadalajara**.

2. Set up and format the presentation for 8.5 × 11-inch Portrait overhead transparency film.

3. Using clip art and digital photographs, apply one or more pictures per slide. If your on-disk clip gallery doesn't have the appropriate pictures, download pictures from the online Microsoft Clip Gallery Live.

4. Include a picture of a jayhawk in the logo that should go on every slide.

5. Design the presentation with an attractive color scheme, logo, background objects, fonts, font size, and font colors.

6. Include at least one picture bullet for the bulleted lists.

7. Save the presentation using the default filename.

8. Print the presentation as a handout with four slides per page.

9. Using the same design and format, create an attractive, legible, single-page poster presentation.

10. Don't include the title slide as one of the slide panes, but rather prepare a title banner that spans the top of the single-page poster.

11. Save the poster presentation using the filename **Jayhawk Poster**.

12. Print the poster onto one regular sheet of 8.5 × 11-inch paper.

Case 4. Group Presentation on a Town or City   You and some of your fellow students have taken jobs as assistants to travel agents at a large local travel agency. The travel agents ask you to work together on preparing information that might be of interest to tourists about a town or city in the United States or abroad.

According to your teacher's instructions, you become part of a three to five person group that will collaborate on preparing a presentation on a town or city. None of the members of the group actually has to be from or live in that town or city, although it might be a good idea to select a location with which one of your group is familiar. You can get further information about the city from travel guides, tourist brochures, Web sites, encyclopedias, and personal visits, all of which are also sources of graphics for your presentation. Do the following:

1. Select a town or city for your presentation, and then get your teacher's approval. If your teacher allows you or instructs you to do so, you can select the city of San Francisco, California, for which your Data Disk contains four photographs. These photographs are JPEG files that begin with the letters "SF". **SFBridge** is a picture of the Golden Gate Bridge; **SFCblCar** is a picture of a cable car; **SFCtyHll** is a picture of San Francisco's City Hall; and **SFDwnTwn** is a picture of downtown San Francisco as viewed from the Twin Peaks area.

2. Gather information about your city and organize it into PowerPoint slides with titles and bulleted lists.

3. Include at least eight slides, not counting the title.

4. Create an original design template for your presentation. Design the template as a multiple-page poster presentation. You might want to design a group or course logo for the presentation. You'll want to use a color scheme that fits the flavor of the town or city on which you are reporting. (If you don't have a color printer, you can use a grayscale scheme, or a color scheme that produces attractive grayscale output.)

5. Include picture bullets in the presentation.

6. Save the design template using the filename **City Template**.

7. Include at least four pictures in your presentation, preferably photographs of your town or city.

Explore

8. Create a title banner to go with your poster presentation. *Hint:* If you don't have access to banner software or a service bureau, you can still print the banner as separate sheets of paper, and then cut and tape the pages together.

9. Save your complete presentation using the filename **City Overhead Presentation**.

10. Print each slide on a separate piece of paper. Mount each printed slide with colored construction paper to give it a colored border.

11. If your teacher instructs, hold a class poster session in which all the groups display their posters to the other class members.

INTERNET ASSIGNMENTS

The purpose of the Internet Assignments is to challenge you to find information on the Internet that you can use to create effective documents. The actual assignments are updated and maintained on the Course Technology Web site. Log on to the Internet and use your Web browser to go to the Student Online Companion to accompany this text at **www.course.com/NewPerspectives/office2000**. Click the PowerPoint link, and then click the link for Tutorial 6.

QUICK CHECK

Session 6.1

1. Advantages: (a) The room can stay lighter, (b) you can more easily face the audience, (c) most classrooms and conference rooms come equipped with overhead projectors, and (d) overhead projectors seem to be more reliable than 35mm slide projectors. Disadvantage: don't look as professional as 35mm slides.

2. True

3. cheaper (less ink), faster (less printing), and the presentation room stays lighter

4. Get to the Background dialog box, select Fill Effects, click Picture tab, and select a photograph file from the disk.

5. The background picture should be dark (if the text is light) or light (if the text is dark) and have low contrast.

6. A film record is a machine used to create 35mm slides. Specifically, the machine exposes the 35mm film, and then you have to develop the film. The film recorder works because it has a built-in camera and a monitor. The monitor displays the PowerPoint slide images, and the camera takes its picture.

Session 6.2

1. Set up the page for banners, and then take the PowerPoint file to a service bureau for printing to large sheets of paper.

2. (a) professional meetings, (b) academic meetings, (c) informal meetings to create poster advertisements

3. A multiple-page poster presentation includes many slide panes and a title banner on just one page, whereas a single-page poster presentation includes one printed page for each slide.

4. Advantages: easy to set up, looks professional. Disadvantages: expensive, takes longer to prepare, cumbersome to carry

5. False

6. Select the action button, open the Action Settings dialog box (from Slide Show on the menu bar), click the Mouse Over tab, and make your selections.

OBJECTIVES

In this case you will:

- Complete a Purpose and Outcomes Worksheet for your presentation

- Complete an Audience Analysis Worksheet

- Complete a Situation and Media Assessment Worksheet

- Create an attention-getting introduction, an advance organizer or overview, and a summary

- Complete a Focus and Organization Worksheet

- Complete a Presentation Visuals Worksheet

- Insert photographs acquired with a digital camera or scanner into your PowerPoint presentation

- Insert graphic, motion, and sound clips downloaded from the Online Microsoft Clip Gallery

- Complete a Presentation Delivery Worksheet

- Copy slides as miniatures to be included on another slide

GIVING A PRESENTATION OF LOCAL FOLKLORE

CASE

Family, Business, or Community Folklore

Folklore is the study of traditions of people, including those that are revealed in popular fiction, customs, and beliefs. Folklore includes myths, legends, stories, riddles, proverbs, nursery rhymes, popular ballads, cowboy songs, and community customs. Folklore is more than entertainment; it tells us how groups of people, view the world, and helps us understand their traditions and history.

Your assignment is to prepare a presentation on one or more stories (or other types of folklore) from a family, business, community, or your school. According to your teacher's instructions, you should do this presentation on your own or as a group.

Here are some examples of the type of stories you might research and present:

- family stories from the George Hamilton family of Sugar City, Idaho. For example, George was traveling in his automobile along a back road near his hometown, when he saw a man whose car was disabled. He helped the man, who then asked George his name. When the man heard Hamilton, he replied, "Are you related to Grant Hamilton? Why, that good-for-nothing owes me $20." George immediately reached for his wallet and pulled out a $20 bill. "The good name of Hamilton is worth more than $20," he said as he handed the man the money.

- business (company) stories from Hewlett Packard. The company prides itself on doing things "the HP way"—meaning that HP has a certain culture, and that culture propagates because of company folklore. For example, when HP faced hard times and a probable 10% layoff, the company officers went to the employees and asked them to take a 10% salary cut and work nine of ten days; in return, they promised no layoffs. This story, known as the "9-day fortnight," became part of the company lore, and is often repeated. Such company folklore breeds employee loyalty.

- community stories from southwestern Utah (red rock desert country). For example, in about 1950, following a road repair, a motorcade of VIPs was traveling the newly paved roadway north of St. George. As a prank, some youth ignited tires and inner tubes inside one of the volcano cinder cones that dot the landscape in this rugged desert area. Because the burning materials were out of sight, the VIPs were frightened, thinking that the ancient volcano was about to erupt. They called in geologists from California before the prank was uncovered.

Do the following:

1. Talk to older family members, long-time company employees, long-time community residents, or alumni from your university. Ask them to tell you commonly told stories. In folklore terminology, the people who supply you with folklore stories are called **informants**.

2. Compile as much information as you can about your informants, including their places and dates of birth, where they were raised, their jobs, marital status (if relevant), religion (if relevant), hobbies, and possibly childhood memories. This information will help you better understand the significance of the folklore they provide.

3. After gathering the stories and the backgrounds of your informants, interpret these stories and reflect upon their significance. To begin, you might ask yourself (or your informants) the following questions: Who generally tells these stories? What are the personality characteristics of the teller? When and where are the stories told? Who is generally the audience for the stories? How does the audience receive these stories? Do they like them? Why? Do they know the stories already and participate in the telling? How are the stories told? (Try to get a feel for the storyteller's tone, dialect, and voice.) How does the informant feel about these stories? What values or cultural characteristics do the stories demonstrate or communicate?

4. Complete a Purpose and Outcomes Worksheet for the presentation.

5. Complete an Audience Analysis Worksheet. Keep in mind that your audience will probably be your classmates.

6. Complete a Situation and Media Assessment Worksheet.

7. Begin preparing a PowerPoint presentation on your folklore stories by creating bulleted lists and, if desired, other paragraphs. Leave space for appropriate graphics.

8. Plan the PowerPoint presentation to include at least eight slides, including the title slide, contents slide, and summary slide.

9. Create an appropriate attention-getting introduction for your presentation.

10. Complete a Focus and Organization Worksheet and organize the text in your presentation accordingly.

11. Create an advance organizer or overview in your PowerPoint presentation.

12. Include a summary recapping the key ideas in your presentation.

13. Using the Presentation Delivery Worksheet, decide on an appropriate presentation style for your presentation.

14. Complete a Presentation Visuals Worksheet. Include at least two pictures that you have acquired by scanning a photograph, or by taking a photograph with a digital camera. Also include at least one appropriate clip-art graphic that you downloaded from the Online Microsoft Clip Gallery.

15. Include at least one motion clip and one sound clip.

16. Design the PowerPoint presentation with an attractive color scheme, background objects, fonts, font size, and font colors.

17. Add appropriate slide transitions and slide animation effects with built-in sounds to your PowerPoint presentation.

18. Copy two or more of the slides to a Contents slide, and hyperlink them to their respective slides in the presentation.

19. Save your completed PowerPoint presentation using the filename **Folklore**.

20. Print the presentation as handouts with four slides per page.

21. Practice your presentation in front of one or more classmates or family members, and ask them to complete the evaluation part of the Presentation Delivery Worksheet.

22. Complete a Facilities Checklist.

23. Set up the presentation room.

24. Give your presentation to your classmates or to some other audience as indicated by your instructor.

In this case you will:

- Complete a Purpose and Outcomes Worksheet for your presentation.

- Complete an Audience Analysis Worksheet

- Complete a Situation and Media Assessment Worksheet for your presentation

- Create an attention-getting introduction, an advance organizer or overview, and a summary

- Complete a Focus and Organization Worksheet

- Complete a Presentation Visuals Worksheet

- Insert photographs acquired with a digital camera or scanner into your PowerPoint presentation

- Insert graphic, motion, and sound clips downloaded from the Online Microsoft Clip Gallery

- Complete a Presentation Delivery Worksheet

- Copy slides as miniatures to be included on another slide

GIVING
A PRESENTATION TO THE DIRECTOR OF A MUSEUM OR HALL OF FAME

CASE

Exhibit Consulting, Inc.

Judith Golovenko is the president of Exhibit Consulting, Inc. (ECI), a large consulting firm with headquarters in Washington, D.C. She recently hired you to help prepare and deliver presentations to museums and halls of fame in the Washington, D.C. area, and in other towns and cities in the mid-Atlantic states. Your assignment is to prepare a presentation explaining the services provided by ECI. You'll give your presentations to directors of museums and halls of fame. (According to your teacher's instructions, you should prepare this presentation on your own, or as a group.)

Some of the services that ECI might provide include:

- arranging traveling exhibits. For example, ECI could arrange for a museum to display a traveling exhibit of artifacts from an Egyptian Pharaoh's tomb, or artworks from French impressionist painters

- negotiating with professional athletes or musicians for personal items to be displayed in a hall of fame

- designing and developing advertising and marketing campaigns for special or permanent exhibits

- providing financial development services to obtain funding from individuals and local corporations

- writing funding proposals to the National Endowment for the Arts, the Federal Council on the Arts and Humanities, the Andrew W. Mellon Foundation, and other public and private grant agencies

- coordinating special lectures from art historians, sports historians, university professors, art curators, or other experts in the field of a particular exhibit

- publishing brochures, guides, slides, postcards, calendars, books, and other print matter dealing with special or permanent exhibits

- coordinating the preparation of audio tours of museum exhibits or halls of fame

- developing family programs and extension programs for museums and halls of fame

Judith asks you to:

1. Visit a local museum or a hall of fame, attend exhibits, look through brochures and other printed materials, view films, participate in other activities associated with a special or permanent exhibit, view the Web pages of a museum or hall of fame, and do anything else you can to learn enough about exhibits to prepare a knowledgeable presentation.

2. Complete a Purpose and Outcomes Worksheet for your presentation.

3. Complete an Audience Analysis Worksheet. Keep in mind that your audience will be the director (or board of directors) of a museum or hall of fame.

4. Complete a Situation and Media Assessment Worksheet.

5. Using the information you've gleaned from your visit and from the above list of services provided by ECI, prepare the text portion of a PowerPoint presentation with at least nine slides, including the title slide, contents slide, and summary slide.

6. Complete a Focus and Organization Worksheet to determine an appropriate organizational pattern for your presentation, and organize the text in your presentation accordingly.

7. Create an advance organizer or overview in your PowerPoint presentation.

8. Include a summary recapping the key ideas in your presentation.

9. Using the Presentation Delivery Worksheet, decide on an appropriate presentation style for your presentation.

10. Complete a Presentation Visuals Worksheet. Include at least one appropriate graphic on each slide. You can obtain your graphics by taking digital photographs of local museums, downloading pictures from Web sites, scanning pictures from art history or sports books and magazines, or downloading graphics from the Online Microsoft Clip Gallery.

11. Using the Presentation Delivery Worksheet, decide on an appropriate delivery method for your presentation.

12. Design the PowerPoint presentation with an attractive color scheme, background objects, fonts, font size, and font colors.

13. Add appropriate slide transitions and slide animation effects with built-in sounds to your PowerPoint presentation.

14. Save your completed PowerPoint presentation using the filename **Exhibit Consulting**.

15. Print the presentation as handouts with four slides per page.

16. Practice your presentation in front of one or more classmates or family members, and ask them to complete the evaluation part of the Presentation Delivery Worksheet.

17. Complete a Facilities Checklist.

18. Set up the presentation room.

19. Give your presentation to your classmates or to some other audience as indicated by your instructor.

TASK	PAGE #	RECOMMENDED METHOD/NOTES
35mm slides, prepare	PPT 3.30	Click File, click Page Setup, click Slides sized for list arrow, click 35mm Slides, click OK, send copy of file to service bureau or click File, point to Send To, click Genigraphics, follow instructions
Action Button, add	PPT 5.21	Click Slide Show, point to Action Buttons, click the desired action button, drag pointer on slide to mark location and side of action button, release mouse button, select desired hyperlink, click OK
Animated GIF, embed	PPT 3.13	Click Insert, click Movies and Sounds, click Movie from Gallery, click desired category button, click desired GIF, click [icon], close Insert Movie dialog box
Animation effects, add	PPT 3.26	In Slide Sorter View, select desired slides, click Preset Animation list arrow, click desired animation effect
AutoContent Wizard, run	PPT 1.14	Click AutoContent Wizard on PowerPoint startup dialog box and click OK, or click File, click New, click General tab, click AutoContent Wizard, click OK
Background graphic, remove	PPT 1.32	Click Format, click Background, click Omit background graphic from master, click Apply or Apply to All
Bullet style, modify	PPT 3.32	Click in text of bulleted item, click Format, click Bullets and Numbering, select desired bullet character and color, click OK
Bulleted item, dim previous	PPT 3.26	Click Slide Show, click Custom Animation, click Effects tab, click desired Entry animation and sound, click After Animation list arrow, click tile of desired color, click OK
CD music, inserting audio track into a slide	PPT 5.19	Place music CD in CD-ROM or DVD disk drive, click Insert, point to Movies and Sound, click Play CD Audio Track, select the starting and ending trak in the Play CD Audio Track section of dialog box, specify other options as desired, click OK
Chart, insert	PPT 3.16	Change slide layout to Chart, Text & Chart; or Chart & Text; double-click chart placeholder; edit information in datasheet; click anywhere outside chart to deselect it
Clip art, insert	PPT 2.12	Change the slide layout to a Clip Art layout, double-click clip art placeholder, click the Pictures tab, click desired picture category, click desired clip art image, click Insert clip
Clip downloaded from Online Microsoft Clip Gallery, apply to a slide	PPT 5.16	Click Insert, point to Movies and Sounds or point to Picture, and then click Movie or click Sound or click Clip Art, click the desired clip, click the Insert Clip button
Color scheme, modify	PPT 3.07	Click Format, click Slide Color Scheme, click Custom tab, change colors as desired, click Apply or Apply to All
Custom Animation effects of objects, add	PPT 5.11	In Normal View, click Slide Show, click Custom Animation, click Effects tab, select object(s) to be animated, set the desired animation and sound, click the Order & Timing tab, set the desired timing, and click OK
Custom Animation, edit	PPT 5.12	In Normal View, click Slide Show, click Custom Animation, click Order & Timing tab, select the desired object, modify its order of animation as desired by clicking [up arrow] or [down arrow], and modify the timing as desired

TASK	PAGE #	RECOMMENDED METHOD/NOTES
Design template, create	PPT 3.07	Change (as desired) color scheme, font attributes, background, and other elements of presentation; click File, click Save As, type a filename, click Save as type list arrow, select Design Template, select desired Save in folder, click Save
First slide, go to	—	Press Ctrl + Home
Format Painter, use	PPT 2.06	Click 🖌
Grayscale, view	PPT 1.32	Click ◪
Help, use the Office Assistant to get	PPT 1.30	Click Office Assistant, click in text box, type question, click Search, click topic, click additional help topics as necessary
Hyperlink, create	PPT 4.16	Select phrase, click 🔗, click Existing File or Web Page button, insert pathname or URL into Type the file or Web page name text box, or click Place in This Document button, select a slide, click OK
Last slide, go to	—	Press Ctrl + End
Layout, slide, change	PPT 2.04	Click Common Tasks, click Slide Layout, click desired layout, click Apply or Reapply
Kiosk browsing, set up slide show for	PPT 5.29	Click Slide Show, click Set Up Show, click Browsed at a kiosk (full screen) option button, click OK
Master, slide and title, modify	PPT 2.05	Click View, point to Master, click Slide (Title) Master
Meeting notes and action items, create	PPT 4.24	In Slide Show View, right-click in slide, click Meeting Minder, click desired tab and add desired items, click OK
Mouse Over Action Settings, apply	PPT 6.28	Select action button, click Slide Show, click Action Settings, click Mouse Over tab, click Highlight when mouse over check box, set other options as desired, click OK
Narration, record	PPT 5.22	Click Slide Show, click Record Narration, click Set Microphone Level button, read contents of the dialog box into microphone, click OK, click Link narrations in check box, click OK, talk into the microphone to record narration, press spacebar to go to next slide, record narration for that slide, continue as desired for subsequent slides, press Esc key, click Yes or No button to save or not save timing
Next slide, go to	PPT 1.31	In Slide View, click ⬇
Notes, create	PPT 1.31	Click in Notes Pane, type notes
Object, link	PPT 4.09	Click Insert, click Object, click Create from file option button, click Link check box, type filename, click OK
Objects, align	PPT 2.10	Shift-click to select objects, click Draw, point to Align or Distribute, click alignment position
Objects, animate	PPT 2.13	Click SlideShow, click Custom Animation, click Order & Timing tab, click object check box, select animation effect
Office Assistant, hide	PPT 1.06	Right-click Office Assistant, click Hide

TASK	PAGE #	RECOMMENDED METHOD/NOTES
Online Microsoft Clip Gallery, download clips	PPT 5.13	Click Insert, point to Picture, click Clip Art, click Clips Online button, click OK, use the Search for text box to search for desired clips, select the desired Search in and Results should be option, click Go button, click the Download button below the desired clip(s)
Organization chart, create	PPT 3.19	Change slide layout to Organization Chart; double-click organization chart placeholder; type personnel names, positions, and other information into boxes on organization chart; add subordinates and coworkers as desired, click File; click Exit and Return to (presentation filename); click Yes
Outline, export	PPT 4.38	Click File, point to Send To, click Microsoft Word, click Outline only option button, click OK, save file in Word
Outline text, demote	PPT 1.26	In Outline Pane, place insertion point in paragraph, click ➡ or press Tab
Outline text, move	PPT 1.21	In Outline Pane, click ⊟ or click a bullet, drag selection up or down
Outline text, promote	PPT 1.24	In Outline Pane, place insertion point in paragraph, click ⬅ or press Shift + Tab
Overheads, prepare	PPT 3.30	Click File, click Page Setup, click Slides sized for list arrow, click Overhead, select desired options, click OK
Pack and Go Wizard, use	PPT 3.31	Place blank, formatted disk in drive, click File, click Pack And Go, follow Wizard
Picture(s), group or ungroup	PPT 2.30	Select picture(s), click Draw, click Group or Ungroup
Picture background, add	PPT 6.12	In either the Title Master or Slide Master window (or in Normal View), click Format, click Background, click Background Fill list arrow, click Fill Effects, click Picture, click Select Picture button, select the desired picture file, click Insert button, click OK, click Apply or Apply to All button
Picture, insert	PPT 2.09	Click Insert, point to Picture, click From File, select disk and folder, click name of picture file, click Insert
Picture, recolor	PPT 6.21	Select picture, right-click picture and click Show Picture Toolbar (if necessary), click 🖼, click Colors option button, click the desired list arrows under New and select new color, click OK
Presentation, open	PPT 1.06	Click 📂, select disk and folder, click filename, click Open
Presentation, print	PPT 1.32	Click File, click Print
Presentation, save	PPT 1.18	Click 💾; if necessary, select disk and folder, type filename
Presentation, save with new filename	PPT 2.04	Click File, click Save As, enter new filename, click Save
Presentation, send via e-mail	PPT 1.34	Click File, point to Send To, click Mail Recipient
Previous slide, go to	—	In Slide View, click ⬆

TASK	PAGE #	RECOMMENDED METHOD/NOTES
Self-running presentation, set up	PPT 5.26	Go to Slide 1, click slide show, click Rehearse Timings button ⬚, advance from one slide to the next with desired timing, click Yes to save timings, set up for Kiosk browsing if desired
Shape, create	PPT 2.19	Click AutoShapes, point to Basic Shapes, click desired shape, drag pointer in Slide Pane to draw and size shape
Shape, flip	PPT 2.20	Select shape, click Draw, point to Rotate or Flip, click Flip Vertical or Flip Horizontal
Slide, copy as image	PPT 5.04	In Slide Sorter View, click slide to be copied, click ⬚, switch to slide or application into which slide image is to be copied, click ⬚
Slide, delete	PPT 1.20	In Outline Pane, click ⬚, press Delete; in Slide Pane, click Edit, click Delete Slide
Slide, hide	PPT 3.28	Click Slide Show, click Hide Slide
Slide, insert from other presentation	PPT 3.05	Click Insert, click Slides from Files, select folder and filename, select desired slides, click Insert button
Slide, insert new	PPT 1.27	Click ⬚, select desired layout, click OK
Slide Master, modify	PPT 3.10	Shift-click ⬚, modify formatting features as desired, click ⬚
Slide Pane, select	PPT 2.09	Click anywhere in slide pane
Slide Show, exit	PPT 1.12	Press Esc
Slide Show, view	PPT 1.09	Click ⬚; press Spacebar or click left mouse button to advance; press Backspace or right-click to go back
Slide Sorter View, switch to	PPT 1.33	Click ⬚
Sound clip, play in background	PPT 5.17	Click Insert, point to Movies and Sounds, click Sound from Gallery (or Sound from File), select desired sound clip, insert the sound clip, click Slide Show, click Custom Animation, click Order & Timing tab, move the media object to the desired position, set the Start animation to Automatically and 00:00 seconds, click Multimedia Settings tab, click Continue slide show option button, click After current slide option button if desired, click OK
Sound file, embed	PPT 3.15	Click Insert, point to Movies and Sounds, click Sounds from File, select folder and filename, click OK
Spelling, check	PPT 2.23	Click Tools, click Spelling
Style Checker, fix style problem	PPT 1.35	Click light bulb on slide, click option to fix style problem
Summary slide, create	PPT 4.15	In Slide Sorter View, select desired slides, click ⬚
Tab stops, add	PPT 4.13	Select text box, click View, click Ruler, click tab stop alignment selector button to select desired tab stop style, click desired location on ruler

TASK	PAGE #	RECOMMENDED METHOD/NOTES
Table, create	PPT 2.15	Change slide layout to Table, double-click table placeholder, set number of columns and rows, click OK, fill in and format cells as desired
Template, apply from other presentation	PPT 4.03	Click Common Tasks, click Apply Design Template, select folder, click Files of type list arrow, click Presentations and Shows, click filename, click Apply
Text, change alignment	PPT 3.10	Click in text or select text box, click a text alignment button
Text box, create	PPT 2.21	Click , click pointer on slide, type text
Text box, move	PPT 2.09	Select text box, drag edge of box (not a resize handle)
Text box, resize	PPT 2.07	Click text box, drag resize handle
Text box, rotate	PPT 2.22	Select text box, click , drag rotate handle
Toolbar, create custom	PPT 4.26	Right-click any toolbar, click Customize, click Commands tab, click Toolbars tab, click New, type name of toolbar, select desired category, select desired commands, drag command button onto toolbar, click Close
Web page, publish	PPT 4.29	Click File, click Save as Web Page, select desired Save in folder, type filename, click Save

Standardized Coding Number	Certification Skill Activity		Tutorial Pages	End-of-Tutorial Practice		
	Activity			End-of-Tutorial Pages	Exercise	Step Number
PP2000.1	**Creating a presentation**					
PP2000.1.1	Delete slides		1.19–1.20	1.38, 1.40	Case Problem 3 Case Problem 4	5 6
PP2000.1.2	Create a specified type of slide		1.27	1.37, 1.38, 1.40	Case Problem 2 Case Problem 3 Case Problem 4	9 2, 12 8
PP2000.1.3	Create a presentation from a template and/or a Wizard		1.13	2.32	Case Problem 4 (in Tutorial 2)	1
PP2000.1.4	Navigate among different views (slide, outline, sorter, tri-pane)		1.08, 1.23	1.37	Case Problem 2	12
PP2000.1.5	Create a new presentation from existing slides			1.35, 1.36, 1.37	Review Assignment Case Problem 1 Case Problem 2	2 1 1
PP2000.1.6	Copy a slide from one presentation into another		1.29	1.38	Case Problem 3	6
PP2000.1.7	Insert headers and footers		1.09	1.35	Review Assignment	11
PP2000.1.8	Create a blank presentation		1.13 2.03			
PP2000.1.9	Create a presentation using the AutoContent Wizard		1.13–1.16	1.38, 1.40	Case Problem 3 Case Problem 4	1 1
PP2000.1.10	Send a presentation via e-mail		1.34			
PP2000.2	**Modifying a presentation**					
PP2000.2.1	Change the order of slides using Slide Sorter View		1.21	1.35, 1.36	Review Assignment Case Problem 2	9 11
PP2000.2.2	Find and replace text		1.17			
PP2000.2.3	Change the layout for one or more slides		2.04, 2.11	2.26	Review Assignment	10
PP2000.2.4	Change slide layout (modify the Slide Master)		2.05–2.07	2.26, 2.31	Review Assignment Case Problem 3	4 7–9
PP2000.2.5	Modify slide sequence in the outline pane		1.21	1.35	Case Problem 3	9
PP2000.2.6	Apply a design template		2.04	2.26	Review Assignment	3
PP2000.3	**Working with text**					
PP2000.3.1	Check spelling		1.17, 1.31	1.35, 1.37, 1.36	Review Assignment Case Problem 1 Case Problem 2	13 5–6, 10 10
PP2000.3.2	Change and replace text fonts (individual slide and entire presentation)		2.06	2.27	Case Problem 1	4

Standardized Coding Number	Certification Skill Activity / Activity	Tutorial Pages	End-of-Tutorial Practice — End-of-Tutorial Pages	Exercise	Step Number
PP2000.3.3	Enter text in tri-pane view	1.17	1.36, 1.37, 1.38	Case Problem 1 Case Problem 2 Case Problem 3	8 4–5, 9 3, 4, 13
PP2000.3.4	Import text from Word	2.02–2.04			
PP2000.3.5	Change the text alignment	2.10	2.26, 2.27	Review Assignment Case Problem 1	6, 18 14
PP2000.3.6	Create a text box for entering text	2.20–2.21	2.27	Case Problem 1	13
PP2000.3.7	Using the Wrap text in AutoShape feature	2.20			
PP2000.3.8	Use the Office Clipboard	1.28	1.36, 1.38	Case Problem 1 Case Problem 3	3 11, 14
PP2000.3.9	Use the Format Painter	2.06	2.29	Case Problem 2	15
PP2000.3.10	Promote and demote text in slide & outline panes	1.23–1.27	1.35, 1.36, 1.37, 1.38	Review Assignment Case Problem 1 Case Problem 2 Case Problem 3	5–7 4, 9 6, 9 8, 15
PP2000.4	**Working with visual elements**				
PP2000.4.1	Add a picture from the ClipArt Gallery	2.11–2.13	2.26	Review Assignment Case Problem 1	11 7–8
PP2000.4.2	Add and group shapes using WordArt or the Drawing toolbar	2.13, 2.18–2.20	2.26, 2.27, 2.29, 2.31	Review Assignment Case Problem 1 Case Problem 2 Case Problem 3	20 11 5 2, 11
PP2000.4.3	Apply formatting	2.06	2.29	Case Problem 2	15
PP2000.4.4	Place text inside a shape using a text box	2.20	2.32	Case Problem 4	4
PP2000.4.5	Scale and size an object including ClipArt	2.07, 2.09	2.26, 2.27, 2.29	Review Assignment Case Problem 1 Case Problem 2	5 2 4
PP2000.4.6	Create tables within PowerPoint	2.15–2.18	2.26	Review Assignment	12
PP2000.4.7	Rotate and fill an object	2.20	2.26, 2.27	Review Assignment Case Problem 1	20 12
PP2000.5	**Customizing a presentation**				
PP2000.5.1	Add AutoNumber bullets	1.10			
PP2000.5.2	Add speaker notes	1.31	1.35	Review Assignment	11
PP2000.5.3	Add graphical bullets	1.10, 2.08			
PP2000.5.4	Add slide transitions	1.10	1.35	Review Assignment	12
PP2000.5.5	Animate text and objects	1.10, 2.13–2.14	1.38, 2.32	Case Problem 3 Case Problem 4	6 2

Standardized Coding Number	Certification Skill Activity	Tutorial Pages	End-of-Tutorial Practice		
	Activity		End-of-Tutorial Pages	Exercise	Step Number
PP2000.6	**Creating output**				
PP2000.6.1	Preview presentation in black and white	1.31–1.32	1.37, 1.38	Case Problem 2 Case Problem 3	15 18
PP2000.6.2	Print slides in a variety of formats	1.32	1.35, 1.36	Review Assignment Case Problem 1	19 13
PP2000.6.3	Print audience handouts	1.32–1.33	1.37	Case Problem 2	16
PP2000.6.4	Print speaker notes in a specified format	1.33	1.35	Review Assignment	20
PP2000.7	**Delivering a presentation**				
PP2000.7.1	Start a slide show on any slide	1.08	1.35	Review Assignment	16–17
PP2000.7.2	Use onscreen navigation tools	1.09	1.35 2.30	Review Assignment Case Problem 3	17 19
PP2000.7.3	Print a slide as an overhead transparency	1.32			
PP2000.7.4	Use the pen during a presentation	2.23–2.24			
PP2000.8	**Managing files**				
PP2000.8.1	Save changes to a presentation	1.18	1.35, 1.36	Review Assignment Case Problem 1	18 14
PP2000.8.2	Save as a new presentation	1.18	1.35, 1.36, 1.37	Review Assignment Case Problem 1 Case Problem 2	2 1 1
PP2000.8.3	Publish a presentation to the Web	1.34	1.40	Case Problem 4	11
PP2000.8.4	Use Office Assistant	1.31	1.35, 1.37	Review Assignment Case Problem 2	19 2
PP2000.8.5	Insert hyperlink	1.34			

Expert Skills

PP2000E.1	**Creating a presentation**			
PP2000E.1.1	Automatically create a summary slide	4.14–4.15	Review Assignment Case Problem 2	16 14
PP2000E.1.2	Automatically create an agenda slide	4.24		
PP2000E.1.3	Design a template	3.06	Case Problem 1 Case Problem 3	8 1
PP2000E.1.4	Format presentations for the web	4.29	Review Assignment	20
PP2000E.2	**Modifying a presentation**			
PP2000E.2.1	Change tab formatting	4.13–4.14	Review Assignment Case Problem 1	 5
PP2000E.2.2	Use the Wrap text in AutoShape feature	2.20		
PP2000E.2.3	Apply a template from another presentation	4.02–4.03	T3, Case Problem 1 T4 Review Assignment	10 5
PP2000E.2.4	Customize a color scheme	3.08	Review Assignment Case Problem 1	3 1
PP2000E.2.5	Apply animation effects	3.30, 3.31	Review Assignment Case Problem 1	11 19
PP2000E.2.6	Create a custom background	3.07	Case Problem 4	4
PP2000E.2.7	Add animated GIFs	3.13–3.14	Review Assignment Case Problem 1	12 12
PP2000E.2.8	Add links to slides within the presentation	4.16–4.17	Review Assignment	17, 18
PP2000E.2.9	Customize clip art and other objects (resize, scale, etc.)	3.13, 3.14	Review Assignment Case Problem 1	7 6
PP2000E.2.10	Add a presentation within a presentation	3.05–3.06	Review Assignment Case Problem 2	9 11
PP2000E.2.11	Add an action button	4.20–4.22	Case Problem 1	12, 13
PP2000E.2.12	Hide slides	3.28	Case Problem 3	13
PP2000E.2.13	Set automatic slide timings	4.23	T3, Case Problem 3 T4, Case Problem 4	10 10
PP2000E.3	**Working with visual elements**			
PP2000E.3.1	Add textured backgrounds	3.09	Review Assignment	5
PP2000E.3.2	Apply diagonal borders to a table	2.17		
PP2000E.4	**Using data from other sources**			
PP2000E.4.1	Export an outline to Word	4.10	Case Problem 2	2
PP2000E.4.2	Add a table (from Word)	4.06–4.07	Case Problem 4	7
PP2000E.4.3	Insert an Excel chart	4.09	Review Assignment	13

Expert Skills

PP2000E.4.4	Add sound	3.15	Review Assignment Case Problem 1	13 13
PP2000E.4.5	Add video	3.13		
PP2000E.5	**Creating output**			
PP2000E.5.1	Save slide as a graphic	3.35	Case Problem 1	22
PP2000E.5.2	Generate meeting notes	4.24		
PP2000E.5.3	Change output format (Page Setup)	3.35	Case Problem 2	2
PP2000E.5.4	Export to 35mm slides	3.35		
PP2000E.6	**Delivering a presentation**			
PP2000E.6.1	Save presentation for use on another computer (Pack 'N Go)	3.31	Case Problem 4	12
PP2000E.6.2	Electronically incorporate meeting feedback	4.24		
PP2000E.6.3	View a presentation on the Web (see PP2000E.9.2)	4.30		
PP2000E.7	**Managing files**			
PP2000E.7.1	Save embedded fonts in presentation	3.31	Case Problem 3	11
PP2000E.7.2	Save HTML to a specific target browser	4.29		
PP2000E.8	**Working with PowerPoint**			
PP2000E.8.1	Customize the toolbar	4.26		
PP2000E.8.2	Create a toolbar	4.26		
PP2000E.9	**Collaborating with workgroups**			
PP2000E.9.1	Subscribe to a presentation	4.29		
PP2000E.9.2	View a presentation on the Web	4.29	Review Assignment	20
PP2000E.9.3	Use NetMeeting to schedule a broadcast	4.41, 4.42		
PP2000E.9.4	Use NetShow to deliver a broadcast	4.42, 4.43		
PP2000E.10	**Working with charts and tables**			
PP2000E.10.1	Build a chart or graph	3.16	Case Problem 1	16
PP2000E.10.2	Modify charts or graphs	3.21	Case Problem 2	16–18
PP2000E.10.3	Build an organization chart	3.20	Case Problem 1 Case Problem 2	14 19
PP2000E.10.4	Modify an organization chart	3.19	Case Problem 1	15
PP2000E.10.5	Modify PowerPoint tables	4.12		

File Finder

Location in Tutorial	Name and Location of Data File	Student Saves File As...	Student Creates New File
Tutorial 1			
Session 1.1	Tutorial.01\Tutorial\Customer.ppt	Customer.ppt	
Session 1.2			Brainstorming for Sales Reps.ppt
Review Assignment	Tutorial.01\Review\Sales.ppt	New Marketing Campaign.ppt	
Case Problem 1	Tutorial.01\Cases\Mailmndr.ppt	MailMinder.ppt	
Case Problem 2	Tutorial.01\Cases\Juica.ppt	Juica Juice Capital.ppt	
Case Problem 3			Personal Liability Insurance.ppt
Case Problem 4			Social Opportunities at...(name of your school).ppt
Tutorial 2			
Session 2.1	Tutorial.02\Tutorial\Incasale.ppt	Inca Sales Presentation.ppt	
Review Assignment	Tutorial.02\Review\Report.ppt Tutorial.02\Review\Apple.bmp	Marketing Report.ppt	
Case Problem 1	Tutorial.02\Cases\4Body.ppt Tutorial.02\Cases\Bodylogo.bmp	4 My Body.ppt	
Case Problem 2	Tutorial.02\Cases\Heather.ppt Tutorial.02\Cases\SouthMnt.bmp Tutorial.02\Cases\Bedroom.bmp Tutorial.02\Cases\Dining.bmp	Heather Condos.ppt	
Case Problem 3	Tutorial.02\Cases\Halloween.ppt Tutorial.02\Cases\Bat.bmp Tutorial.02\Cases\Witch.bmp Tutorial.02\Cases\Ghost.bmp Tutorial.02\Cases\Skull.bmp	Hannah's Halloween Design.ppt	
Case Problem 4			My Activity.ppt
Tutorial 3			
Session 3.1	Tutorial.03\Tutorial\MachPicc.jpg Tutorial.03\Tutorial\Clapping.wav Tutorial.03\Tutorial\Fanfare.mid		Annual Report.ppt Inca.pot (design template)
Review Assignment	Tutorial.03\Review\Benefits.ppt		Supplemental Benefits.ppt
Case Problem 1	Tutorial.03\Cases\SBouquet.bmp Tutorial.03\Cases\SBouquet.ppt Tutorial.03\Cases\SBouquet.wav		Sweet Bouquet.pot Sweet Bouquet.ppt
Case Problem 2	Tutorial.03\Cases\Safety.jpg Tutorial.03\Cases\Safety.ppt Tutorial.03\Cases\Cordova.jpg	SafetyFirst Overheads.ppt	
Case Problem 3	Tutorial.03\Cases\TravLogo.jpg Tutorial.03\Cases\Hone.jpg Tutorial.03\Cases\TelAviv.jpg Tutorial.03\Cases\OldJeru.jpg Tutorial.03\Cases\Galilee.jpg Tutorial.03\Cases\Masada.jpg Tutorial.03\Cases\Giza.jpg		Middle East Tours.ppt
Case Problem 4			Sporting Goods.ppt
Tutorial 4			
Session 4.1	Tutorial.04\Tutorial\Proposal.ppt Tutorial.04\Tutorial\Table.doc Tutorial.04\Tutorial\Expenses.xls	Inca Proposal.ppt Inca Expenses.xls	
Session 4.2	Tutorial.04\Tutorial\NewOff.ppt	New Office.htm	
Review Assignment	Tutorial.04\Review\NEComp.doc Tutorial.04\Review\Graph.bmp Tutorial.04\Review\Sales.xls	Competition in the Northeast.ppt	
Case Problem 1	Tutorial.04\Cases\CLCFDoc.doc Tutorial.04\Cases\CLCFPres.ppt Tutorial.04\Cases\CLCFData.xls	CLCF Success Data.xls CLCF Presentation.html	Introduction of CLCF Marketing.ppt
Case Problem 2	Tutorial.04\Cases\XPres.ppt Tutorial.04\Cases\XIntro.wav Tutorial.04\Cases\XPencil.tif Tutorial.04\Cases\XSales.xls	XPressions Product and Services.ppt XPressions Outline.doc XPressions Sales.xls	
Case Problem 3	Tutorial.04\Cases\Debby's.ppt Tutorial.04\Cases\DebLogo.tif Tutorial.04\Cases\DebChart.xls	Debby's Gym and Spa.ppt	
Case Problem 4			Report on (Country).ppt

File Finder

Location in Tutorial	Name and Location of Data File	Student Saves File As...	Student Creates New File
Tutorial 5			
Session 5.1	Tutorial.05/Tutorial/TradeSho.ppt Tutorial.05/Tutorial/CoSummry.ppt	Tutorial.05/Tutorial/Inca at Trade Tutorial.05/Tutorial/Show.ppt Tutorial.05/Tutorial/Inca Company Summary.ppt	
Session 5.2	(Continued from Session 5.1) Tutorial.05/Tutorial/ProdMap.jpg Tutorial.05/Tutorial/Bldgs.jpg Tutorial.05/Tutorial/Tuesta.jpg Tutorial.05/Tutorial/Arias.jpg		
Review Assignments	Tutorial.05/Review/GenInfo.ppt	Tutorial.05/Review/Inca General Information.ppt	
Case Problem 1	Tutorial.05/Cases/Heart.ppt Tutorial.05/Cases/Heart.jpg Tutorial.05/Cases/Arteries.jpg	Tutorial.05/Cases/Rehab Heart Program.ppt	
Case Problem 2	Tutorial.05/Cases/GrndCan1.jpg Tutorial.05/Cases/GrndCan2.jpg Tutorial.05/Cases/GrndCan3.jpg Tutorial.05/Cases/GrndCan4.jpg Tutorial.05/Cases/GrnCan.ppt		Tutorial.05/Cases/Scenic.ppt
Case Problem 3			Tutorial.05/Cases/Game.ppt
Case Problem 4			Tutorial.05/Cases/MyJob.ppt
Tutorial 6			
Session 6.1	Tutorial.06/Tutorial/IncLogo2.jpg Tutorial.06/Tutorial/IncaBkGr.jpg Tutorial.06/Tutorial/IncaOver.ppt Tutorial.06/Tutorial/Inca35mm.ppt	Tutorial.06/Tutorial/Inca Overheads Workshop.ppt Tutorial.06/Tutorial/Inca 35mm Slide Presentation.ppt	Tutorial.06/Tutorial/Inca Overheads Template.pot Tutorial.06/Tutorial/Inca 35mm Slides Template.pot
Session 6.2	(Continued from Session 6.1) Tutorial.06/Tutorial/ Inca Multiple-Page Poster.ppt Tutorial.05/Tutorial/NextBtn.jpg Tutorial.06/Tutorial/PrevBtn.jpg	Tutorial.06/Tutorial/Inca Multiple-Page Poster.ppt Tutorial.06/Tutorial/Inca Banner.ppt Tutorial.06/Tutorial/Inca Single-Page Poster.ppt	Tutorial.06/Tutorial/Inca Web Presentation.ppt
Review Assignments	Tutorial.05/Review/ZincBean.ppt Tutorial.06/Review/PintoBns.jpg Tutorial.06/Review/IncLogo3.jpg Tutorial.06/Review/BkgrDNA.jpg	Tutorial.06/Review/Zinc-Rich Beans 35mm Slides.ppt Tutorial.06/Review/Inca 35mm Bean Template.ppt Tutorial.06/Review/Zinc-Rich Beans Overheads	
Case Problem 1	Tutorial.06/Cases/BkgrTree.jpg Tutorial.05/Cases/ParkSign.jpg Tutorial.06/Cases/Bullet.jpg Tutorial.06/Cases/ParkShow.ppt Tutorial.05/Cases/ParkJog.jpg Tutorial.05/Cases/ParkPic.jpg Tutorial.05/Cases/ParkRivr.jpg Tutorial.06/Cases/NavNext.jpg Tutorial.06/Cases/NavBack.jpg	Tutorial.06/Cases/Canyon Glen Slide Presentation.ppt	Tutorial.06/Cases/Canyon Glen Slide Template.pot Tutorial.06/Cases/Canyon Glen Web Page.html
Case Problem 2			Tutorial.06/Cases/Palm Multiple-Page Overhead.ppt Tutorial.06/Cases/Palm Single-Page Overhead.ppt
Case Problem 3	Tutorial.06/Cases/Jayhawk.ppt	Tutorial.06/Cases/Jayhawk in Guadalajara.ppt Tutorial.06/Cases/Jayhawk Poster.ppt	
Case Problem 4	Tutorial.06/Cases/SFBridge.jpg Tutorial.06/Cases/SFCblCar.jpg Tutorial.06/Cases/SFCtyHll.jpg Tutorial.06/Cases/SFDwnTwn.jpg		Tutorial.06/Cases/City Template.pot Tutorial.06/Cases/City Overhead Presentation.ppt